Reclaiming Leisure

Reclaiming Leisure

Art, Sport and Philosophy

Hayden Ramsay

First published 2005 by
PALGRAVE MACMILLAN
Houndmills, Basingstoke, Hampshire RG21 6XS and
175 Fifth Avenue, New York, N. Y. 10010
Companies and representatives throughout the world

PALGRAVE MACMILLAN is the global academic imprint of the Palgrave
Macmillan division of St. Martin's Press, LLC and of Palgrave Macmillan Ltd.
Macmillan® is a registered trademark in the United States, United Kingdom
and other countries. Palgrave is a registered trademark in the European
Union and other countries.

ISBN-13: 978–1–4039–4703–1 hardback
ISBN-10: 1–4039–4703–1   hardback

This book is printed on paper suitable for recycling and made from fully
managed and sustained forest sources.

A catalogue record for this book is available from the British Library.

Library of Congress Cataloging-in-Publication Data
Ramsay, Hayden, 1964–
    Reclaiming leisure : art, sport, and philosophy / Hayden Ramsay.
        p. cm.
    Includes bibliographical references and index.
    ISBN 1–4039–4703–1 (cloth)
        1. Leisure–Philosophy. 2. Leisure–Social aspects. I. Title.

GV14.R36 2005
790'.01–dc22   2005042060

10   9   8   7   6   5   4   3   2   1
14   13 12 11 10 09 08 07 06 05

Transferred to digital printing in 2006.

Contents

Preface

Leisure and recreation are among the great topics of classical philosophy. Disposal of our private time – the time in which we can most be ourselves, without unwanted impositions or moral scruples – raises deep questions of who we are, what we value, and how we should live. But in modern societies, many people when faced with the opportunity for leisure and recreation simply do not know what to do, or do something inappropriate (like more work), or something unsuccessful in terms of achieving lasting recreation (like buying more). With the victory of the consumerist lifestyle, this is now a largescale social problem affecting the ways in which entire communities respond to leisure time. Questions of who we are, what we value, and how we want to live as a society are more pressing than ever, and this pressure will increase with growing affluence, more work, and more consumerism.

Contemporary philosophers have occasionally looked at leisure, but have hardly ever taken advantage of the philosophical legacy, or of work on leisure produced in more recent disciplines, such as sociology and leisure studies. The present work is not a contribution to these newer subjects, and would not claim to do justice to their insights. It does, however, attempt to revive the topic of leisure as a philosophical one, and to suggest that connections between philosophy and other academic disciplines might lead to valuable new work in this area.

In presenting an account of leisure and some of the implications of this account this work stands foursquare in awe of the classical philosophical tradition, and of those analytic commentators who have worked to explain and interpret the classics for modern readers. To help to inspire clear thinking and deeper reflection on leisure is the book's simple aim.

I am grateful to the editorial and production staff at Palgrave Macmillan, and to two anonymous referees. I was helped by the marvelous library staff at Kuring-gai Campus, University of Technology Sydney. I am also grateful for many suggestions to Bishop Anthony Fisher OP; to John Weretka for advice on music matters; to Peter Zwaans for research assistance on sport, and to John Paul II Institute for Marriage and Family Melbourne for supporting Peter's work; and lastly, to Steve Lawrence for a great conversation about ethics and Aussie Rules Football. All views expressed and all errors remain my own.

Hayden Ramsay

Introduction

Affluent people today spend significant time and money on stress-relief, anti-tension therapies, anxiety cures, and other self-help and self-pampering strategies. Stress and tension are very real in people's lives. And with their cure now the subject of a major industries, we are all increasingly suggestible to diagnosis of these lifestyle-sicknesses. Treating our anxieties by philosophical thought is certainly rarer than responding with spas and luxuries.[1] Indeed, few philosophers have taken our daily stresses seriously since St Thomas Aquinas explained that he felt sure that this problem had a spiritual cause.[2] I feel sure that Aquinas was right.

Aquinas did not intend his spiritual diagnosis just as a call to go to church more often (though some studies suggest that is bound to help people de-stress[3]). Rather, he had in mind a summons to rediscover the contemplative depths of our lives: to appreciate more what makes life meaningful, and to invest the time and energy that is most truly ours in a serious encounter with this source of meaning. Aquinas agreed with the ancient Greeks that for lasting and effective 'stress relief' and 'tension control' we need to reclaim leisure from a world that would eat it up in work, or in trivial and unsatisfying amusements.[4] Today, this approach means reclaiming leisure from those who have long sought its commodification and so contributed to the slump in its recreational potential.

Aquinas stands in a noble line of leisure philosophers who have reflected on the fact that people, like land and animals, need regular rest and re-creation. Foremost here is Aristotle, the main source on pre-modern or contemplative leisure. Then come the gracious Romans, in particular the Stoics, Marcus Aurelius, Seneca, and Cicero, who combined political office with a metaphysical approach to the nature of

1

things and a courageous, leisurely stance in the face of the unalterable. Next in line are the Christians, who decided to follow the Jews in combining the day of rest with the day of worship, cannily recognising that if Sunday is not a holiday people are less likely to worship, and if not a holyday, less likely to take leisure time with their families. Later Christian leisure thinkers and practitioners even more shrewdly recognised that leisurely contemplation and spiritual detachment are also compatible with precise division of the day for purposes of prayer and physical work. After the composition of St Benedict's great Rule, contemplative leisure and necessary work are officially compatible, at least on the Christian account.

Thomas Aquinas unites the classical approach of the Greeks with the discipline of Benedict and St Augustine, regarding prayer, study, and work. A man of little free time himself, Aquinas showed that serious contemplation and thoughtful religion are each other's best support: that philosophising and theologising belong together in a well-balanced search for truth; that they contribute equally to an integrated vision of the highest life. After the middle ages, leisure tends to become the preserve of the 'leisured classes', the moneyed minorities and educated elites of the Renaissance; until even this ideal trickles out under the force of the Reformation which brought new and rigidly disciplined attitudes towards work and time. In the post-Reformation period, pockets of leisure survive: for example, in seventeenth century innovations in drama and lyric music. The succeeding centuries of Enlightenment and industrialisation ushered in the industrial cities, the beginnings of consumerism, the market, and, eventually, the growth of mass leisure (as well as mass everything else).[5]

Contemplative leisure seemed to have all but vanished from life and philosophy by the mid twentieth-century when the topic was given new life by the advocacy of Josef Pieper and the insight of Johan Huizinga. Huizinga paid serious attention to the concept of play, a concept with an important role in any theory of leisure. He argued for play's source at the roots of human experience and its continuing presence in all important social and cultural institutions.[6] Huizinga documented the playful nature of much that we take seriously today. He also explained how inappropriate growth in seriousness can attack the natural human sense of playfulness, thus undermining the deep, evolutionary origin and meaning of many of our activities. Meanwhile, Josef Pieper, concerned equally to save civilisation from post-World War Two totalitarianism and from trivialisation, argued that leisure is a spiritual attitude, not simply the disposal of our free time in whatever we can afford or for our preferred (and possibly low-grade) pleasure.[7] For Pieper, leisure requires and enhances an inner calm and silence that is truly contemplative – that is, open to reality and to new possibilities. Leisure is the very opposite of work, busyness, and the effort required by our social roles and others' expectations.

So Huizinga argued that play affects all culture, though our modern culture is over-serious; while Pieper argued that leisure affects all culture, but our modern culture is over-frivolous. Though very different in approach and aims, the two thinkers agree that the play and leisure most modern people experience are trivialised, dehumanising, and unproductive of the rich cultural experience that individuals and societies thrive upon. They agree too that play and leisure are activities that require no justification beyond themselves: they consist in stepping aside from the daily logic of means-end production, from all external pressures and justifications, and choosing enjoyable activity free from any need for outcomes.

In play and leisure we can reach the freedom which consumerist society still dreams of, mythologises, even fetishises – but meet it not by buying better things or adopting a socially approved lifestyle, but by our willingness to encounter and be changed by the deep meaning of the natural and personal world around us. Play and leisure remind us of the possibility of existence apart from the daily round, life beyond the anxieties of work and need. Thus they present us with the possibility of a lasting recreation: a genuine 're-creation', in which we rest, renew ourselves by activity personally chosen (and hopefully much enjoyed), and then face again the more demanding parts of our lives. Play and leisure mean freeing ourselves, legitimately and enjoyably, however briefly, from demands – even the demands of duty – and so receiving the share in recreation that we all need for a fulfilled life.

The thought of Pieper and Huizinga influences the argument of this book in a number of ways. I will argue for a classic account of leisure and so will critique some trends in contemporary leisure, including some particular leisure activities. I agree that contemplative leisure is worthwhile for its own sake, and I also argue for the leisure status of other activities worthwhile in themselves. But I do not think, as they do, that every activity worthwhile in itself is a leisure activity. Leisure activities are the normal means to recreation, and that cannot be said of every activity worthwhile in itself: most healthcare, relationships, and prayer is worthwhile in itself but not normal means to recreation.

Activities such as listening to music, writing a diary, or practicing gymnastics are, however, worthwhile in themselves as ordinary means to recreation. Moreover, they are also activities performed through a playful engagement with the world, a reflective engagement with the world, or both: people who perform these activities play as they do so and/or gain some insight through their leisure. On my account, then, leisure activities are our normal means to recreation, and play and reflection are the major features of leisure.

Recreation consists first in rest and recovery, which are promoted (though not exclusively) by play; and secondly, in rejuvenation and renewed understanding of our commitments, which are promoted (again, not exclusively) by reflection. Leisure activities then are those activities chosen for their own sakes that are also normal means to rest and renewal. The connection with recreation, and not their intrinsic worth, is what identifies activities as leisure.

I will speak of 'reflective leisure'[8] and sometimes 'playful leisure' to describe the two main features of activity that is our normal means to recreation. It will be important here not to downgrade play, or to idealise reflection. Gifted, hard working people do play: they spend time in activity that is simply refreshing and restorative; and ordinary, hard working people do reflect: they do spend time thinking about the value of their activities and relationships, the importance of these to their lives, and indeed the importance and meaning of their lives. It is important too to remember that not all recreation comes from leisure: rest can also come from sources other than play; rejuvenation can come from sources other than reflection. But leisure is the normal means to recreation, and few people are gifted or interested or fortunate enough to receive sufficient rest from, for example, sleep or personal relationships, or sufficient rejuvenation from religion or self-analysis or work.

At first encounter, the notion of playful leisure may be widely acceptable (though in fact it challenges many of the norms of today's leisure 'industry'); whereas the notion of reflection may seem detached from ordinary life and ordinary leisure. Perhaps charges of elitism cannot be avoided altogether here: reflective leisure does, after all, imply an immense change in popular social attitudes.[9] Part of my response to critics here will be to argue for reflective leisure on the basis of a 'natural law' approach to human nature and welfare. Thus I will not simply introduce reflective leisure as another option: I will offer some philosophical justification for the approach, as others recently have sought to offer sociological justification for it. Furthermore, I will continue to explore the justification of reflective leisure through consideration of a more reflective (and playful) approach towards the particular leisure activities of reading, travel, music, and sport.[10]

We find our modern lives stressful and rushed not because of insufficient leisure, but because of insufficient playful and especially reflective leisure. So successful is the consumerist system within which most of us live, and so extensive its reach, that it forms a *total logic* – a system one cannot buy into without buying in totally, like certain religions, relativism, Marxism, nihilism... We cannot be just 'a bit' consumerist, because accepting consumerist logic and vision means accepting that today's item is tomorrow's waste, that all life's needs arise from and are satisfied by purchasable items; that I, the subject, am essentially a market object, a 'player', the consumer, or producer, or both. Being consumerist just about some things is not possible because commodities are specially designed to require other commodities, replacement, and support services; and being consumerist only occasionally is not possible because access to commodities requires massive social involvement in more basic commodities. Thus clothes, money, education, food, and a myriad other consumerist goods – as well as a particular understanding of oneself and of other persons – are all required for a bushman to walk into a city convenience shop to buy a sandwich.

In ways I will go on to discuss, the total logic of consumerism impairs our realisation of our full human potential and our pursuit and enjoyment of important human goods. I agree with Pieper (and with leading sociologists and cultural theorists of leisure such as Geoffrey Godbey, John Kelly, John Robinson, Sebastian de Grazia[11]) that mass commodified leisure undermines human well-being and diminishes our leisure lives; and I attempt to justify this view with a philosophical account of human nature, leisure, and recreation. This account of human nature will also include a more appropriate, if more restricted, role for commercial transactions and ownership.

It is interesting, and somewhat poignant, to recall today another philosophical call for increased leisure from the era of Huizinga and Pieper, but a call that echoes a very different philosophical tradition. In 1932 Bertrand Russell published an essay 'In Praise of Idleness'.[12] Russell believed that the early twentieth century saw many people unemployed and many over-worked because of a perverse over-estimation of the value of work. He argued that the leisure to follow personal interests that was possessed by the few ought to be more highly valued and more justly distributed throughout society. As people grew in their understanding of the intrinsic worth of leisure, both in terms of simple pleasures and of higher activities, Russell thought that both work and leisure would be less gobbled up by the wealthy few, and more equitably shared among all the able-bodied and able-minded: less over-work, less unemployment, less stress.

Whatever of this specific proposal, it had the merit of reviving in English-speaking societies the idea that leisure properly promoted can help to address major social problems and to relieve the sufferings and stresses of those affected ('leisure as a public good'). After Russell, there was indeed a vast democritisation of leisure opportunities, riding largely on the back of post-World War Two peace and (eventual) prosperity. The advent of shortened work hours and mass leisure did at least mean a break for many from over-long hours, and the possibility too of new entertainments and additional relaxation. But we can applaud more just and safer work arrangements while still lamenting the continuing neglect of (and perhaps even decrease in) opportunities for meaningful leisure. Today, we should be speaking up not in praise of idleness, as Russell thought, but in honour of leisure: we should promote doing things for their own sakes, playing without gaining, and reflecting on our lives so that we can grow in freedom, insight, and happiness.

Recent study of leisure has been largely the preserve of leisure studies professionals, sociologists, psychologists, sometimes healthcare professionals. It was once a central topic – for Aristotle, the central topic[13] – in philosophy. Despite the often superb efforts of several decades of leisure theorists, leisure-related social problems, such as stress and mass anxiety, continue, and continue to puzzle. Mass, consumerised leisure has been a mixed blessing, and consumerised cures for the stress consumerism causes hardly help. So it is timely to look again at what philosophy has said about leisure in general, to critique some contemporary leisure activities, and to suggest philosophical justification for a more playful and reflective leisure life. In what follows, I will be arguing for leisure as superbly recreative, a great joy, and a key to effective exercise of many of our most important human capacities.

My approach will be to recall in Chapter 1 some philosophical views of leisure, from the ancients to the present day. This will help to establish leisure as an important part of philosophical thinking and to locate my suggestions about reflective leisure within the history of philosophical thought on the topic. It will also help to give philosophical credibility to the revival of leisure called for by Pieper, and by cultural theorists and sociologists such as de Grazia, Godbey, and others.

In Chapter 2, I discuss the concept of leisure and relate it to reflection, recreation, play, relaxation, and fun. This chapter will include argument against consumerist leisure, discussion of contemplation and of other leisure activities worthwhile in themselves, and introduction to some of the contemporary leisure literature.

In Chapter 3 I borrow some ideas from recent natural law thinking on human nature and discuss briefly our most important capacities. One of these capacities is recreation. I try to clarify this capacity and to justify the role of reflective leisure activity in achieving recreation. I also describe the form of virtue that applies to leisure and the contribution our leisure lives make to our happiness. Chapters 1 to 3 carry the weight of the philosophical analysis of leisure.

Having made my own view clear, I next discuss four popular leisure activities: reading, travel, sport, and music. I examine these activities because they have high recreational potential and serious stress-breaking power. I suggest some ways in which they have suffered diminishment, particularly by the total logic of consumerism, and make some suggestions about how we can act to protect these activities from further risk and make them more reflective. These chapters give some description of the nature of each activity, describe the ways in which it is currently pursued, and suggest certain virtues and vices of current thought and practice in each case.

In Chapter 8 I discuss the relationship of leisure and work and discuss some ethical issues in balancing the two within an individual life and a society. Mihalyi Csikszentmihalyi has argued that most people now find their most challenging and rewarding experiences not in their leisure time but at work.[14] This suggests that a new account of the relationship of the two is necessary – an account that suggests some practical steps for reclaiming leisure, while protecting the proper autonomy of work, and promoting a healthy balance of the two.

Finally, in Chapter 9 I discuss the performing arts and their status as leisure. Making sport, travel, and so on more reflective is up-hill work: doing the same for the arts should be easier. Yet some people who support the arts are suspicious of classing them as leisure or discussing their recreational appeal. To some, this risks down-grading aesthetics to popular entertainment. But on a view such as reflective leisure, relating art to leisure does not involve the difficulties that consumerist leisure raises. I describe a possible relationship, and suggest that it may be beneficial both for art and leisure.

Pieper once seemed a lone, civilised but rather idealistic voice on leisure, contemplation, and culture. Today, thanks in large part to excellent work in leisure studies and sociology, Pieper, and through him Aquinas and Aristotle, contribute once again to mainstream leisure thinking. Contemporary philosophers, however, are fairly silent on this new development. My hope is to make a contribution to the revitilisation of philosophical thought on leisure, and, more generally, to philosophising in the style of Aristotle, Aquinas, and their modern defenders, such as Pieper.

To sustain hope in a new leisured age, including a turn towards contemplation, takes courage and patience given the total logic of consumerism. By their nature, total logics are a monopoly: they seek to dominate the field and to see off all other contenders. But although its success is extraordinary, it is not likely that consumerism is the system that will permanently dismiss all other forms of social life and fully explain culture to itself. One alternative to consumerism is Huizinga's play; another is Pieper's reflective life. One great power that play and reflection share is the fact that they have – and can have – no justification outside themselves. They stand or fall by their own intrinsic appeal to those who learn of them and come to practice them. Experience and history suggest that, contrary to the dominant total logic, the appeal of play and reflection is still profound; and when the two are combined, that appeal may be irresistible.

1

Philosophers on Play

Philosophical work on leisure, play, recreation, and even reflection, is a contemporary rarity. In this respect, philosophy has travelled far from its roots, for leisure was an important concern for many great philosophers of the past. In order to establish the philosophical significance of leisure and some associated concepts, and to introduce some of the ideas and distinctions that I will later rely on, I here consider some of this history. This brief look at the philosophical legacy of leisure will also help to establish playful and reflective leisure as ideas with some philosophical pedigree and potential.

I have chosen to focus on Aristotle, Aquinas, Kant, Wittgenstein, Gadamer, and some senior thinkers in contemporary philosophy. These sketches reflect some ideas and traditions that I will later draw upon; but I think they also give a reasonably representative flavour of the range of philosophical responses to leisure. A fully representative discussion of leisure theory today would of course include important new work in sociology and leisure studies. But my aim here is to look at a little of the philosophical past, so as to focus in coming chapters on the philosophical future.

Aristotle: contemplation

The rather austere figure of Aristotle may seem hard to reconcile with the worlds of leisure and play. But not only are these ideas central to his practical thought, he is also a thinker steeped in the empirical and the social; a man sufficiently young at heart, after all, to be appointed to tutor the young Alexander the Great. As A. W. Price has pointed out, he is also the man who manages to get erotic love even into the dryness of formal logical proofs in the *Prior Analytics*;[1] the man

too whose attributed works include a treatise discussing the uses of
bear fat, spontaneous combustion, ghosts, and the gestation period
of elephants. Aristotle is the very opposite of an armchair philosopher:
he is more likely to be found in his leisure hours crawling along
beaches looking for sea slugs and standing on hilltops studying the
direction of the winds, correcting his theories by nature itself rather
than by indoors philosophising (ironic certainly, for someone who
argues that leisure is best spent in contemplative reflection).

It was of the greatest importance to Aristotle to argue against identifying the ethical life with a successful public life or a life of private
indulgence.[2] His point may seem obvious, but perhaps it still needs
arguing in every generation. Aristotle explains that the ethical life is
the life that most excels as a human life; the life in which the activities
and virtues necessary for fully human existence are best practiced. But
he does not think that a good life is all hard work and no play: sheer
pleasurable indulgence may be a childish end to live for, but true happiness requires time for leisure and its attendant relaxation and pleasures.[3] In fact, the central purpose of social and political life and of its
constitutive activities (business, military, government and so on) is the
building up and encouragement of leisure opportunities.[4] There seem
to be three clear ways in which a good human life involves leisure.

First, Aristotle argues we cannot engage in any activity continuously
without periods of leisure, what we might call 'recreational leisure'.[5]
The dedicated scholar, family man, or public figure needs time away
from the serious focus of his daily life. This allows for recovery, attention to personal needs, relaxation, and the opportunity for fresh
insights into his primary activities. Leisure here sometimes functions
as a purely external means (like money, opportunities, or liberty) to
continuing primary activities. But leisure also has an internal relationship to these activities: we can choose a leisure activity that serves and
perhaps increases the form of primary activity upon which we focus; so
politicians may choose to read political biographies, families to picnic
and play football together, scholars to read quality fiction and watch
good films.

In its second sense, leisure is not instrumental, but a constituent of
the good life itself. Leisure not only functions recreationally, but 'of
itself gives pleasure and happiness and enjoyment of life.'[6] According
to Aristotle's ethical theory, good people value and seek fulfilment of
their whole being (body, mind, imagination, sociability, sexuality, spirituality etc.); thus they make choices in accord with the virtues that
best shape each part of their being for fulfilment. But such virtuous

choosing requires a certain freedom from constraints and necessity (slaves in Aristotle's Greece lack leisure because they suffer complete constraint and dependence, hence their incapacity for fulfilment generally); it also requires a relaxed, calm frame of mind: 'enjoyment of life', or what we might call today a sense of well-being.

People flourish in the rational, balanced exercise of the virtues, and such a life requires freedom from pressing material concerns and constraints, a sense of ease and an interest in one's own life and future, and the leisure to deliberate options and to form and see through commitments.[7] As Elizabeth Telfer, writing on Aristotle, says, we need 'time in which people can do what they think worth doing for its own sake...[time] properly spent only if their activities are really worthwhile.'[8] Ethical leisure is necessary for growth in virtue, and it is increased by the practice of the virtues in activities which have value in themselves.[9] Leisure is therefore part of the complex good that we are to pursue for a fulfilled human life. Men and women concerned about their happiness and that of others have good reason to choose and to support 'ethical leisure'.

There is a third sense of leisure in Aristotle. Here, leisure is neither purely recreational nor a single component of the complex good life; rather, leisure is the capacity to reflect on the good, including the human good, on first principles, and on the meaning of the universe generally.

Aristotle famously makes a case for the activity of contemplation as the highest form of happiness.[10] He suggests that contemplation is sheer activity, or activity performed entirely for its own sake and for no end beyond its own continuation; it is also semi-divine activity in which the mind continuously and effortlessly engages with the highest objects.[11] He thinks this activity is the natural outcome of genuine leisure,[12] for contemplation is the natural condition of a rational being who has escaped everyday human limitations and worries and has fulfilled daily needs and responsibilities. When we are freed from pressing mundane concerns we are most truly at leisure and will then contemplate what is not quotidian: the higher things. This philosophical contemplation offers us absorption in, and a sense of identity with, the principles by which all things are explained.[13] Due to the utter satisfactoriness of this experience, our liberation from the mundane is extended, and we experience an easy and deeply fulfilling maintenance of this state in which our thoughts are at one with their lofty objects. Hence, 'contemplative leisure' has higher recreative potential than recreational leisure: if the latter is stopping for a much-needed sandwich at a filling station, the former is being invited to a banquet with the guests you have always wanted to meet.

Aristotle thinks contemplative leisure ('*theoria* gracing leisure'[14]) is the ultimate purpose of good human living, the true end of all our individual efforts and social interactions. Achieving contemplative leisure is our deepest happiness and the natural goal of politics, business, soldiering, scholarship, family life, and so on. For here we are free from all practical cares and anxieties; we express fully the most distinctively human (yet also most god-like) aspect of ourselves – our minds; we comprehend something of the highest truth about the universe; and we rejoice and are restored by the most blessed of human experiences.

Modern people often talk as if contemplation, if it occurs at all, is opposed to practical sense and practical activities: contemplation is other-worldly and only for the eccentric, gifted few. But practical persons – persons who live in the ordinary social world and aspire to lead morally good, valuable lives – have some good reasons for choosing contemplation in Aristotle's sense.

First, it is arguably the most perfect, enjoyable, and restorative leisure. Secondly, it is an important insight of Aristotle that virtue aims ultimately at freeing us from absorption in ethical reflection and practical decision-making.[15] We are not practical purely for the sake of becoming more practical. Rather (at least, for everyone apart from moral philosophers), where virtuous habits are developed, they liberate us from the effort of repeated ethical deliberation so that we can more easily enjoy the substantive human goods that are the point of ethics, such as socialising, art, worship, family life and contemplative leisure. Thirdly, whereas in all other human activities we continue to experience the anxiety of need and the urgency of finitude, in contemplation our activity responds to and increases our freedom from everything else. In contemplation alone, we are most utterly ourselves, neither constrained to serve nor concerned with need, but just present to ourselves as rational creatures whose activity is fully worthy of our reason. The freedom this offers, and the rational vision of life lived so as to be oneself, to be free, is surely attractive to busy practical reasoners.[16] Thus contemplative leisure is a coherent end of a genuinely practical life, something busy people might hearken after.

Contemplative leisure is Aristotle's main contribution to the philosophical history of the topic. Leisure involves turning from work, freeing oneself from striving after needs; thus it means opening oneself up reflectively to the world, contemplating at leisure – and without anxiety or urgency or an eye on the clock – our nature, our happiness, our place within the universe, and the universe's relation to God or the gods. This intellectual or even spiritual sense of leisure is what most who write on Aristotelian leisure have in mind. But I think it is important too to note that for him, the concept of leisure also includes recreation/restoration, and the facilitation and development of virtue. His view of leisure is an ideal that is psychologically realistic and ethically relevant, as well as intellectually, and perhaps religiously, satisfying.

Aristotelian leisure no doubt raises as many questions as it answers: what is the precise relationship of contemplation to the more familiar and knockabout leisure activities? Can leisure, particularly in this contemplative form, really be the key to all human happiness? Which contemporary leisure activities are likely to promote, and which to impede, leisure in each of Aristotle's three senses? I will answer some of these questions in my discussions in the following chapters. Aristotle is antidote to views of leisure as trivial, under-achieving, irrelevant to 'higher', activities; he is inspiration for leisure as an alternative to the social trivialisation spread by consumerism's apparent victory.

Aquinas: achieving bliss

Aristotle's work on leisure and contemplation is endorsed and developed by Thomas Aquinas. As a Dominican friar, contemplation and prayer, and the leisure to pursue them are of great personal importance to St Thomas. His most important works are texts designed to help young students of philosophy and theology and other beginners in faith to contemplate. This is not only a matter of helping them with their formal studies. Aquinas had particular devotion to the young not only as a beloved teacher but also as companion and counselor: he would send the novices of his Order off on picnics and advise them to rest and hold parties, at least from time to time. A vignette of this philosophy of life is found in his brief *Letter to Brother John: concerning how to study* (for Thomas, the key to study turns out to be understanding how to live).[17] Aquinas is also the author of wonderful contemplative hymns, in which people are exhorted to spend time with God in prayer since the wisest use of leisure is striving for sanctification.

Aquinas traces the leisure/contemplation link not only to Greek philosophy but also to early Christian tradition. He discusses St Augustine who explains that 'the love of truth seeks a holy leisure, the demands of charity undertake an honest toil.'[18] St Gregory agrees that leisure is needed for love, especially love of truth, but warns that 'there are some so restless that when they are free from labour they labour all the more, because the more leisure they have for thought, the worse interior turmoil they have to bear.'[19] Instead, we should seek to have the mind naturally pure and restful, so that we are ready for contemplation whenever an appropriate opportunity arises. Aquinas adds considerably more by way of a developed notion of contemplation; but he writes too on the play element in leisure. Play for him is good in itself and necessary for human happiness. And, as Aristotle too argued,[20] play has its own special virtue – *eutrapelia*.

Play has two elements: appropriate pleasure, and the relaxation or rest which comes after labour.[21] The theme of leisure time oriented towards rest after labour is common in Aquinas: 'leisure and play and other things pertaining to repose are pleasant, inasmuch as they banish sadness which results from labour.'[22] His main suggestion for the 'order' or direction of leisure is that within leisure activity, pleasure should be directed towards recreation and rest, and not *vice versa*. Does this mean that leisure and play are only instrumentally good, good only because their enjoyment makes relaxation more likely? It seems not, for in dealing with this objection Aquinas suggests that playful actions have no end beyond themselves – though the pleasure which partly accompanies and partly composes them does have the end of recreation and rest.[23]

Some may think play unworthy as a good in its own right, a frivolous use of leisure time that might be better spent, but in the Prologue to his *Commentary on Boethius's De Hebdomadibus* Aquinas strongly disagrees: 'playing has no purpose beyond itself; what we do in play is done for its own sake.'[24] So play not only offers rest from labour and preparation for further goal-directed activity; it also brings to fruition the human being's natural playfulness. Thus people who do not seek leisure, play, and the rest and pleasure they bring will suffer harm, and not just disinclination to continue working.

An important indication of the respect Aquinas has for leisure and play as necessary for happiness is his discussion of the virtues and vices that pertain to fun and games.[25] As he generally does, Aquinas lines up a formidable array of objectors to his own position: Ambrose, Chrysostom, Aristotle. He counters their objections to the very notion of virtue and high standards in play by appealing to the authority of Augustine: the wise man seeks not only work but also relaxation through playful words and deeds.[26] Since the life of the bodily senses is as natural to us as the intellectual life, one who lives for a time exclusively for the mind will then require to turn to sensory pleasures, on pain of weariness of soul. Playful words and deeds stir up pleasures that can refresh the soul, or inappropriately sought, can add to the soul's burdens. Thus it is important to take leisure rationally and to develop the special virtue that governs playfulness so that we are not tempted to waste leisure or to indulge in harmful pleasures. Whether we engage in play frequently because of the tiring nature of our work and other commitments, or only occasionally as an expression of our natural spirit of fun and play-fulness, play performed in accord with the virtue of *eutrapelia* will bring its own reward of a 'happy turn of mind' in the agent.[27]

Aquinas touches here on a matter of great importance to all who deal with play as part of leisure: namely, its status as activity not directed beyond itself. There are two senses in which play is not end-directed. First, like all necessary human goods, play is not directed towards any more ultimate end than itself: it is *itself* required for our happiness. But secondly, there is a special sense in which playful acts consist in doing things just for their own sakes: for unlike other activities that are ends in themselves (creativity, study, religion, friendship and so on), playful activities have no purpose beyond their activity. We create to produce a beautiful or useful object, study to know the truth, worship to praise God, form friendships to give and receive love; but when we play, we simply play. If we are playful, we do not play to win, or to exercise, or to enjoy ourselves: we play simply as an expression of playfulness. Play is rationally directed but directed at no other object; and when we enjoy our play and find it relaxing so much the better.

This notion of play as activity directed but not directed beyond itself – the enjoyment of actions simply because of what they are – offers insight into the notion of acting for something 'in itself'. This can be a difficult idea to grasp and to communicate: the very idea of a final end is so hard for many people to grasp today that it can seem almost impossible to teach philosophy students the theory of practical reasoning. But because play is so familiar, and un-threatening, it is particularly useful for illustrating that acting for the sake of truth, love, health, friendship, integrity 'in themselves' is not to aim at ('subjectivist') getting, or to stand before a valued good end with an ('objectivist') aspiration to it, but is rather to respond rationally to a connection we already have with that good. The most important goods are neither personally selected goods, nor remote, Platonic goods, but the flesh-and-blood goods of Aristotle.

Play represents activity that is not directed towards ends, but activity in which we rationally decide not to let reason have the whole say. In play, reason grasps that it is part of our nature not always to be scrupulously rational but sometimes just to abandon ourselves to the enjoyment of activity. The activity to which play bears most resemblance is of course contemplation, in Aristotle's sense of becoming one with the contemplated object. Aquinas brings fresh insight into the contemplative life, and it is for this as much as for his analysis of play that he is significant in the development of reflective leisure.

Aquinas is passionately in favour of the contemplative life, but argues for a contemplative existence beyond Aristotle's imagining: contemplation of truth is certainly higher than practical activity in service of daily needs, but passing on to others the truths contemplated is higher still; hence, the highest life is the active life of teaching (for Aquinas, the apostolic life).[28] This is not to argue that contemplation is valuable only as a means to teaching; for what is taught is what is contemplated, and it is taught precisely so as to encourage and direct greater contemplation; for Aquinas thinks that perfect happiness, for everyone, will only be found in endless, blissful contemplation of God.[29]

Of course, during earthly life this degree of continuous and perfect contemplation is not available; or perhaps available only to a few, such as St Paul who was snatched in rapture and temporarily granted the Beatific Vision.[30] Nevertheless, a paler version of happiness is possible for those who, like the philosophers and mystics,[31] commit themselves to study, understanding God and the highest things, and practising virtue amid the cares of daily life.[32] But such contemplative happiness will require once again liberation from practical and bodily necessities, and the leisure to reflect without threat or force.[33]

Kant: happiness and self-development

Kant does not enjoy a reputation as a warm or sociable man, but he seems to have understood the importance of recreation and amusement (at least in theory!) and cultivated these as best as he could: even in his lectures, the young Herder, a great thinker of the future, found Kant to be witty and entertaining. Past interpretations of his works portrayed him as a philosophical misanthrope, a man suspicious of pleasure; that is quite false, as any unprejudiced reading will show. Conviction that there is much more to moral obligation and virtue than securing and dispersing pleasures is not being a kill-joy about the appropriate place of pleasure in life.

Kant is the thinker who puts the unconditional value of the person at the base of ethics and politics; he elevates respect, freedom, and community life to the status of moral truths. In doing this, he creates the moral space within which everyday personal and social life – including leisure activities – can flourish, licitly and enjoyably. His theory is not a severe, Protestant ethics of duty but a true modern 'Stoicism' that requires us to honour ourselves, take our pleasures rationally, and develop to the full all our natural gifts and talents. Such a philosophy will not deny the value of a reasoned leisure. This will not, however, be leisure to contemplate, but leisure, in the first place, for pleasure and relaxation, and secondly, to prepare for our obligatory social contribution in ways that are natural and congenial to us.

Kant's conception of human happiness is based on the satisfaction of desires or inclinations.[34] Happiness is understood physically: it is being satisfied with my physical state. Inclinations are not wicked but a sign of lack and dependency, of something currently missing, and wanted; thus their satisfaction, and so our happiness, is acknowledgement of our dependency and incompletion. Achieving happiness has no positive implications for human freedom and dignity; in fact, it is a mark of human limitation and can be a cause of suffering and indignity.[35] Thus living for no more than happiness would be a life unworthy of rationality and moral agency; it would be world-conditioned living, not living in accord with a free response to objective values. Instead, we should live and choose for the sake of the objectively valuable moral law and its current embodiment in the reasonable choices of the free people and communities – choices that will often appear to agents as burdensome, precisely because of the universal human inclination towards personal happiness.[36]

Happiness should not be our principle of action, but it is clearly an aspiration of our nature and plays a part within our overall good. Kant criticises the Stoics precisely for exaggerating the self-sufficiency of moral worth and ignoring the role of personal happiness in our final end.[37] Happiness is a 'natural end': our goals cannot but include our own happiness.[38] It is because we inevitably seek happiness that seeking it is no part of our duty: 'an obligation to enjoyment is a manifest absurdity.'[39] Nevertheless, though not morally worthy, seeking happiness is good. And when sought in harmony with our obligations, happiness serves (along with morality) as part of the complete human good. Being as happy as we morally deserve to be is, for Kant, the highest good of all.[40]

As happiness plays such a significant part in ethics, Kantians cannot be kill-joys.[41] Kantians have no reason to repel feelings, fun, or play – nor do they encourage these only for the sake of encouraging people to do their duty.[42] Rather, they respect and pursue the affective life, and subordinate it, when they do, only to the necessary demands of moral law and human dignity.[43]

In practice, Kant thinks that we should enjoy some pleasurable aspects of sentient life because we *deserve* this enjoyment as the result of our morally permissible life and deeds; we should enjoy other pleasures because we *need* this enjoyment as part of our natural happiness; and other pleasures because without good feelings, particularly about our fellows but also about ourselves, we would take little *interest* in moral ends at all.[44] Neither here nor elsewhere does Kant discuss leisure in any detail. But it seems clear that leisure activities are morally unexceptional forms of the pleasurable sentient life; that leisure is often deserved by morally good people; plays an important part in our natural happiness; and promotes our moral efforts in various ways. Thus we should enjoy leisure, subject to, and subordinate to, the demands of the moral law.

Another major theme of Kantian ethics is the cultivation of our talents and gifts. We can consider this either from the perspective of satisfaction and happiness, or moral obligation and human dignity. Self-improvement is sometimes undertaken simply for the satisfaction it gives us (people today will talk about 'sense of well-being'). Satisfaction through developing our physical and mental powers, overcoming barriers, maturing intellectually, and so on, is of no specifically moral worth for Kant; again, it is part of our natural happiness. But self-development is tied up with the performance of our moral obligations in various ways.[45] For where someone does develop his intellectual, artistic, inter-personal, and other gifts, there is likely to be greater sensitivity to moral issues and appropriateness of moral response.

Our specifically moral obligations are not fully discharged just by avoiding adding to others' difficulties: however just our choices and our institutions, many people would still be left vulnerable if we did not all cooperate in acting kindly towards each other, and making intelligent decisions about the satisfaction of our common needs. Thus we have a moral obligation to make some social contribution, and it is reasonable to tailor our contribution by our individual gifts, tastes, and talents. Thus we should each make some effort to discern how best to use and develop our talents so as to support others, and we should organise our social lives to include this.[46] Talent-developing as a moral response is related to but distinct from talent-developing for personal satisfaction and happiness: the second is inevitable, though it should still be an occasion for self-improvement and not for vice; the first is part of rational self-control and compassionate response to the universal demands of moral law.

Some may object to the idea of a moral obligation to use our leisure opportunities in ways that will improve us, or allow us to do 'our bit' (sport done for the sake of building community spirit or training for future military service; country walking for stirring up environmental concern; cinema going for mental stimulation and improvement; hobbies developed to make useful products or sustain craft skills; and so on). But the idea is not that we have duties to recreate, in ways possibly against our wills, so as to be able to make a social contribution; rather, we have duties to cultivate gifts and talents we have already been blessed with and so already incline towards, and to make the fruits of their exercise available to those who would benefit from them. This is compatible with human dignity and autonomy: Kant would not seek to coerce the reluctant participant into games; but he would think that someone with natural sporting talent, background, and inclination would be the best sort of person to encourage in physical development and skills for their own welfare and that of the community.

Thus the justification of leisure is a matter of our natural endowments, our own needs and interests, and the justified interest of the community in the self-improvement and public spiritedness of its members.[47] Leisure is neither solely private nor public, but, in true Kantian style, is part of the rational individual's response to universal moral law and our shared vulnerabilities. Leisure is part of natural happiness since it satisfies inclinations, and part of our rationality since it develops self and sustains community. It also plays an indirect role in determining the quality of our lives, since the highest good is enjoying the natural happiness that we morally merit.[48] The good life will include leisure both for instrumental reasons (gaining happiness) and intrinsic reasons (serving moral law by developing talents), as Aristotle thought it would, but for very different reasons.

Wittgenstein: game-playing

The character of Ludwig Wittgenstein is about as far from that of the playful philosopher as it is possible to get. Two things redeem his play life: his veneration of and joy in classical music,[49] and his lifelong passion for westerns and detective stories.[50] But compared to his one-time friend, A. J. Ayer (a party-animal philosopher indeed), Wittgenstein is seriously deficient in jocularity. But Wittgenstein's thought is important in philosophy of leisure for at least two reasons. First, he is the philosopher of games *par excellence*, writing his philosophy in playful-forms that affect the actual substance of his thought. Secondly, the change in Wittgenstein's thinking from viewing language as an independent, abstract entity (the 'picture theory of meaning') to viewing it as a tool of human ingenuity, benefit, and delight ('language games') indicates modern philosophy's growing respect for such cultural realities as play, games, and other skilled performances, and the turn from subjective experience to social reality in order to explain meaning. With Wittgenstein, leisure activity is not for contemplation of eternal truths, but is a basic social reality; and it is the reality of games he adopts as key to the explanation of behaviour.

The history of Wittgenstein's gradual conversion to games as the reality that underlies language and so social communication itself is a wonderful tale which others have told.[51] The key concept is language game. This can be a purposeful use of language, for example, to command, request, assert, translate; but it is more properly an engagement in an activity structured by one of these sorts of language usage.[52] We not only ask questions, issue orders, assert facts: we also demonstrate an interest, assume responsibility, teach a class, close a deal; and it is what people actually do that Wittgenstein thinks philosophy should pay attention to. We perform activities, and do so successfully if we are grammatically competent language-users and socially competent game-players.

The theory of social life as linguistic life and of language use as game playing is an apparatus that applies the notion of play throughout the whole domain of purposeful human activity: all structured human activity is playing the language game that defines that particular activity. This raises two questions. Are Wittgenstein's language games really play? And if they are, what then is the language game that is play as we ordinarily understand it? Which 'playing' is leisure activity, as opposed to (playing at) commerce, family life, study, religion?

On the first question, 'game' can be an analogical term: language has a number of significant features in common with games (rules, social relationships, meaning, universality, adaptability and so on), therefore game playing is an excellent analogy for linguistic usage. On another reading, however, it is game playing and not language that is the primary concept: game playing is basic social reality. Here, language is the most significant species of game playing, and activities that use language are 'language games'. The more communicative the linguistic activity (that is, the more – and more diverse – people it addresses), the more perfect it is as game playing. On the first view, language 'games' are not play, though they have significant features in common with games and can be profitably explained as game playing; on the second, they are play – they are the most important form of game playing.

So is a language game only analogically play, or is it real play? The answer for Wittgenstein is 'both and neither'. For part of the genius of his account of play is the attempt to manoeuvre between the essentialist claim that all play has something in common that makes it really play and the nominalist claim that the only feature acts of play have in common is that we call them 'play'. The Wittgensteinian critique of this dichotomy consists in his notion of family resemblance.[53]

He asks what is common to all games, and he answers 'nothing' – but neither are all games arbitrarily so called; there are genuine similarities between various types of games but no one set of features which every game must possess. Thus football is like chess in involving two sides and a rule-book; and football, but not chess, is like lacrosse in requiring teams; and chess, but not football, is like tennis in having no fixed time span; and lacrosse is like hockey, but not football, in using a stick.... We can compare this to the 'trees' of resemblances between members of a family: they may share no single common 'essential' feature but neither is their relationship merely 'nominal': there are significant similarities and unique patterns of relationship between groups of members. Also, games are not bounded: there are no rules circumscribing the set of games or the territory of play. Thus modern diplomacy, politics, fantasy, romance, war, sport, commerce, indeed all decision-making, is often explained and often conducted as game; and actual games modelled on these primary activities are also popular.[54]

The answer to our question, then, is that language games are not 'merely analogies', nor are they 'really' (as opposed to just analogically) games. They share a family resemblance with certain other games and they can be as much – or as little – game playing as can football, banking, or political debates. And that is as much of an analysis of fun and games as Wittgenstein thinks we can give.

Then what of the activity of playing itself: what differentiates the (game of) playing games? Wittgenstein seems to think that the activities we describe as language games are based upon more primitive language games that are typical of our childhood play. Our childhood games become more sophisticated as we develop and construct relations between the concepts they utilise and between the games themselves. The whole family of games (including language games) is a development of this very basic form of game playing and it, if anything, is Wittgenstein's concept of play.

There is an important, if subordinate, role for this primitive game playing throughout adult life. Mastering sophisticated language games does not remove the need to continue just playing. In fact, the need to maintain and develop our skills at and interest in sophisticated game-playing and the need to tackle new forms of game due to our own and the world's progress means that the creativity, flexibility, and enjoyment of childhood games has an important place in adult life. Their value may only be instrumental, but real games and play have a structurally unique role. One particularly important reason for Wittgensteinians to play is that it keeps in shape our skill at following rules – a skill which involves intellectual dexterity and moral sensitivity as we try to combine respect for the principles underlying rule-governed practices with our responsibility for keeping the practice relevant, morally acceptable, and humanly fulfilling.[55]

Further insight into just what Wittgenstein understands by play comes from his *Remarks on Frazer's Golden Bough*. Wittgenstein objects to Frazer's attempts to make tribal customs intelligible to western people. He argues that this is to assume there are theories or beliefs underlying ritualistic practices, and this is precisely to miss the lesson that ritual teaches us. Wittgenstein's point is not that ritual is done for no reason, but that the reason involved is contained and expressed in the profound ritualistic significance of what is being witnessed, and to theorise about this is to eliminate it. Religious rites are not tokens of God-appeasement: they are themselves the enactment of actual sacrificial events; tribal rites are themselves expressions of fundamentally important realities, just as are the rites of the city-dweller's religion (confessing sins, venerating a relic, praying, adorning an altar etc.).[56]

Ritual is more serious than child's play, but we can learn something about play from ritual. The adult continues through hobbies, sports, and so on to practice and develop skills first explored in childhood games; so too he continues in symbol, liturgy, and what Wittgenstein calls 'magic' to express his primitive understanding that skilled human activity has value beyond its utility – an understanding so fragile it is easily lost as we 'mature'. The human gifts – intellectual, imaginative, passionate, social, physical – developed through play are also the gifts celebrated in ritual. Play and ritual are different activities belonging to the family of games, but they are more than just two more games: for play has as its object increase of our capacities for game-playing in general; and ritual expresses our acknowledgement that there is at stake in game-playing something of intrinsic value. The response to this value in sophisticated adult habits of game-playing is the closest Wittgenstein comes to reflective leisure.

Gadamer: play and festival

Hans-Georg Gadamer is best known for his significant work in hermeneutics; but he is an expert too in the interplay of philosophy, language, and literature, and his work on aesthetics has important insight into the nature of play. Again, Gadamer may not seem an obvious choice on leisure, for there is something formidable about the man and his work. Yet he was one of those Germans who elected to stay in their country through the 1930s and not to offer support to the regime (though he seems not to have spoken or worked against it either). He did attempt to keep ideology-free philosophy alive through the dark days. He taught even in his hundredth year, drawing great crowds, and discovering in retirement a new interest in travel, mainly through finally accepting invitations to speak at US universities. His thinking on play is the antithesis of the logician's dissection; in some ways, he helps us to place leisure in the humane and spiritual context Pieper had developed for it.

In *The Relevance of the Beautiful* Gadamer tackles the difficulties modern painting and music pose for many lovers of traditional art. He suggests this is not an isolated phenomenon peculiar to art, for 'in our daily life we proceed constantly through the coexistence of past and future. The essence of what is called "spirit" lies in the ability to move within the horizon of an open future and an unrepeatable past.'[57] But the gulf is perhaps greatest in the case of contemporary art, for here we are attempting to reconcile the modern notion of art as an autonomous activity (the subject of Kant's 'disinterested delight') with the older notion of works produced not just for the sake of art, but as expressions of faith, political principle, family status, and so on. To reconcile these two notions Gadamer suggests we turn to the more fundamental human experiences of play, symbol, and festival.

Like Pieper, he thinks culture is inconceivable without play. Play is not simply 'freedom from particular ends', which would be sheer randomness, but what Gadamer calls 'free impulse'.[58] The essence of play is free movement between poles which direct the movement but are not final goals of the activity. Aristotle explained living things as self-movers; play is simply self-movement directed to no particular end: 'a phenomenon of excess, of living self-representation'.[59] Human play, however, is characterised by reason and thus self-discipline and order, so in our play it is generally 'as if' purposes were involved. In fact, we do intend things in play but what we intend is not 'conceptual, useful or purposive'. So play is free movement, self-representation, and an opportunity for reason to structure non-purposive activities for us.[60]

Play is also a sort of communication for Gadamer. Those who witness play cannot help but 'go along with it' in some way; those who spectate are not mere observers of play but become participants. Thus play unifies otherwise solitary individuals. This thought has important implications for philosophy of art, and our concepts of symbol and festival.

Art (the 'play of art') is meaningful and so is to be explained by an account of symbol – not for Gadamer a simple matter of representation, but a question almost of sacramentality, of capturing some reality: 'the work of art does not simply refer to something, because what it refers to is actually there.'[61] This symbolic meaning will only be apparent to the viewer if he is already part of the relevant constituency or community and makes the intellectual and spiritual effort necessary to apprehend and be changed by the work. Art requires this communality, and seals it.

To understand this further, Gadamer investigates the notion of holding or celebrating a festival. In festivals we cease work – all activity that separates and divides us – and gather together to praise and enjoy what unites us. Festivals take us out of normal time into festive or liturgical time. Art has a festive character, for good art imposes its own time frame on us, moving us freely by means of our shared symbolic tradition.

Gadamer's aesthetics here touches on a number of important issues of play. But in particular, he suggests that the play of art allows us to catch sight of ourselves, to notice what we truly are, what we are really doing, and what we might be. Like leisure, art invites us to reveal ourselves. But Gadamer thinks that play and playfulness are more serious matters than leisure: 'is it not an illusion to think that we can separate play from seriousness and only admit it to segregated areas peripheral to real life, like our leisure time which comes to resemble a relic of lost freedom?'[62] Play should not be confined to leisure, for there is too little of that and often it is time trivialised. Also, play can be unwelcome, frightening, and sinister, not leisurely at all; for what is intended is the free play of individual spirit and this may take us where we would not choose to go. Play may take up our freedom but run with it beyond the region of our own free choice. Thus play can mean self-transcendence and freedom beyond leisure.

Recognising that play reconciles freedom and restraint (the 'ontological dignity' of play) clarifies that play is not separate from real life and is close to art. Those who play and know the importance of what they are doing can escape both mundane aspects of nature and the frivolous pleasures of society. Thus good playing can extend the sense of reality throughout our lives and introduce us to the importance of art. It can help not only to reclaim leisure from triviality, but also to open up freedom's proper reach, even beyond leisure, throughout the activities of civilised life.

Williams, Nagel, MacIntyre: life's meaning

Williams, Nagel, and MacIntyre are three of the most important philosophical writers of the last (and the previous) generation. Each is a fine speaker and an important public intellectual, as well as a university teacher. But the notion that we should know something of their hobbies and leisure interests so as to help us to understand their thought on leisure would probably seem odd to each of them, and to most other philosophers today. It helps to understand the genesis of Aristotle's view of leisure to know that he spent leisurely hours in empirical research, that Aquinas spent leisure time in prayer, Kant in self-disciplined habits and excellent teaching, Wittgenstein in private reading and viewing, Gadamer in taking to expanding his horizons late in life. But contemporary philosophy's 'professionalisation' means that there is a strong separation between scholarly public work and private life. It would appear rude for a stranger to phone up a professor of philosophy at home and ask what he did with his spare time; bizarre to suggest we need this kind of knowledge to help us to appreciate his philosophy. Whether this professional, and distinctly 'non-leisurely', approach to philosophy is a good or a bad thing can only be judged by the depth of insight thinkers attain relative to their predecessors.

Analytic moral philosophy is quite seriously hampered in dealing with topics like leisure (or work, religion, family, friendship, commerce and so on) by its self-definition as the study of metaethics, normative ethics, and applied ethics. Topics such as leisure tend to be ignored, or relegated to specialist applied ethicists, or treated as subjects of occasional addresses in festschrifts and the like. Moral philosophers could learn much from ancient and medieval ethics, for which study of substantive, real life topics such as leisure is of great importance. But the divide is not as great as it once was: key ancient and mediæval concepts (flourishing, virtues, practical reason, conscience and so on) have had a good effect on recent analytic moral philosophising, and with these concepts comes discussion of related practical topics.

Williams, Nagel, and MacIntyre are at the forefront of using traditional concepts to oppose the sterility once characteristic of twentieth century ethics. They have helped to revive philosophical questions about the meaning of life, and a broader conception of ethics than the once standard moral frameworks of deontology and consequentialism offered. The (very different) visions of the good life they argue for all include a role for non-moral but valuable activities such as leisure.

Bernard Williams's *Ethics and the Limits of Philosophy* gathers together a number of insights from Greek practical thought and directs them towards an expose of modern morality and modern moral thinking. Building on some groundbreaking work of Elizabeth Anscombe, Williams suggests a distinction between ethics and morality: 'morality should be understood as a particular development of the ethical, one that has a special significance in most Western cultures.'[63] Socrates' Question had been 'What must I do to live well?' But there is a difference between living well and doing right. Doing right – which Williams understands as following the obligations of universal morality – is certainly one important response to Socrates' question; but it is a response that Williams thinks we should scrutinise and ponder well. Moral philosophy may not be the best way in which to think ethically. A more all-round good life may be a finer thing than a faultless moral life.

Williams does not systematically identify the actual features of a good life, but it is clear from his discussion that it will be a reflective life, a life of virtuous activity, a life too that includes welcome social attachments, and goods such as work and leisure that are necessary for the development and enjoyment of a human life. The good life will be composed of choices directed towards such objectively good ends, rather than choices that merely satisfy individual wishes, or possession of objectively good things without personal choice of these as our ends.

Williams's conception of the good life thus includes not only morally required activities, but activities in whose performance we are at ease and self-sufficient: activities we choose, and choose because they achieve what we can recognise as substantive good for ourselves or others. The classification of ethics as seeking the good life and morality as seeking the obligated (good, though restricted) life makes it possible to identify leisure – an activity in which we are very much at ease and self-sufficient – as a central ethical activity.

On the other hand, Thomas Nagel's presumption is in favour of the obligations of universal morality over those of the good life more broadly construed; though he acknowledges some creative tension between the impersonal standpoint of morality and the other demands made upon individuals.[64] Sometimes, however, the moral life will be a worse life than its alternatives. Then the most we can say is that we hope the reasons for acting morally will always outweigh our other reasons. There is one criticism by Williams, however, which Nagel is keen to see off: Nagel thinks following universal moral obligations does not require alienating ourselves from our deepest projects and commitments, as Williams believes. Nagel thinks that to hold this is to fail to understand the seriousness and significance of morality: morality should enter deeply into everyone's serious projects and personal commitments. Ideally, the moral life is not an alternative to the good life but the most human and fulfilling version of the good life; a life in which everyone can reconcile their personal tastes and habits with the demands that are made of all persons.

Nagel's view is not, however, a denial of the non-moral aspects of the good life; in fact, in attempting to address the grand question of the meaning of life Nagel strongly rejects identifying oneself solely with morality.[65] Such dreams of escaping from 'subjectivity' are as hopeless as the alternative of identifying ourselves solely with the subjective viewpoint and attempting to jettison morality. If I am to judge my life to be of any significance at all, I require the objective, as well as the subjective, viewpoint. We are all necessarily aware of both detachment and engagement, burning interest and cool indifference; we are creatures of an 'absurd' tension between the universal and the particular, the public and the private.

Since this gap is unavoidable, the project of self-integration must be our life's work. In the attempt to reach an integration that allows for tranquility and happiness, two issues become very important to us: first, the moral life in which we wrestle with questions of our own interests and the interests of others; and secondly, those activities in which we can briefly step aside from the public/private gap. Nagel turns here to a form of reflection – not for him the contemplation of timeless truths (for this would be to fall back into the universal and public). Rather, he thinks that by reflecting on a particular, concrete thing and allowing it to absorb us completely – as we do in aesthetic response, for example – the difference between objective and subjective viewpoints may temporarily lose its significance.[66] 'Particular things can have a noncompetitive completeness which is transparent to all aspects of the self.'[67]

This is a different understanding of reflection from the Aristotelian tradition, for with Nagel we step aside not only from our everyday activities, but also from the contemplation of timeless truth and realities: we require leisure from work *and* from contemplation so as to lose ourselves in objects. The value of this reflection is that it heals the self and makes it possible to live on the edge of an abyss without distress, at least for periods. Thus we can experience a certain integration and hold that life has some meaning, that it is not utterly absurd. Yet Nagel's position is uneasy. For him, leisure is needed urgently, like a drug; we are far from the ease of reflective leisure, and very far indeed from the sense of play that accompanies it.

Other contributors to contemporary ethics have a more positive vision for leisure. Alasdair MacIntyre argues that games and other play are examples of 'practices'.[68] Practices are marked by internal goods: goods obtainable in no other way than engagement in that particular practice. The external goods a practice affords (goods also obtainable in other ways) are always someone's possession and thus potential objects of competition; but with internal goods, 'it is characteristic of them that their achievement is a good for the whole community who participate in the practice.'[69] Practices also include standards of excellence ('virtues'), and require obedience to rules. Growth in excellence and better understanding of the rules develops our grasp of and love for the goods and ends at stake in the practice. This in turn will lead to evolving mature and open relationships with fellow practitioners and so contact with the developing history and tradition of the practice. Entering practices meaningfully, then, is entering relationships and traditions, and engaging in them in excellent ways – in particular, MacIntyre thinks, by respect for objective excellences such as justice, honesty, and courage.

On this account, games and other leisure activities have a clear and important role in the good life: 'tic-tac-toe is not an example of a practice in this sense, nor is throwing a football with skill; but the game of football is, and so is chess.'[70] MacIntyre here avoids a grand, metaphysical conception of the human purpose and of our individual goods and ends. He argues that what we are is largely what we inherit. The practices, relationships, communities, and traditions that are our history are also our present, and so indicate in broad strokes what our futures will be like; and these activities will include at least as many leisure activities as work activities: after all, twenty first century jobs such as

IT consultancy are less a practice and a tradition than football or choral singing.[71] Furthermore, it is clear from his most recent work that MacIntyre sets great store by the importance of play in our development as thinkers and agents.[72]

MacIntyre argues that engagement in practices and traditions brings unity to a life because one's life thereby tells a story intelligible in terms of those engagements, involvements, relationships, and past experiences. In other words, human life has a narrative structure: each life is unified by the plot of the story that it tells.[73] To be a story-telling animal is to live out a tale that has not yet reached its end; we are always testing and developing the ends of our stories and, to some extent, the very rules by which our stories can proceed. This is perhaps the most play-like aspect of MacIntyre's thesis. If we are not existentially free for MacIntyre, then neither are we mechanistically determined: narrative has genuine inventiveness and indeterminacy but coherence, and this is close to the sort of free-play discussed by Gadamer and Huizinga.

MacIntyre's preferred term for the activity of story-tellers is 'quest': a journey with an end which the journey itself must help to define. Quest is perhaps the most serious sort of play we face.[74] Quests are enthralling (everyone loves the stories of the Golden Fleece, the Holy Grail, the fountain of youth, lost treasure, the new frontier, the Lord of the Rings and so on). Quests are exciting to take part in (at least when we are young), to recount, and to hear about. Active human life is an adventure: uncertain in its outcome, requiring inventiveness and high standards of virtue and skill, shared with others, and governed by rules that are adjudicated by authorities which have the living traditions of the questors genuinely at heart. Human life, in other words, is a particular form of drama: a play of sorts. And if our drama has no pre-fixed purpose, no metaphysically constraining goal, it is (like all play) a story told purely for its own sake, absorbing, often fun, sometimes a little somber, and quite serious.

Many other great philosophers have written about leisure. The figures chosen here are meant only to illustrate something of the history, potential, and the pitfalls, of thinking about leisure in western philosophy. In Chapter 2, I present an account of leisure and relate it to various other relevant concepts, and to the main alternative view: consumerist leisure. Then in Chapter 3, I will discuss the place of leisure in our lives and our happiness, and thus offer some philosophical justification for accepting my account. We will then be in a position to examine various popular leisure activities, and also leisure's relationship to work and art.

Although I make most use of ideas derived from Aristotle, Aquinas, Pieper, and Huizinga, the thought of other thinkers introduced in this chapter – on contemplation, bliss, satisfaction and talent developing, games, festival, and life's meaning – will have some part to play in my argument.[75]

2
Reflective Leisure

One approach to reflective leisure would simply note that today 'leisure' means something very different, that the world has moved on and leisure developed in ways that take account of new realities and modern societies' needs. That the world has moved on from the 1950s and leisure changed radically is undeniable.[1] The move has been towards readier access to leisure, encroachment of certain leisure activities (for example, TV watching and shopping) over more and more of our lives, identification of key fashionable activities with leisure activity, and more immediate, guaranteed fun through leisure. Yet mass leisure, because it has largely depended upon making money for providers who sell leisure opportunities to consumers, has also diminished choice and obscured the appeal of leisure activities that cost little and may give few quick thrills, but do provide longer term investment, a gradual sense of understanding and contentment, and sustained personal recreation.

Pre-consumerist leisure often required fewer external resources and relied more upon utilising and developing people's inner resources – imagination, will, intelligence, wit, love. A busy life or a life of deprivation can often be borne if people can find pockets of leisure in which the anxieties of buying and selling, the pressure to work, and the fear of serious loss are neutralised by play, or gathered up into our reflection, pondered, and better understood or accepted. The commercialisation of leisure has meant an ideological move from simple play and sound reflection; that is, from inner resources, wise use of personal time, investment in knowledge, and delight and wonder in our daily lives. The move has been towards fun and fashion, pampering rather than developing, lifestyle rather than living, buying into activities that are more isolating, though easily repeatable. In short, we have commodified leisure.

31

The main justification for this change is 'democratic': 'this leisure is available to all', and 'this is what the people want.' In fact, what mass leisure has meant is vastly expanded opportunities to buy from providers (a natural outlet for our post-WW II 'disposable income'), and reduced social encouragement of activity that has no price tag but that serves personal needs for understanding, growth, rest, and renewal.

Despite consumerism's reach, people continue to rebel against the idea that they are slaves of the market: people deny that their vision is reduced to the commercial opportunities made available to them; deny that their every value can be represented in cash-or-status terms. Most people still want to see themselves as in charge, bold, and individual; as better educated, more probing, more autonomous than their forebears. It is fortunate that we do still possess something of this vision and self-image, for it means that reclaiming leisure is still a possibility. It is of course already a reality for many people: some do try for a more reflective leisure within a generally hostile society, or hear of it from inspiring teachers, pray for it, or urge it upon their children. Reflective leisure is not yet an alien concept. But since its appeal depends upon a sense of the incompleteness of consumerism, consumerism's vast scope and power do too often make reflective leisure appear dull, elitist, idealistic, even to people who claim not to be committed consumerists. Similarly, play is made to appear wasteful, trivial, embarrassing, even to people who claim not to be work-obsessed.

Unmasking consumerism is largely a matter of altering people's perception of what now appears natural, or at least inevitable: like changing people's beliefs about God, it is more a matter of perception than accepting philosophical proofs. The first task then is to shed some light on consumerism – to strip a few layers from familiar 'reality' – and then to propose playful and reflective leisure as aspects of a different way in which people can think and live.

Consumerism

Consumerism is the main experience of social life and basis of social understanding for many, many people. Most of us take consumerism's burdens and benefits for granted. It has brought astonishing benefits to whole populations: safe, reliable, and available food and water; easily available healthcare and hygiene; mass produced buildings, furniture, clothes, and tools that free us from personal manufacture; easy transport and communications; instant internetted communication; and on and on. No one can deny these benefits; my interest, however, is in the burdens also brought by such an empire. The consumerist experience is complex. First, it is exposure to and belief in an ideology: acceptance of a simple and convincing explanation of how society works and what is important; an explanation that captures the wishes and hopes of a powerful majority of people. We meet ideologies everywhere, and it takes determination to identify and question them, especially given their connection with powerful constituencies and vast majorities, and more especially when they seem to have great explanatory power or provide comfort and security.

But consumerism is an economic imperative as well as an ideology: it is a theoretical economic position and set of policy positions. Because people in consumerist societies need to take part in that economic system in order to survive, they are required to live by and protect the rules of the system. This economic system would be more economically vulnerable than it is, more open to question by theoretical economists and policy analysts or even by ordinary people, if it stood alone. But combined with the supporting ideology, consumerist economics becomes immensely stronger, fortified as it is by the beliefs and activities of millions of people. Similarly, the ideology by itself without the supporting economy would lose appeal and coherence: the critiques of moral thinkers – from radical socialists to the Pope – would have much more effect if the ideology were not also supported by global economic reality. When the irrepressible force of the free market and consumerist political ideology meet, the result is compelling and seems irrefutable.

Consumerism's strength lies not just in its benefits and its welcome by millions. Consumerism is strengthened by what I will call its 'total logic'. By total logic I mean a number of things. First, the term refers to a set of beliefs that seeks to give serious answers to the most fundamental questions. Some belief systems may be unreflective, have no body of serious argument and no historical development behind them, or may not address questions believers themselves hold to be important: a total logic, however, refers to serious beliefs about important matters. Secondly, total logic refers to a set of beliefs that form a system: beliefs are not only compatible, but are logically connected so as to form a consistent vision or philosophy that unites the serious answers it offers to important questions. Thirdly, because it refers to a consistent vision or world view, a total logic is the basis of its adherents' practical evaluations. Ascribing to a world view means recognising a certain body of belief as providing one's basic reasons for action – and excluding other beliefs from such a role.

Not all worldviews exhibit a total logic. Thus some people endorse and act for the sake of more than one world view: one can be a political conservative and a Buddhist, attempting to identify, or perhaps increase, the overlap between the two. Others endorse a world view but only allow it to affect their decision making occasionally: for example, certain Christians today. Yet others endorse only some propositions of a world view, for example, those free masons who enjoy the philanthropy but not the cosmology, or skeptics in the classroom who happily trust in the laws of gravity and the highway code when in the outside world. In their own terms, these world views allow for partial endorsement or occasional observation. With a total logic, however, we meet a world view which, as we shall see, we cannot combine with any other, must always act upon, and must endorse in its entirety. These 'musts' are genuine: partial acceptance of a world view that possesses a total logic is not acceptance of that world view at all.

The two most common types of total logic are ideological world views and world views supposedly based on divine revelation. The most obvious instance of the latter is Catholicism. Catholics believe in doctrines that provide serious answers to the most important human questions, form a world view, and have thoroughly worked out relations to their beliefs and activity. Moreover, they hold these beliefs because they believe that the doctrines are revealed by God through Scripture and the teaching of a God-founded Church. Belief in divine revelation entails not just inerrancy, but also scope for the world view: picking and choosing certain Catholic beliefs, combining Catholicism with other world views, or choosing just when I am willing to act on beliefs is not being Catholic. Instead, it is selecting some other criterion of belief and action over a world view which claims already to provide all necessary criteria.

Ideological total logics also depend upon a set of doctrines offering serious answers to fundamental questions, a world view, and a practical stance. Those who believe in such ideologies accept the world view because it seems to explain the workings of society and captures the wishes, assumptions, and hopes of the dominant majority to which the believer belongs, or aspires to belong. Marxism would be a good example of such a total logic held by many people back in the twentieth century.

The clearest example of an ideological world view today is consumerism. Consumerists appeal to bodies of social and political thinking to justify the answers they give to the most important human questions as serious answers. These answers always assume it is good to extend commodities and services over all areas of human life and culture; they also stigmatise non-material activities, choices, and lives as not sufficiently serious. Close personal identification with material goods and ambition for more and better goods is always seen as right; social aspiration based on this is worthy and represents admittance to a privileged lifestyle based on wealth and certain forms of expenditure, with loss of youth, looks, and health the only spectres at the feast – though even these can be prolonged with wealth. Thus consumerist answers can pay lip-service (at best) to values that are not commodities and choices that are not for enhanced social status through on-going and ever-greater participation in material consumption.[2]

Because they believe in an ideology, consumerists also have a particular view, explained by the principles of their ideology, of what the most important *questions* are: these generally concern how to improve one's material and social position, how to acquire dignity and status through ownership, how to reduce deprivation and indignity by protecting oneself against material poverty, and how to extend one's rights to purchase, use, transfer, and so on. The answers to these questions form a simple system that appeals to the clear, self-regarding instincts that help to account for the ideology's success. And the whole system in turn provides a very simple ethical and political stance: hedonistic, egotistic, advancing personal ownership, and disregarding existential questions unless asking, answering, encouraging, or ridiculing them has some commercial or status value. Contracts and collaborative activities can be dressed up as altruistic and communitarian, but under consumerism they too are self-serving.

Consumerism cannot be combined with any other world view. It may sometimes appear that we can be a consumerist Buddhist, consumerist Socialist Worker, consumerist Calvinist; but in fact, consumerism eats up the partner world-view. That is, it treats Calvinism itself as another commodity to be 'used' when it does not challenge consumerist status and values, and otherwise to be set aside. Also, we cannot be occasional consumerists. Consumerist goods are designed to alter the way in which we satisfy and even identify our needs. This means that losing a commodity makes it very hard indeed not to replace it. For example, I buy a plastic pen, and so come to write within a certain time-scale based on the pen's quality and reliability; I adapt my work, my expectations, and the expectations of others around this item; but the item is manufactured to have a certain life-span and when that expires, given the new expectations, I have good reason to replace it; also, during its lifespan, the pen requires various other items (refill, new clip) each of which locks me in to other replaceable commodities; and when the pen breaks down, I am required to take it to a shop that sends it to a factory that... Being a consumerist means being a full-time consumerist.

Finally, one cannot be consumerist only about certain items. Any one act of consumerism involves us in countless other and earlier transactions. Thus a simple act like buying a pen requires me to have earned money, but also to have bought paper, to have read books, worn clothes, eaten food, obtained an education, and taken part in countless ways in the dominant consumerist culture. A man who attempts to be non-consumerist for one day a week will find his 'perfect', consumption-free Sunday structured by consumerist sub-logics regarding food, reading matter, transport, clothing, entertainments, and so on that he must observe on this and the preceding and following days.

Consumerism is not only an ideological total logic; it is also an imperialising ideology. That is, the system is successful not only in locking people in to it, but also in colonising more and more of human life, human value, and human experience. So used are we to the appearance and effect of consumerism at the heart of family life, sport, the arts, religion, healthcare, that many of us now hardly ever question its legitimacy. Irritability or embarrassment are often felt, but these are among the emotions that last only a short period. Even new ethics is crafted by some thinkers to serve the interests of the vast Empire, for example, 'preference-satisfaction utilitarianism'. And, like other total logics, consumerism immunises against criticism. Critics of consumerism are tagged as benighted at best, communist at worst, enemies of human happiness in any case. Anyone who wants to raise questions from within is now likely to have to use consumer tools (for example, internet chat rooms) to do so, and may very well be compromised in the process.

Occasionally, public intellectuals worry about 'the market' rearing its head where it should not. But consumerism was exhibiting strong imperialist tendencies long before the 1980s expansion of the free market. Expansion of the market is a development of the economic consumerist system; the ideology of consumerism was already hell-bent on conquest of territory twenty years before.

I use 'imperialising' here as an evaluative term; it implies a judgement on my part. 'Total logic', however, is not an evaluative term. Belief in certain experiences of divine revelation may be good and belief in certain ideologies may be good, thus a certain total logic may be good. But belief in consumerist ideology is not good. Aspects of the ideology may have saved lives and answered dreams; elements of rationalist economics may have given a new start and raised aspirations; but when we combine consumerism's total logic with its substantial beliefs that the reasons for action are commercial opportunities, that free choice is adaptation to fashionable options, and that the standard of value is whatever earns more money for rich providers and future consumers, then consumerism is exposed. It has barred or limited access to key aspects of human experience; it has perverted society's understanding of freedom to choose; it has diminished our practical reasoning, in particular about ultimate ends and appropriate means; preyed on gluttony and greed; and it has blunted our understanding of happiness, so that only the very simplest utilitarianisms are today descriptive of social reality. One small part of this destructive total logic is the commodification of leisure.

Consumerist leisure

The story of leisure in the twentieth century turns upon the rejection of eternal realities and spiritual truths. With no God, cosmic answers, or first principles there is nothing worthy of contemplation; leisure, then, quietly drops the contemplative ideal and dedicates itself not to other reflective experiences that divert us from our daily burdens, but instead to securing interesting and enjoyable experiences that are within our price range or, preferably, just above it.

If we do not believe in God, ultimate values, or an afterlife, then naturally we will hope for heaven here and now, and commercial leisure provides the simplest sort of heaven – the opportunity amidst cares and uncertainties for comfort and excitement without having to set aside our everyday props of transactions and commodities. By the time Pieper came to offer his diagnosis, leisure had already been transformed into purchase of trivialities or tranquilities, with this new development often justified in a strained version of Aristotelianism as our reward in our 'own time' after the rigours of daily work.

Consumerist leisure has a nice face and a nasty face. The nice face expresses increased freedom and individual choice. Leisure is our free time, time that is structured by us without unwelcome constraints. This echoes the Aristotelian tradition that we work so as to enjoy leisure. In modern leisure we are said to meet ourselves (or at least our own wishes), exercise choice, and are creative or responsive, as opposed to merely obedient to employers. This nice face, however,

soon clouds. Aristotle's leisure was not infected by any total logic, ideological or revealed; hence, standing back from necessity was an adventure and a challenge, the opportunity to use freedom for the sake of
contemplation, an encounter with one's own true self and with ideas
that really matter. But consumerism means that it is now very difficult
for people to stand outside necessity. When work ceases, there is the
demand and urge to use its fruits to buy, repair, replace, and engage
with fellow workers in the leisure industry. This industry has fully
understood the total logic, and now provides endless opportunities for
us to have leisure time ('quality time') without feeling the need to
avoid commercialisation, or to seek our true selves, or any other truth
outside the familiar borders of purchasing and advertising. Thus the
most popular leisure activities in the US today are visiting shopping
malls and watching TV.[3]

So the nasty face of consumerist leisure expresses acquisitiveness,
possessiveness, what the ancient Greeks called *pleonexia*: the desire for
more than one's appropriate share. Work is both cause of and imposi-
tion upon the drive to buy, to use, and to buy bigger. All time outside
work is time to seek leisure that escapes the obligatoriness of work,
but in fact it makes work, for purchaser and provider. We are never
away from commercialised work and its environment. Al Gini writes:
'Simply put, we have become addicted to the fruits of our production...We have deconstructed Aristotle's adage "the purpose of work is
the attainment of leisure" to the far baser notion "I work in order to
consume and possess."'[4] The paradox around obligation-free leisure
time is the driven quality, the compulsions and obsessions around purchase and use, to which many people are vulnerable due to the sheer
vastness and success and ease of consumerism. For those relatively
immune, there is self-doubt and others' scorn at their lack of participation in the malls, cinemas, fashions, and leisure complexes. Bizarrely,
in 'sophisticated', commodified leisure, adults are returned to the days
of childish play and dependency, unwilling, and perhaps eventually
unable, to aspire higher than towards the proffered excitements and
comforts.

The freedom shown by the nice face is the value that consumerist
ideology is most proud of protecting and serving. But as all first year
philosophy students learn, freedom is not being told 'okay, you're free
to choose whatever you want'. Freedom is not just familiarity and
dexterity with the structures of practical decision making: it is understanding that life includes time in which we are alone with ourselves
(and perhaps our God), liberated time unburdened by external

pressures and with no obligation except for the rational creature's unavoidable obligation to think seriously about the truth of things. In sacrificing meaningful freedom, consumerist ideology has failed to protect its own highest value.

In search of a satisfactory account of freedom within a classic account of leisure, Martin Davies describes the way in which good leisure will grant us a world of our own. This is something that should matter for each of us because 'in contemporary society the private realm is a dismal sphere of frustration, boredom, and neurosis.'[5] Our modern stresses may be relieved if we can recover leisure as commitment to time and choice that are truly ours, not others' convenience or profit; leisure that nurtures interests of deepest importance to us, and that represents our honest attempt to be ourselves and not to reflect the restricted fare provided by those who decide what we should want.

But even if we can describe the concept of a better leisure, of what use is it if no one wishes to adopt it? How can it compete with the seductive and easy offers on the consumerist menu? The answer is that it cannot. In diagnosing the leisure crisis decades ago, Sebastian de Grazia wrote that 'the commercial spirit, in business and government both, has no interest that any such ideal [of leisure], without spending attached to it, should come to prevail.'[6] And De Grazia explains that this situation cannot be improved by offering the commercial world better arguments, for 'if [the life of leisure] could be justified in terms of the state, then we could speak of its function. If we could do this, the life of leisure would no longer be free. It would have a determined relation to the state. It would become a state functionary.'[7] We cannot justify anything like contemplative leisure to the contemporary world, for talk of buying, selling, status, fame, power, money – all of the contemporary justifications – would cancel out its reflective status.

I believe that we have to accept de Grazia's position, and I will argue in Chapter 3 that the only way in which to propose a radically different leisure today is to reject the total logic of consumerism. This claim will no doubt sound utterly unrealistic to most ears – though it may well be possible to retain *some* of the up-sides of consumerist economies and polities in a new conception of leisure. We can begin here by indicating that wanting to revive what I call reflective leisure is not as unreasonable as some might think. One way in which to do this is to argue that consumerist leisure is simply not working and that a choice to continue as we are may be too costly; another is to reclaim for modern leisure the notion of ideals; a third is to argue that modern people are not actually happy with consumerist leisure at all, and thus may be more open than is imagined to discarding the ideology.

To take these three ways of arguing in order, first everyone agrees that stress and tension are serious modern problems. Whereas once these were suffered by people with antecedent mental disorders or episodic depressions; today they are suffered by many people much of the time. Yet recent research suggests that Americans have more free time today than thirty years before: that people have greater leisure potential, yet still feel rushed and tired.[8] This suggests that stress and tension will not be reduced by more consumerist leisure. We are repeatedly exhorted to buy more and more holidays, treatments, trips, entertainments; but it is not lack of contemporary leisure opportunities that creates mass human dissatisfaction: it is the altered attitude towards life that commodified leisure, as one part of the total logic of consumerism, represents and encourages. I will argue in the next chapter that contemporary leisure has significantly undermined our potential for fulfilment, and that the most serious element of this has been impeding our share in recreation. The cost of consumerist leisure on our psyches and happiness is good reason to revisit our commitment to consumerism and so to investigate reflective leisure.

Secondly, Gerald Fain discusses the fact that leisure is now synonymous with any free time activity or relaxed state; instead of offering an ideal for life, leisure is just enjoying what industry sells us.[9] He asks, can we really afford to reduce the noble ideal of freedom to live as one chooses to spending time and money on commercialised pleasure? Fain's is an important attempt to reconnect with the Aristotelian tradition by reminding people of the need for and the power of ideals. Cyril Barrett too distinguishes the idea of leisure as free time and rest spent doing what I want and doing it for its own sake, from the ideal of leisure, which includes contemplation, creativity, and play.[10] For these writers, 'ideal' does not mean 'idealised', 'idealistic', 'impractical': it means 'inspiring', 'inexhaustible', 'always worth striving for'.

Even Aristotle recognised that few mortals could give most of their time to contemplative leisure, and even they would need some friends, material satisfactions, and 'time out'; but at least every mortal can commit himself never to choose what is incompatible with the ideal of contemplative leisure. No one needs to choose what directly conflicts with the high ideals of reflection, study, and time free from daily chores; no one needs to choose so as to disqualify themselves from this activity, or to hinder others from achieving it, or to obscure its appeal. Ideals are actually best, not worst, when they are high: for high ideals are not remote; in fact, they are closer to people's hearts than ideals just a few notches above the everyday. Few people can continue to live by their own best standards unless those standards are fixed to some ideal, and yet that is a thought alien to contemporary consumerism whose 'ideal' states are easy, reachable, replaceable, and always negotiable.

Thirdly, John Kelly and Geoffrey Godbey have argued that even if people are happy spending their leisure time watching TV or visiting shopping malls, the debate does not stop there.[11] Their research indicates that people value leisure activity more highly when there is sustained commitment to development of skills and knowledge, and social communication and interaction. Here, they cite Mihalyi Csikszentmihalyi's important work on the concept of flow, the optimal psychological experience that gives meaning to life and which Csikszentmihalyi's research indicates modern people are twice as likely to find at their work than in their leisure activities.[12] Furthermore, they cite evidence that people are much less attracted to and satisfied by commodified leisure than anecdotal evidence suggests.

Kelly and Godbey's argument is important. If they are right, then consumerist leisure has already begun to lose its grip. If so, this is probably because of (very) slowly dawning dissatisfaction with consumerist ideology itself, rather than a positive attraction to a more reflective ideal of leisure. Yet these tendencies will support each other: a more challenging and spiritually uplifting leisure life will help to question the dominant ideology, and a desire to escape the total logic will create new needs for the human spirit to be challenged and deepened. Having argued that leisure must be a life of discipline not just consumption of trivial experiences, Kelly and Godbey conclude: 'It must also produce and reflect the spiritual impulse. The transition to a society of leisure dreamed of by humans for centuries, is today not so much a matter of technological advance but of understanding the basis upon which the universe, all life within it, and even our very selves can be celebrated and are therefore sacred.'[13] If there is already sociological evidence that people are more open to such an ideal than before, there is certainly reason to set out the ideal in some detail and to suggest justification for a more reflective leisure that can stand as alternative to consumerist leisure.

Reflective leisure

My alternative will consist of: *leisure activities*, which, since they stand outside our work and daily pressures, will be opportunities for *play* and *reflection*; the goal of *recreation*, a part of human nature and an element in well-being, and achieved ordinarily through leisure activity; and experiences of *relaxation* and *fun*, which are by-products of play and at their most satisfying when play and reflection combine in our leisure choices. After discussing these ideas, the next chapter will consider in more depth the relationship between leisure, recreation, and other parts of our well-being.

As others have argued, leisure is a way of life, not a period of time;[14] and although we all need rest and recovery after busyness, resting is not a way of life; thus there is more to leisure than just playing so as to rest. Aristotelian leisure focuses on activity, and particularly the activity of contemplation as the highest way of life. Paradoxically, in contemplation, we are most truly active, least passive: we are open to, potentially, all truth and all meaning, and we move naturally from simpler to deeper and more lasting understanding of the world. The ancients and medievals recognised that leisure mattered because leisure prepares and then sustains episodes of such contemplation which transform our lives and prepare us for spectacular, transcendent versions of happiness.[15] Clearly, many modern people lack any such vision. But the essence of what the ancients Greeks called '*theoria*', and the religious express in their attitudes of awe and reverence in the presence of God and things consecrated to God, is still available to us in our modern world. Classic leisure is an ideal that may still be attractive to busy people.

After the six days of Creation, the Bible tells us God rested and contemplated the goodness of all he had created. Josef Pieper writes: 'In leisure, man too celebrates the end of his work by allowing his inner eye to dwell for a while upon the reality of the creation. He looks and he affirms: it is good.'[16] Pieper's point is that the choice for leisure is the choice to engage for a while in activity which pays attention to the world, including the little parts of the world we have achieved or contributed to by our own labour and choices. Contemplative leisure is enjoying things just as they are, taking delight in creation, and in our own choices and personal creations. In *Happiness and Contemplation*, Pieper writes that contemplation consists in silent perception of reality, intuitive knowledge of what is present, and accompanying amazement.[17] It is a spiritual attitude, a sense of inner calm that requires discipline, but a discipline that brings joy and ease – the very opposite of the discipline of servile labour and painful effort. In leisure, we abandon the immediate and the material, the contemporary, the urgent troubles of ourselves and others, even the urgency of our moral dilemmas. We spend a short time simply reflecting in wonder and delight on all that the world contains, and on the human potential for belief, understanding, wisdom, and moral choice.

Pieper's view is not one of 'time out', abandoning responsibilities, putting our heads in the clouds. Leisure is not doing nothing: 'not a Sunday afternoon idyll, but the preserve of freedom, of education and culture, and of that undiminished humanity which views the world as a whole.'[18] In other words, leisure is trying to understand the world, and that understanding will open up reflection on our obligations and why they matter. Leisure that is reflective will interrogate the practicalities of how we live. Robinson and Godbey conclude their study of 'the surprising way Americans use their time' by suggesting that we need to learn to appreciate more, consume less, become conscious of the good things around us, and the limitations of the past that modern societies have now overcome. They agree with Pieper's Aristotelian insight into the need for more leisurely pondering in our lives, and they broaden the impact of his insight with their discovery that with more leisure time today, we all feel more rushed. The false promises of consumerist leisure, and our consequent lack of realism about human life, suggest we now need leisure that is both more contemplative and more realistic.

Abandoning contemplative leisure has made us less realistic. Consumerism has taught a mentality that expects 'hassle-free personal relations, limitless material possessions, and a world unfolding to meet our personal agendas.'[19] When, inevitably, we fail to receive this, the anti-contemplative mentality is not capable of accepting this wisely and exercising mature agency, but instead turns to childish passivity. We feel victimised, confused, unable to cope, not getting what we want. Compared with this neurotic modern response, thoughtful, quiet reflection on our circumstances and our fates puts us in charge, reminds us of what is good about modern life, how blessed modernity is, and prepares us to carry on. Pieper's spiritual reflection represents reasonableness, empowerment, and realism here, not naïve idealism.

Aristotle's contemplative ideal consisted in beholding with wonder the basic truths and the principles that explain all things. This is excellent leisure, for we are active (in the intellectual encounter) but also tranquil (in the insight gained), and we are free from the external pressure to work out answers and solve problems that we find in everyday life and in our non-leisure activities. But what makes contemplation excel as leisure is not the contemplative's gazing at truth, but his understanding the significance of that truth for his life. Contemplation equips us to reflect on our lives, not with the hurried, anxious thought of everyday reasoning, but by introducing 'big-picture' thoughts, and considerations of meaning and purpose which our everyday lives do not normally allow us to entertain. Contemplation gives people a broader context within which to explore their lives and choices, a sense of meaning that allows for recovery and revitalisation.

Contemplation of truth is perhaps the most rewarding reflective activity, for it means that our reflection on life's meaning is likely to be profound, sustained, and accurate. Few can sustain such contemplation. Nevertheless, if few of us are contemplatives, most of us can reflect on life's meaning through activities other than contemplation which share a reflective core with contemplation. Most people can reflect upon the meaning of their lives through activities of making, enjoying, relating, appreciating, or doing. The reflective life can be sustained through a range of activities that provide us with freedom from the everyday world, worthwhile activity, and episodes of tranquility.

These activities include *study*: both in the act of studying and as a result of study students can engage reflectively with the meanings that other thinkers have sought to communicate about the world and so develop new understanding of their lives; *creative writing*: in writing we clarify and record our reflections in such a way that our thoughts are communicable to reflective readers; *prayer* and spiritual meditation: here, we may reflect on God as answer to (all) questions of meaning and on transcendence as context for all our efforts; *love and friendship*: being in love, and enjoying love and friendship, is a continuous reflection on the significance of relationships;[20] *creative artistry*: art is a mystery of imagination and reflection in which artists identify deeply with something outside themselves and refocus their, and our, perception of reality through their meditation; *responding to beauty*: aesthetic response to nature or art is recognising that things mean something, that they are not just organisations of parts and pigments but have symbolic meaning; *exercising*: moving so as to cause and enjoy a sense of power, repose, fitness, or beauty in our own bodies is often a natural beginning of reflective thought, thus many thinkers think as naturally 'with their feet' as in their libraries.

Some qualifications are in order here. Of course these reflective activities are not always undertaken for the sake of recreation – they also serve family life, health, religion, work – but one good reason for undertaking them, and for increasing their reflective element, is recreation. Furthermore, we can become absorbed in our favourite leisure activity in such a way that no conscious reflection is taking place at all. Generally, such leisure is play, and is certainly useful for personal recreation. But if all our leisure is play and none of it is reflective, the recreational potential of our leisure will diminish. Entertainment and relaxation are no substitutes for a big-picture sense of our lives and their significance, for they bring us no sense of encountering our true self or being active in ways of great importance to that self. Finally, of course people can also have reflective episodes when performing all sorts of non-leisure activities too, from buying fish to repairing the car. But what distinguishes reflective leisure activities is that they are best done reflectively, and are the normal means to achieving recreation. Because they are free, not part of the logic of consuming and owning, not constrained, these activities are ordinarily performed thoughtfully, and so ordinarily means towards personal integration and renewal.

Reflective leisure is naturally suspicious of consumerism's attempt to decrease-or-commercialise reflective activities. Of course, many activities in life are rightly instrumental (making dinner, building a house, teaching someone to read and so on), but consumerism's effect is to instrumentalise *all* activity and to do so by making the only ultimate end (temporary) satisfaction in possession and status. Hence, reflective leisure is opposed to consumerism, rejecting both the inappropriate extension of instrumentalisation and the ultimate end which consumerism seeks to impose.

Others too have attempted to retain the basic Aristotelian ideal and to modify it. My argument differs from most of these attempts in that I also suggest in Chapter 3 justification for reflective leisure. Here, I will briefly relate my view to some other revisions of the Aristotelian ideal.

The most significant modern contribution on leisure is Pieper. But Pieper is attempting much more than a critique of consumerist leisure. His basic argument is that culture itself depends upon leisure, and that leisure depends upon openness to the divine. He affirms the validity of Aquinas's interpretation of leisure as union with God, and the need for religious worship (the 'cultus') in order to make this spiritual activity part of people's daily lives. Pieper thus attempts major social critique of our (doomed) attempt to build a culture without contemplative leisure and our attempt to build a post-Christian culture. In doing so, he presents an ideal of philosophy, freedom, and peace, and an ideal of reflective insight that challenges the common view that most people are capable of nothing more than amusements. These ideals amount to a passionate defence of individual human dignity in the face of totalitarianism and commodification. For these reasons, Pieper's book is one of the great classics of modern philosophy.

Pieper calls society to leisure so as to uphold culture, and the culture he wishes to uphold gives first honour to religion and finds true wisdom in spiritual experience. My own view is that the practice and experience of religion entails contemplation, but that reflection, which is intrinsic to contemplation, occurs in other activities too. Thus we can extend genuine, reflective leisure to the non-religious (and likewise, not all religious activity is contemplative). I have some sympathy here with John Hemingway, who writes that Pieper's Thomism can over-strongly colour his interpretation of Aristotle. Hemingway argues that Aristotle sees the purpose and value of leisure as *developing the citizen*, as well as producing contemplation: leisure frees us from the mundane and sets up the drive for personal excellence, to which character and activity will then respond.[21] My concept of reflective leisure better accommodates Hemingway's point than does Pieper's by extending reflection, the essence of contemplation, throughout other social (and practical) activities (and relationships).

When Pieper wrote he had in mind Marxists who glorified work and saw leisure as decadent activity of the unjustly rich, post-WW II capitalists fired with the work-ethic who equated leisure with vice and godlessness, and the new middle classes, understandably open to all the trivialities of affordable amusement after the dark days of the 30s and 40s.[22] Thus he could argue then that religion was the only social arrangement that made true leisure possible. Today, Marxists are rarer, and the middle-classes are more likely to agree with Aristotle that we work to get leisure, than with a Calvinist work-ethic. Thus even a purely religious justification of leisure would now require a different argument from Pieper's.

Elizabeth Telfer in a classic article also suggests revision of Aristotelian leisure. In what she describes as the 'Aristotelian view': 'the proper use of leisure is the practice of activities worthwhile in themselves.'[23] Telfer argues that for Aristotle, only contemplation of eternal truths has this status; but that this can and should be expanded to include the non-instrumental activities of scholarship, the arts, and personal friendships – and also, that these activities ought to be engaged in by us in our leisure time because of the pleasure that is part of pursuing them. Thus revised, Aristotelian leisure embraces activities done because they represent a 'final end' for us rather than serve some of our other final ends. For Telfer, however, our final ends are complex: they may, for example, include other people's well-being; moreover, ('instrumental') activities that are done for results may also be regarded as final ends, 'if we abstract from the result and consider the nature of the activity employed.'[24]

Telfer here makes significant inroads upon the view that in Aristotle's ethics the distinction between servile ends and ends in themselves is sharp; she also opens up an intriguing approach to the work/leisure relationship (see Chapter 8). My account of reflective leisure differs from her account in two main ways.

First, though I agree that genuine leisure activities do not serve external purposes but are done for their own sakes, I argue that this is not what makes them leisure. There are many activities done for the sake of their own internal ends without thereby being 'candidates for leisure activities';[25] for example, healthcare and hygiene, learning to read, completing a work project, starting a family, caring for the marginalised. None of these is a leisure activity, though each is or may be done purely 'for its own sake', in the sense of for those goods for which such activity is naturally suited. These activities are involved in realising other parts of our nature than recreation, therefore they are not leisure. Secondly, Telfer determines whether an activity is merely useful or an end in itself by appeal to how the agent sees his activity and how others judge it.[26] But unless some more basic criterion is given, leisure here will not be determined by the nature of the activity but by personal judgement; that is, 'Aristotelian' leisure will be indistinguishable from consumerist leisure. I offer as the criterion of reflective leisure its relationship to human nature, and in particular to our capacity for recreation (Chapter 3).

A similar difficulty occurs with Al Gini's view. Gini transforms Aquinas and Pieper on leisure into the weekend-freedom to do whatever we choose.[27] He is insightful on the ways in which our weekends have become over-structured, too full of busyness with which we attempt to make up for the 'pain and emptiness' of the week. But he takes no strong stand on the trivialisation of leisure – so long as our choice helps us to relax and to enjoy freedom. Gini is for the Pieper critique, but not for his solution.

Gini is certainly worried about the loss of some dimensions of leisure through increasing commercialisation: not reflection, but solitude, and a 'secular Sabbath' as a time of rest and openness to new possibilities[28] (his practical examples of this are having meals together, and getting better sleep). Yet he can see value in commercialised leisure too:

we work hard, have little time off, want an interesting experience which we do not have to work hard for ourselves; therefore, why not just pay up?

Gini's work represents a potential difficulty for attempts to revive a notion of classic leisure. 'Freedom from cares for the sake of freedom to contemplate' is easily reduced to 'freedom from cares'; in other words, classic leisure can become just a less busy version of (North-Eastern US, small 'l' liberal) consumerism: take more time out, do your own thing; certainly aspire to activities that are worthwhile in themselves, but use consumerist leisure discriminatingly as a supplement.

I think many would find this a reasonable compromise, but I also think that most people are more reflective than Gini gives them credit for, that there is much more to leisure than play, and that opportunities to rejoice in the fresh, simple things that he mentions are more than just rest breaks for modern people. They are recreational not just in the sense of rest, but also as an opportunity to clarify our thoughts on how we should live. I think Gini's view of dipping into consumerist leisure also fails to understand the effect of a total logic upon our lives and choices. I too use travel agents to help me to plan my holidays, since opting out of the consumer economy is not presently possible. But I would much rather have different destinations, modes of travel, fellow-travellers, accommodation, timetables, and so on; and I recognise that none of that will change in a consumerist world, except in ways that ultimately earn even more money for wealthy business owners. But such a world can change; and no doubt, like all worlds, one day will change.

Geoffrey Godbey offers the following definition of leisure in *Leisure in Your Life*: 'living in relative freedom from the external compulsive forces of one's culture and physical environment so as to be able to act from internally compelling love in ways which are personally pleasing, intuitively worthwhile, and provide a basis for faith.'[29] Pleasure, intuition, and a spiritual basis are important qualities, and compelling love serves to raise leisure activities above the degraded or trivial. Godbey's definition again focuses on activity that is worthwhile in itself. But in failing to include a reflective dimension he makes insufficient common cause with the Aristotelian tradition, and so provides no compelling reason why one might not take part in consumerist leisure much of the time if this is one's own free choice and one is reasonably relaxed and stress-free.

R. T. Allen, however, does find common cause between chosen activity and Aristotelian tradition.[30] He suggests extending Pieper's critique by peeling off the structural features of Aristotle on contemplative leisure and finding them in, for example, art and craft, so long as this is done for the joy of making and delight in the exercise of skills. And he also notes Pieper's observation that if leisure means what is worth doing for its own sake, then that thing must be logically connected to meaning in (and perhaps, of) life. Thus Allen comes closest to my view that leisure has best recreational potential when it facilitates reflection on the meaning of our lives and choices.

Recreation

Reflective leisure, which combines freedom from pressures, activity for its own sake, and reflection on meaning, has excellent recreational potential. People sometimes speak of recreational sex, drugs, partying, relationships; but the most effective way of achieving deep and lasting recreation, as opposed to simple fun, is reflective leisure. Few writers distinguish leisure from recreation.[31] But I suggest that leisure is activity with the goal of recreation, and that recreation is a basic human capacity, part of our nature. It may seem strange to argue that leisure is undertaken for no external end and undertaken only for the internal goal of recreation.[32] But to say leisure is done for no alien end *is* to say that it is recreational, either as play or as reflection. Successful leisure activity achieves recreation, literally the re-creation of our selves after the time, effort, and alienation of work and providing for our daily material needs.

Recreation refers to 'making new'. This includes rest and recovery, but also revitalisation, the sense of new life. Rest, restoration, and recovery after effort mean returning to where we were before we expended ourselves on the effort; this is important, and it is most naturally achieved by playful leisure activity. But recreation also means renewing oneself, gaining new insight and heart, and so starting from a fresh position; this is the natural result of reflective leisure activities. Just as human creation seeks analogies with divine creation in which God brought wonders into being from nothing, so human recreation celebrates within our daily lives the double culmination of this process when God *rested* from labour and when, in the Christian account, the Son of God *renewed* creation by rising from death. Recreation as an autonomous part of human nature only becomes clear in the Christian era; thus in pre-Christian times leisure was often assumed instead to actualise our potential for religion or contemplation of the truth.

Recreation can be achieved in various ways. For example, some people gain substantial recreation through their work, their faith, through various of their friendships, their family life – anything that gives fresh insight into how we live and fresh motivation for what we do. These activities may also form parts of our leisure lives in various ways of course, but they need not: our share in religion, friendship, and so on may be neither playful nor reflective. Recreation may come even through what may be difficult, enforced, or unwelcome experience of family or friends, exercise or work. It may come too without our realising it or aiming at it. But ordinarily recreation comes through leisure activity, and when it comes through reflective leisure, it will generally be profound, extensive, and lasting. For here we achieve a new perspective on our lives and efforts through our own reflection that is sustained or produced by our own favourite activities.

Recreation as an ultimate life-goal is not an unfamiliar thought for modern people. But recreation as literally re-creating the self, fashioning step by step a revitalised self, may be a notion one step too metaphysical for some tastes. Yet all of us will be aware sometimes (even if only in times of distress, or of recovery from distress) of the experience of gaining in strength and growing in insight, and of starting out again, never just the exact same self, but renewed. I suggest this recreative experience is not a 'therapy' we need only episodically, but a natural and on-going human need; something that should play a part in every busy and tense life. Reflection is certainly a rarer habit today than hitherto; though perhaps the contemporary phenomenon of 'counselling' provides a sort of vicarious reflection. Many people will turn to reflection, like prayer, only when in need or fear. But people who do get a taste for reflective leisure activities and experience their recreational boost may pause more often to enjoy life and to reflect peacefully but thoughtfully on what they do and what it means.

If reflective leisure and self-renewal sound too heavy compared with familiar and undemanding consumerist pastimes, we can recall that reflective leisure is unlikely to support lasting recreation if it is pursued in the spirit of moral duty, therapy, or religious obligation. Leisure is activity that shifts us from the world of work, necessity, and burden. At its best, reflective leisure means that our control, though effective, does not consist in constant self-monitoring and feverish seeking for a 'cure'. Reflection is free precisely because its progress exceeds our control; it succeeds where we hand ourselves over and cannot quite guess the result. This means that the best reflective leisure is where adults give themselves over happily to play as well as pondering.

Play

Play is perhaps as basic to our lives as anything can be. Healthy, normal humans who are 'doing nothing' will actually have thoughts drifting across their minds and will be directing the movements their bodies make even in repose, for no particular purpose but just after their own fashion (when we add a pen to this, the movement is known as 'doodling'). This most basic experience of playful thought and action is deeply natural to us, forms continuities between us and other members of the animal kingdom, and serves our growth and development as independent thinkers and agents. Alasdair MacIntyre writes: 'Play is important because it is exploratory, because it releases those who engage in it from the pressures of felt need, because it extends both the range of activities found worth pursuing for their own sake and the range of pleasures that can be taken in such activities, and because in moving from the kind of playfulness exhibited both by humans and dolphins to more sophisticated forms of play we move from animal intelligence to specifically human reasoning.'[33]

Johan Huizinga argued that play is 'free activity standing quite clearly outside "ordinary" life as being "not serious", but at the same time absorbing the player intensely and utterly.'[34] Or as Gadamer puts it: 'Play fulfils its purpose only if the player loses himself in play.'[35] Play is turning from 'the seriousness of purposes'; it is spending some time in activity that seeks no further purpose beyond itself. It is seriously important that we play, and play well and often, in our daily lives;[36] but we cannot take the activity too seriously when playing. There is innocence, absorption, enthusiasm, and delight in all play: 'in play all that is gay, lovely, and soaring in the human spirit strives to find the expression which a man of spirit and of enthusiasm is also seeking to attain.'[37]

Play has sometimes been thought of as closely connected to the spiritual life, a mode of union with God (who creates, and redeems, in absolute 'free play'). Hugo Rahner writes that 'all play...is an attempt to approximate to the Creator, who performs his work with the divine seriousness which its meaning and purpose demand, and yet with the spontaneity and effortless skill of the great artist he is, creating because he wills to create and not because he must.'[38] Rahner's idea here is that play is activity that is significant, but non-utilitarian; and its significance for us rests above all in its integration of spiritual with bodily life. Like God's Creation, which was quite free yet highly significant, human play integrates freedom with physical activity in ways pregnant with meaning but serving no utilitarian end.

Given how much of our lives we adults spend inside a network of purposes, sub-purposes, instrumental purposes, and puzzling out the logical and practical relations between all these, it is invigorating and consoling to take seriously this idea of acting purposively but with no further purpose in mind. Reflecting on our need for playing games, Rowan Williams, Anglican Archbishop of Canterbury, writes: 'Games are unproductive. The point is not to make anything out of the common activities agreed, but to perform the activities themselves.'[39] By playing, we are carried out of daily logic and open to things that matter in themselves and that have thrilled us in youth: 'play is about awe, wonder, rapture, and enthusiasm.'[40]

Although it has no purpose beyond the act of play, play has structure and significance. In fact, some think play is related to many important aspects of daily life and is the natural base of cultural ritual, symbol, and myth.[41] Part of Huizinga's fear for modern cultures is that they have become over-serious and lost interest and delight in the worlds of play and ritual; certainly, maturity often seems to narrow the horizons of play, limits the ability to giggle, impoverishes delight. But, paradoxically, when our institutions abandon the connection with play and become more serious, they then become more flippant: modern cultures that lose interest in play and symbol become more childish; modern people more likely to self-indulge with trivial or sensational recreations rather than seek out new and stimulating forms of play. For Huizinga, our culture must recover the freedom and intensity of play which is such a deep part of our nature and which helps us to recognise our true place within the natural and animal worlds.

The modern impulse is to separate reflection (intellectual, mature, difficult, cultural) from play (physical-emotional, infantile, easy, natural). But the distinction is false. As Huizinga shows, play is everywhere: it is adult, often sophisticated, and responsible for the direction of our major cultural institutions. And as Pieper shows, reflection is natural: it requires no special equipment, flows as easily as faith and hope, and reflects our true nature as rational. Our separation of the life of the mind and the life of the body here reflects a dualism few think stands up to philosophical scrutiny, and few experience as their personal reality. Of course, play can – and often should – occur without reflection, because play is freedom and that extends to simple, thought-less acts too. But a life devoted to play without reflection (or *vice versa*) would mean impoverished recreation.

I have argued that reflection occurs through various 'physical' activities, such as creativity and friendship, as well as through contemplation; and Huizinga has shown that play occurs within our major cultural and intellectual activities, as well as within physical activity. Thus reflection and play are not opposing parts of human experience. Moreover, they come together most naturally in leisure, for when we reflect in freedom from external needs and demands, we are least constrained, most 'at play'.[42]

Play can of course occur as non-reflective leisure too. Our leisure can be restful and enjoyable, without reflection. Play's power to recreate is never as deep without reflection, but sometimes it is appropriate for people to seek renewal through play, or at least to begin the process this way. This is most obvious in the case of healing depression, bereavement, and other forms of personal break-down in which life has lost meaning for the sufferer. We sometimes speak here of people 'falling apart': the faculties and parts of the person to some extent have lost integration, ceased to function as aspects of a whole person. Leisure, at first playful and then reflective, may have an important role to play in putting people back together.

Personal break-downs often begin with shock, hysterics, trauma, and then may develop into depression with loss of activity. Aquinas well characterised such depression as a spiritual problem. We tend to overlook this because we pathologise or psychologise unhappiness in the language of twentieth century medicine and therapies, but Aquinas believes that the true problem with depression is deeper than psychological unpleasantness or chemical imbalance. He writes that to be depressed is to 'be hindered in one's own movement by some weight'; to be unable to initiate thought or activity for oneself due to the experience of a great burden pressing down.[43] It is a de-pression of soul, a sorrow that stops us from moving, weighs us down with apathy.

Aquinas spends one whole question of the *Summa Theologiae* on the remedies for depression. He advises a whole programme of personal renewal, beginning with new pleasures, the presence of friends, tears, sleep, hot baths, and finally the contemplation of truths.[44] All Aquinas's remedies bear relation to new movement of spirits and the body, energy, novelty, stimulation, hope. We are to find ways of diverting ourselves in order to return movement and activity to our depressed limbs and souls. Friends, pleasures, bodily remedies, and rest are all to be used to get us moving again. In particular, contemplation, in which we reflect on the truth, receive hope for the future, and love to embrace it, is to be encouraged.

At the low-point of depression, Aquinas describes a state of *acedia*, a lack of movement and activity so extreme one is unable to do anything.[45] Acedics gradually lose their interest in anything that is good at all, anything that speaks of the love of God. This is the most extreme depression in which people are so burdened that moving towards any imagined good becomes unbearable; at this dangerous point *acedia* can pass into sheer despair.[46] One potent indicator of *acedia* is inability to work;[47] thus we can sometimes treat acedics by returning them to meaningful work. A good way in which to begin this is to introduce some simple activity the person can initiate for himself. Thus forms of play which do not over-stretch the person, but do allow him to act, and which may in due course allow him to begin to reflect on the issue and not to dodge it, are effective. Successfully motivating someone with well thought-through leisure can help to return to him, through activity and then reflection, the possibility of meaning in his life.

When we attempt to revive depression sufferers by play, and, ultimately, reflection, it may be best to begin with the parts of the person that are easiest to move. The senses are very naturally moved towards bright colours, pleasant smells, sounds, and so on. Thus it may be easiest to revive movement by first introducing forms of play that engage the senses – simple things such as flowers in the room, perfumes, gentle music, attractive foods, massage, getting your hair done. In play, we seek no external purpose; so we can simply enjoy the activation and release of the sense powers, and the muscles and sinews in which they are located. Playing with the senses encourages jaded appetites; so recovering sensory stimulation and pleasure through play can be a beginning in healing depression and *acedia*.

From here, we can move to reorienting the emotions. Grief counsellors know that in grief or depression what people often need is not more knowledge or companionship (they may well need less of both of these) but something like well-chosen play and diversion that helps the emotions to operate in healthy, non-distressing ways. In a recent book on child bereavement the authors write: 'play is a natural, safe and constant part of children's lives. It grounds them. Play and various art forms allow children to express feelings that they may not be able to express verbally because of their developmental stage.'[48] Similar points hold too for adults: when feelings are stunted and our natural lives and development frozen by grief or depression, carefully chosen forms of play can help people to relax and so express emotions in ways that are familiar or more bearable.

With a return to movement and function in the senses and emotions, a next step might be to reinvigorate the imagination. All good play engages the imagination – allows us to form images that are informative and pleasurable and to reassemble these images in ways that are creative and revealing. Part of the cure of depression and *acedia* is being able to imagine an alternative life in which one still lives with the burden yet, despite it, can now see possibilities for goodness and love. When we move from renewing the senses and emotions to the imagination, we are approaching forms of activity that are more obviously cognitively directed. Thus reviving a weary or over-burdened imagination and freeing it from habits of compulsively entertaining sorrowful images should respond best to a mixture of reflection as well as play. So there is a role here not only for playful activities but also for reflective leisure activities (contemplation, writing, creativity, prayer and so on). Consumerist leisure, however, is particularly unhelpful here since it tends to be unimaginative, at best masking pain with thrill or monotony.

When the person has begun to function again imaginatively as well as emotionally, we can encourage good habits of willing: strength not only to look at images of the future but also to perform acts of will aimed at their pursuit. Play once again can assist here; in fact, what was once called 'character building' play probably has much more to do with will-building, giving 'back-bone', rather than virtue. The competitive dimension of play, especially games, may also help to recover will at this stage, since it teaches determination, endurance, the will to succeed. Meanwhile, as Kant argued, skilled play, because it encourages self-improvement, will also communicate the idea of self-respect and the sense of dignity that can come through exertion, perseverance, and success.

With so much of the person recovered, full reintegration and a return to normal life should be possible. This occurs when we can accept habits of reflection in which we face up to the meaning of our situation, our life, our activities from here, and the meaning of the world in which we must now live with our memories. In these final stages of the re-creation of the person from breakdown, stages that are not just therapeutic or recuperative but genuinely renewing and revitalising for the rest of life, play will give way to the more sophisticated forms of reflective leisure in which we finally face and accept our future.

Relaxation and fun

Almost all writers on the topic agree that modern people need to relax more; we have to address the collective and individual build-up of stress. 'No matter what we do to earn a living, we all see the benefit of leisure, lassitude and inertia.'[49] But as Gini explains here, increased relaxation is very difficult for many of us. Building on Robinson and Godbey's work, he notes that people today actually brag about being busy. People have more leisure than they believe they have, and boast about their belief that they are over-worked. Eventually, people living like this have a crisis. They realise their leisure lives are currently more about recuperation and rehabilitation than recreation, and they make a change. But, as Gini recounts, this often occurs only after a warning from the cardiac surgeon. Modern life is too busy; but leisure cannot be used simply as healthcare compensating for bad living: we must look to our leisure lives to unwind and to laugh, not just to preserve our health from the effects of busyness.

The most effective way to achieve relaxation and fun, is to unite them and seek them together: thus entertainment should not be exhausting or draining, and relaxation should not be slothful or self-satiating. Reflective leisure activities, such as study, writing, creating, appreciating, enjoying relationships, experiencing physical strength and calm, can be relaxing and great fun; but they can also become dull and tiring, lose their appeal, and even add to life's burdens. This is so when (reflective) leisure activities take place frequently or for substantial periods of time without play.

Sometimes people find themselves seeking reflective leisure as a duty, grudgingly, reluctantly, resentfully, too often, or too rarely. When this is so, 'leisure' may become tiring, aggravating, burdensome, and our reflection unproductive, repetitive, unimaginative. Without doubt, consumerist leisure has helped to encourage the phenomenon of exhausting, predictable, mind-numbing, or over-stimulating leisure – leisure achieving nothing worthwhile by way of recreation. Moreover, the great emphasis in commercial leisure of activities directed towards youth can pressure young people, and others who think young, into certain forms of leisure as fashion or in response to the social expectation to 'keep up'. When leisure appears in any of these ways as obligatory activity or activity subservient to external ends (others' expectations, their approval, their acceptance of us, our socially-constructed self-esteem), it ceases to be playful, and so its powers to relax and give fun decrease. Needless to say, such leisure is then unlikely to produce significant recreation, but is likely to add to stress and frustration.

Where people are concerned that life has insufficient rest or enjoyment, they obviously need to play more. For adults, playing is more attractive and rewarding where well integrated with leisure activities that also allow us to reflect on what we are doing and how it fits into the broader pattern of our lives. For most adults, play can only be sustained where integrated with creativity, study, relationships, exercise, spirituality. Our very human thirst for relaxation and fun reveals a genuine recreational need; and it is a need best catered for by playful activity that is also thoughtful.

The concept of reflective leisure cannot be justified within and by consumerist culture; it is difficult enough to justify playful leisure within this culture. In Chapter 3 I will suggest some philosophical justification for reflective leisure. This justification will also offer some reasons for rejecting or at least questioning consumerism, including consumerist leisure. I recognise that questioning is unlikely to happen amongst most in the consumer culture for very many years. But it is possible; and it will probably happen at some point, since it is unlikely that any ideological total logic could determine culture permanently.

3
Reflective Leisure and Recreation

The big question for my thesis is asked by John Hemingway: 'is Aristotelian leisure compatible with liberal democracy?'[1] Hemingway argues that it is not. The possibility of leisure in modern democracies depends on the ability to consume; reflective leisure is the antithesis of consumption; therefore, it has no place in our modern democracies. Modern leisure ideas and practices are passive and individualistic. Reflective leisure radically challenges these notions of self and value, and our understanding of work and leisure, and thus can have no foothold in our democracies.

I do not think this is right; but what is true is that reflective leisure cannot flourish in our democracies while they are subject to the stranglehold of consumerism. As Sebastian de Grazia argues, a non-commercial justification of reflective leisure would not be listened to in consumerist society, and a commercial justification is not possible. The only possible justification is a philosophical one. Such a philosophical justification can be offered from within, and to, liberal democracy, just so long as the justification responds to consumerism and indicates an alternative role for commerce, purchase, and ownership – a role which leaves human dignity intact and outlines another version of the human good.

In the last chapter, I gave some reasons for thinking that replacing consumerist leisure with playful and reflective leisure, though an enormous shift, is not an absurd proposition. In this chapter, I will suggest that reflective leisure is justified by its role within a philosophical conception of human nature and well-being. These ideas are developed from contemporary work in natural law theory – in particular, from work on human capacities and goods.

A version of natural law theory is one of only two credible hopes for unraveling the total logic of consumerism today. The other possibility is adopting postmodernist beliefs and activities, which include reject-ing consumerist society, and all other ideologies and dogmas too. I will not here give reasons for rejecting the postmodernist option, since it makes no provision for a revival of classic leisure, which is my topic. The postmodernist turn and its implications have in any case been effectively critiqued by others.[2] As an alternative to consumerism and a justification for reflective leisure I offer a natural law argument which, I believe, is fully compatible with the major values and institutions of modern democracies.

Human nature

Most people would probably agree that a life entirely devoid of recre-ation would not be a happy life. But many would also think that a life including only a very little recreation might well be worth living. For example, if a person is deeply contented in the areas of family and friendship, knowledge, work, or religious faith, some would argue that receiving only minimal recreation would not detract from his overall fulfilment. The argument might run: 'of course we all need a little recreation – but being deficient in recreation is far less important than having no friends or an appalling education or being spiritually dead; if I am deeply committed to and fulfilled by my family, study, friend-ships, faith, some especially fulfilling career, or humanitarian work, then the fact I hardly ever enjoy leisure or play, and receive recreation rarely, if at all, will not detract from my overall well-being.'

To discuss whether this downgrading of recreation and the leisure activities that serve it is reasonable, I will first consider some of our most basic human capacities: those capacities whose exercise is required for our well-being. I will suggest that recreation is one such capacity, and that it is of importance for our well-being generally, since recreation indicates on-going renewal of all our basic human capacities in integrated functioning. For this reason, reflective leisure, which is the ordinary means to recreation, has an important role to play in our lives. Quality leisure enables recreation and so is a means to our living happily.

Aristotle argued that to understand what a thing is we first look at what it does:[3] if a man wants to find out what a washing machine really is, he should squat down and observe how a good machine functions, try to discover the sort of activity characteristic of well-functioning washing machines. When we know what something characteristically does, we can infer from this knowledge of its distinctive capacities, the capacities that functioning things of that sort possess and in whose exercise things of that sort flourish. In other terms, knowing something's characteristic activities is grasping its full potential, its potential for activation, or in the case of a living thing, flourishing. If in this way we ponder characteristic human activity, we ought to be in good position to identify the distinctive capacities that will be exercised in a flourishing human life. We ought to be able to give an account of human nature. We can then discuss whether recreation is one such capacity, something necessary for human functioning and happiness.

Talk of 'capacities' embraces both presently operating ('occurrent') and generally operable ('dispositional') powers. In discussing human nature I mean to include both of these, and also those capacities which specified individuals may never have had but which are 'normative' – a sign of health and wholeness – for members of that individual's species. Thus, for example, hearing is 'natural' to a person congenitally and irreversibly deaf since hearing is a capacity exercised in a healthy, whole human life, and tragically missing from this life. Likewise, the ability to reason is 'natural' in an embryo or a new-born child not yet sufficiently developed to exercise this power distinctive of that species. With each important capacity, there are certain activities in which that capacity is ordinarily (and so effectively and reliably) exercised. I will argue that leisure activity ordinarily exercises our capacity for recreation – a mark of every whole and healthy human life.

To identify human nature with whatever is distinctive of our species does not mean that human nature includes everything that is unique to human beings. Some of our unique capacities may be (purely or partly) responses to local conditions (such as western, modern commerce), or temporal developments of more basic species capacities (for example, tool-making as a development of our capacity for work), or responses to contingent crises which the whole species has undergone (for example, the effects of the alleged defect Christians call 'original sin', such as our capacity for warfare). To discover what is *distinctive* of us, we need to know what is essential to us: human nature consists in those capacities without exercise of which (any) human life will be unfulfilled and human well-being compromised or threatened. But does this not mean we are here presupposing a concept of the human being and the fulfilled human life, and so presupposing rather than proving the capacities that are essential to us?

The question of 'presupposition or proof?' arises in any attempt to identify essential human capacities: how can you identify our central capacities without first having the concept of the human being, and how can you have this concept without first identifying our central capacities? There are a number of ways of responding to the question.[4] One is to hold that the concept of a human being and so of what is essentially human is arrived at not only through philosophical reflection on theories of human nature but also through self-reflection: reflection on our experiences of leading and planning a life, forming and balancing commitments, integrating central values, making choices, comprehending encounters and relationships, helps to clarify what it is to be human and what is essential to human life.

Such explorations may be 'phenomenological', in the sense of reflecting on the quality of experience and the objects of conscious experience as a reliable guide to truth;[5] or they may be 'logical', in the sense Aquinas has in mind when he discussed our self-evident knowledge of the ultimate objects of our choices and activities. For Aquinas, certain objects are comprehended as choiceworthy without the endorsement of justifying practical argument, since these objects are themselves the foundations of all such justificatory arguments.[6]

The logical method is followed by the 'new natural law' school, which focuses on identifying the basic human goods that make intelligible our choices. These basic goods represent ultimate and irreducible parts of our nature, investment in which is the goal of all deliberate human acts.[7] While deeply sympathetic to the revival of natural law thinking, especially this version of it, I believe the new natural law school insufficiently accounts for the complexity of our nature and the actual structure of our practical reasoning by describing human goods as either 'basic' (intrinsically choiceworthy termini of chains of practical reasoning, guarantors of intelligibility) or 'instrumental' (chosen for the sake of basic goods, mere instruments whose value resides in their facilitation of our sharing in basic goods).

Even a slight 'phenomenological turn' suggests that we do not regard all non-basic goods purely instrumentally. I may go to gym 'for the sake of' the basic good of health, but I would not choose to take a health-pill (or perform a different healthcare activity) that gives me the same increase in health. For exercise is not for me just a means to health: it is the particular way of sharing in the basic good of health that, for me, has greatest importance (I see myself in this way, am committed to this healthy choice and its continuation, have a specific quality of satisfaction from working out, have an understanding of health that is conditioned by the importance, and the satisfaction, of exercise to me, and so on). Exercise is not only my *means* here; it is health-*as-I-invest-in* it.

Thus I think that realisation of certain parts of our human potential results in goods that are *neither* basic goods (because they are explained by their share in yet more basic goods – as exercise or eating well is explained by health, or delighting in well-performed music is explained by appreciation of beauty, or growth in articulacy is explained by truth, and so on), *nor* merely instrumental goods (since exercise, eating, joy, and linguistic competence are direct realisation of parts of my potential, not mere means). We might, for the sake of a name, call them '*quasi* basic goods' or 'q-basic goods'.

Because my aim in this chapter is to describe our nature so as to locate recreation within it, I do not argue here for a position in the debate over the best list of basic human goods; nevertheless, I do think that the new natural law will increase its philosophical respectability if adherents adjust their classification of the human good by adopting a more sensitive self-reflection than Aquinas's *per se nota* test by itself allows for. If we apply the results of phenomenologically sensitive self-reflection, as well as philosophical reflection on available theories of human nature, I believe we can identify a sufficiently concrete notion of the human being to make some suggestions about the essential human capacities.[8] In doing so, I provide a view of human nature and indicate the (q-basic, and basic) human goods we enjoy through exercise of the capacities that form that nature.

Emotion, perception, language, will

Many people today are pre-philosophical dualists: they believe we are composed of two separate substances, body and consciousness, and that some powers belong to the body while the most important powers belong to consciousness. I think that the form of a human life is substantially that proposed by Aristotle in works such as *De Anima* and *Nicomachean Ethics* and discussed by Aquinas in his commentaries on these, thus I will make use of this view (my view, however, could hardly be described as 'Aristotelian'!). My account begins with some powers particularly associated with the body: emotion, perception, communication, and will. It would clearly be false to describe any of these as 'non-psychological', but I identify all four as parts of our bodily nature since they are tied up with the body in important ways.

The benefits or goods received by exercise of these four capacities are q-basic, not basic, goods. Though these capacities are important parts of individuals' lives and their exercise essential for human well-being, they are not exercised for their own sakes', but for the sake of realising other parts of our nature (we do not feel, sense, talk about, and will just for the sake of doing so). Thus the goods we share in by exercise of these capacities are not ultimate goods, but good because of the yet more basic goods which we share in by receiving these q-basic goods.

To be emotional or passionate about something is to make the sort of judgement about that thing that produces one or more of the following: feelings, sensations, desires, physiological symptoms (increased heartbeat, rapid breathing, blushing, and the sniffly-nose phenomenon).[9] The judgement we make helps to differentiate the actual emotion we are experiencing. A judgement, for example, that *I wish I had that* marks a different emotion (envy) from a judgement that *I, not she, ought to have that* (jealousy). Emotions are states in which we are affected by the world and the ways in which we perceive the world. But they are not purely passive states, or simple sensations like itches and tickles: they are primarily evaluative, though they give rise too to a range of changes in feeling and so can affect conduct. A paradox of the emotions is that though emotions are evaluations, forms of thought, they are traditionally regarded not as psychological but as bodily powers. Why is this?

First, consider the concept of angels. These are disembodied intelligences, intellectual beings upon whom the world cannot impinge. Thus they experience no emotions, since emotion is a way of being affected by the physical world and called to judge that world by features of the world that elicit our judgement *whether we wish this or not.* Emotions are bodily powers because they involve the world changing us, making fresh demands on us, affecting the way we see reality, and this requires a body. Emotions are not angelic but embodied experiences.[10] Secondly, an adequate emotional life is open only to people who take seriously the power of emotions and our responsibility to develop them in ways that control their power to overwhelm us (and harm others). This requires us to appreciate how dramatically we can be affected by the *products* of the emotions (feelings, sensations, activities, desires, physiological symptoms) and not just their *objects* (the states of affairs over which we pass judgement in experiencing the emotion). It is because of the physical origin of the emotions in sensation and reaction, and the physiological impact of the emotions upon us that they are regarded as bodily powers.

The power of sense perception is of course common to animals. Animals' sensory powers depend upon their sensory apparatus, which undergoes change when the animal encounters external objects (and perhaps, in the human case, when we encounter our inner thoughts).

This apparatus is part of our bodies, and our perception is affected by the health and efficiency of our sense organs.

Human perception, however, is intelligent, as well as bodily. We perceive things as morally significant, beautiful, funny, virtuous or vicious, and so on. This combination of sensory experience and cognitive attitude in our perception in turn develops our senses of beauty, humour, morality, selfhood, reverence, and so on – the non-animal, or rational senses. For example, perceiving things as beautiful involves sense pleasures and judgements that the object is significant; these reinforce each other and so dispose us to notice this sort of thing in the future. Such a sense of beauty is perhaps perception at its most rational: the closest we can come to recognising truth through having sensory (rather than purely cognitive) experiences.

Our bodily powers also include communication. Communication *per se* is often thought of as a cerebral or verbal matter. But in fact, as Herbert McCabe for one suggests: 'all shared, vital activity is....some form of communication.'[11] All purposive animal behaviour communicates something (irritation, feelings, deep seated desires, needs, inclinations, preferences, habits, goals, beliefs and so on). Human beings, however, uniquely among the animals, can communicate not only information and desires, but also the meaning of these communications: thus truly human communication is reflective, or linguistic. Distinctively human communication is expressive of rational thought and symbolic in nature; it forms a language, which means that, unlike other animals, we can create, modify, and extend the very means by which we communicate.[12]

McCabe suggests that linguistic communication is a new and radically different way of being an animal;[13] but it is still a way of being an animal: human communication is a power not just in, but of, the body. Thus our language is an extension of the power of bodily communication which we share with all animals. Language may be communication through structures the human animal chooses and invents, but it is not non-bodily communication. It is because of the way our bodies, and in particular, our brains, are made that we can create our own media of communication. Thus linguistic communication is another part of our bodily potential. With the emergence of human beings, living bodies take on new communicative potential (for one thing, truly communicative life – community life as opposed to pack living – becomes possible).

Will is a fourth bodily power. In the German philosopher Schopenhauer's formulation, we know our bodies in two distinct ways: as objects, and as 'objectified will', as subjects.[14] Our bodies are the way in which our will to achieve things becomes actual in the world and thus we know our bodies not just as physical things, but also as the external effect of interior wishing and striving. The body is conceptually linked to willing, tied up with the meaning of willing; as Elizabeth Anscombe once argued, the most basic sign of wanting something is trying to get it.[15]

We cannot, however, *reduce* the will to the body; or *vice versa*, despite the extravagant hopes of Schopenhauer and other Romantic idealists. For it is conceivable to know one's will, and even to exert will, in the absence of any bodily activity: this would be the condition of post-mortem human souls, ghosts, or sci-fi disembodied intelligences. The body's primary act may be the physical expression of our wishes; but it is not the will's primary act to express our bodies.

There is temptation to regard willing as a purely psychological matter. Will is motivation; thus people have strong wills, act wilfully, are weak willed, exert their wills over others, and so on. This purely psychological willing is the experience I have when I try, unsuccessfully, to raise my broken arm. But this psychological experience of unsuccessful will – *volens interruptus* – is not the primary experience of will; the primary experience is the practical one of being attracted by some perceived good and inclined to respond. Willing is not just the response, if any, to some stimulus or directing inner power, but orienting ourselves towards what we find desirable. Thus willing is a moral or 'practical' capacity, not a purely psychological phenomenon;[16] and thus for Aristotle and Aquinas, the most important quality for a good will is not strength but justice, the virtue which raises the will to the good of people other than ourselves (justice gives us a will for the 'common good'[17]).

How does this moral dimension of willing relate specifically to the body? To will the good of another is first to see him as I see myself – embodied as well as rational, with all the characteristics of human vulnerability and human dependence. When I see another as sharer in my/our human nature in this way, an impartial reason will recognise that what I believe good for me to do for me is generally also good for me to do for him. Justice simply directs the will from its natural tendency towards the agent's good to a cultivated tendency towards others' good as well, and so to the common good. Justice does not transform the 'natural' will from its bodily focus to a sort of moral transcendence of the body; rather, it extends our body-centred care and concern for ourselves to similar concern for other selves – to every*body*.

Reflection on philosophical theories of human nature and on one's own life and experiences suggests that a human being is an emotional, perceptive, linguistic, and volitional being. Exercise of these four body-centred powers is essential for human flourishing. When we do actualise our nature in these ways, we share in certain benefits or goods: *emotional sensitivity* and *tranquility*; *sensory awareness* and *delight*; *verbal fluency* and *expression*; personal, moral, and political *insight*. Such sensitivity, awareness, fluency, and insight are truly good, but good because they are particular ways in which individuals share in yet more basic human goods (such as friendship, knowledge, art, family, and so on; about which more below).

No specific correlating activities exercise these capacities and so secure these goods (there is no ordinary and always effective way to develop feeling, heighten perception, communicate successfully, or will ethically). However, social interaction is particularly important for exercising each of these powers; and since they are bodily powers, bodily (including neurophysiological) health is essential too. Furthermore, without the capacity for rational thought, all four bodily powers would be either inoperable or unstable: sustaining emotion without rational direction, perception without rational reflection, language without rational belief, and will without rational desire would be either impossible or chaotic.

Above all, we should recognise that this is a different account of emotion, perception, communication, and will from that presumed by consumerism (and by consumerist leisure). Emotion here is judgement of reality capable of intelligent guidance and improvement: not excitement, preference satisfaction, or unquestioning response to a narrow range of stimuli. Perception is adopting intelligent perspectives on the world and delighting in its sensory impact: not a stimulation-mechanism to be manipulated by advertising, peer pressure, and envy. Communication is the imaginative creation and use of various means of conversation: not passively receiving or even swapping simple messages about superficial matters via user-pays media. Will is striving for the good and lifting one's mind to the common good: not merely acting upon or asserting impulses and adding to the 'demand' that in turn affects 'supply'.

Sensitivity and tranquility, articulation and expression, awareness and delight, and personal, moral, and political insight are human goods that are necessary for well-being, and sought or obtained through activities such as interaction, basic healthcare, and rational thinking; not through consumerist activity – though reasonable commercial transactions may of course be properly involved in our interaction, healthcare, and rational thinking. These goods are the results of people recognising, respecting, and realising their potential for emotion, sensory perception, communication, and will. They are unlikely to be experienced where people's central values are commodities and upward mobility through self-identification with possessions.

Imagination, intellect, sociability, sexuality

Imagination is both the creation, from perceptions and memories, of images which can then be stored in readiness for subsequent thought; and the capacity for creative work. This latter 'artistic' operation of imagination is peculiar to human beings. Imaginative people or people of creativity are not people of fancy: they deal in fictions but fictions are not mistaken, fantastical views of reality, but reality depicted in a way that helps us to understand some new truths about it. Our capacity for creating and appreciating fictions and art may well be a relatively late human development in which simpler inclinations for knowledge and for attractive and beautiful things came together. Thus the move people sometimes make from popular culture to high, artistic culture may not be so much a move to 'real' art from something of a lesser order, but rather the development of an increased role for reason and imagination within the primitive response to the attractive and meaningful: people satisfied with popular culture have not (yet) combined the basic inclinations for knowledge and for attractive things.

In its other work of creating and storing images from our perceptions – a capacity we seem to have in common with at least some other animals – imagination also involves reason. Once our perception of some object is complete the object can be stored as an image so that when we return to the image mentally, we are able to ponder and make judgements about the object: intellect can 'abstract' from the object we imagine those of its features that are universal and so thinkable.[18] For example, from the smell of wet fur I construct and store an image of my wet cat which, later, I may call to mind in order to work out from general features of wetness and catness how the animal got a soaking, what soaking does to cats, and so on.

Because images can exist without our currently thinking of them, or perceiving their objects, they are transitory phenomena: they come *from* perceptions and are headed *towards* cognitions. This sometimes causes people to assume that imagination is less real or reliable than sense perception or thought. But images do have real existence and significance of their own. It is true, however, that the real purpose of imagination is to provide from perception the wherewithal for thinking: strictly speaking, we do not need images in order to perceive; but they do provide indispensable material for the operations of human reason. That material, however, does not just serve to inform reason but also works to influence the quality of our reason; for example, in someone with a healthy imagination, imagination works to stop reason from becoming 'cold', and the person from being overly rationalistic.

Intellect, together with will, constitutes mind – the part of us that many believe survives death. People sometimes confuse reason with intellect; but all human capacities, and not only intellect, are shot through with rationality: many are open to rational direction, others affect reason's operation, even if not affected by it. It is true, however, that intellect is the part of human nature most transparent to reason. Logical and discursive thought is either rational or irrational: there is no non-rational or a-rational thinking.

The nature of intellect is an enormous subject. But at its core is the relation between our ability to understand the essences of objects – to see things as intelligible, as what they really are – and our ability to understand principles and to apply them to the things we think about so as to understand them. These are closely related abilities: after all, things are as they are because of the first principles that explain them. But just how these two abilities inter-relate in our everyday thinking, from the highly conscious to the barely conscious, is a deeply controversial matter.

The nature of reason is a similarly vast topic and there is no real philosophical consensus on the nature and scope of rationality.[19] I have suggested that reason is not simply one other part of human nature, but a pervasive factor in a fulfilled human life and a key to successfully realising other parts of our nature. Perhaps we can say the major work of reason is comprehending natural limitations to our thought and choice, and then studying the implications of these limitations for our thinking and choosing. Rational beings recognise laws, logical and moral, which specify the furthest extent of the conceivable and the desirable; increase or growth in rationality is increased knowledge of and commitment to such laws. Thus increase in rationality would involve greater understanding of the laws of reason and better application of these laws in thought and action.

There are certainly close ties between rational activity and the activities of intellect; the connections between our grasp of essences and principles and our understanding and application of rational laws are complex, though contemporary philosophers show much less interest in this than do scholars of the ancients and medievals. We should therefore note the privileged bond between reason and intellect, but avoid reductionism here: not only intellect but also emotions, imagination, will, and communication depend on rational laws.

The human capacity for sociability is perhaps the least contested part of our nature. Aristotle was the first to suggest that not only are we social by nature, but our nature is sociable – participation in organised social life is intrinsic to human nature and so part-constitutive of flourishing.[20] Most of the interaction in which social life involves us is fairly impersonal: the cooperative and bureaucratic acts of citizens. But our social nature also expresses itself in a range of personal relationships, which Aristotle analyses in the eighth and ninth books of the *Nicomachean Ethics*.

He suggests that the highest form of personal relationship is close friendship, in which people who are virtuous and each other's social and intellectual equals grow to love each other's good.[21] Both sociability in general and the capacity for close friendship are parts of our nature. People can of course choose to opt out of particular societies and can renounce their citizenship; but if this includes attempted de-socialisation, self-ostracism, and rejection of all close friendship, then the person is harmed in ways for which no increase in other forms of good can compensate him.

Sexuality may run even more deeply in our natures than sociability. Humans alone make societies; but sex is something we share with most other animals, and with many plants. Sex therefore connects us with wider than human (or animal) parts of nature, and in this sense is a very old, very basic part of our make-up. Being sexed is one of the most primitive signs of our natural bond with other living things. If this is so, then sex in the natural sense of masculinity and femininity, or what politicised accounts call 'gender', runs very deep indeed in our natures – deeper than race, ethnicity, culture, creed. Sex in this sense is not preference: it is the capacity, whether realised or not, for meaningful, intimate union with the other sex, and for making a family out of that union. Human fulfilment requires coming to understand and act upon the urge for sex and for making a home.

'Having sex' is not essential to fulfilment: choosing celibacy is a perfectly natural response to sexuality, not a tragedy (though being 'left on the shelf', or jilted, or embittered by celibacy may be); but understanding and making choices about marriage and family is essential to our happiness. Even people with same-sex attraction do not thereby have a ready-made stance of anti-marriage and anti-family: that comes, where it does, only with culture and deliberate decision. Same-sex attraction could even offer some people different opportunities to share in, support, encourage (even if not contract) marriages, as well as personal roles in (their own and other people's) families, and different duties to provide for family life in general. Thus the capacity of sexuality is not the human potential for (having) sex; it is our potential for discovering and following ways in which we can engage in married and family life.[22] An implication of this is that haters of the other sex, marriage, or family will lead diminished lives.

Imagination, intelligence, sociability, and sexuality are parts of our nature that have to be appropriately realised for fulfilment. Exercising these capacities is productive of human goods of *creativity and appreciation of beauty, truth and understanding, love and friendship,* and *marriage and family*. These are *basic* goods: they are good in themselves; it requires citation of no other good than appreciation (or truth, or friendship, or family) to explain the value to us of a certain related activity. Activities that most naturally and effectively exercise these capacities and so give rise to these goods include: artistry and appreciation of artistic and natural beauties; study, learning, and contemplation; socialising and self-sacrifice; love-making and home-building.

Yet again, this view of human nature is rather different to that assumed by consumerist society or ideology. On my account, imagination is aesthetic activity or creating and storing images for future thinking: not exploitative stimulation of the fanciful or the over-familiar. Intelligence is knowledge of essences and principles: not instrumental reasoning about how to get more and increase status. Sociability aims at the reciprocal love of the virtuous: not just the pleasure-sustaining or utility-sustaining relationships of the commercial and fashionable worlds. And sexuality is our potential for permanent union and genuine domesticity: not promiscuity, 'recreational sex', and an expensive house.

The basic goods of creativity, appreciation, truth, friendship, and family are not commodities, and they cannot be sought as such. They slip from our grasp when we place price tags on them and apply the logic of 'upgrade here for a bigger and better offer'. They are the results of action that directly realises our capacities for imagination, intelligence, sociability, and sexuality.

From vitality to transcendence

There are, finally, some other significant, though perhaps more philosophically controversial, aspects of human nature. First, to engage in activity we must live – not just in the sense of being alive and surviving but also having reasonable hope of continuing health, safety from accident, and security from attack. Human life, health and security are essential to human flourishing.

But to live in this sense, and even to flourish in the other parts of our nature outlined above, would still be to lack something. A good human life is not one in which our capacities are exercised either in rigidly ordered, pre-programmed sequence, or in disordered chaos. Rather, our capacities are unified into clusters by circumstance and choice, and our discrete acts are formed into habitual and goal-directed plans and activities. Thus we have various second-order capacities for bringing unity to the exercise of the more primary parts of our nature.

Although we belong to the rational species, we are routinely less than perfectly rational in our choices. Outright irrationality may be rare, but periodic unreasonableness is common. The attempt to review and unify choices to ensure that our chosen goals constitute a reasonable plan of life and that our activities cohere with these goals is traditionally called '*phronesis*': planning a life and living in accord with a good plan.

Phronesis is the quality of reason which means agents can judge well how to live and what to choose. It was almost dealt a death blow by early twentieth century philosophy, which reduced it – where it mentioned it at all – to strategy, caution, self-interest; but it has made a good recovery in recent philosophical literature. *Phronesis* implies realising our nature in ways that reflect and support a reasonable plan of life: not simply aiming to share in important goods, but doing so in coherent activity that is compatible with our long-term and serious goals.[23] As I suggested above, reason has a special status in achieving well-being – a status confirmed by the fact that the self-reflection in which we identify the basic structures of our well-being is itself a paradigmatically rational activity. Reason is ineliminable from every deliberate human thought and act;[24] it therefore has a necessary role not only in identifying our capacities, but in determining the order in which we should realise them.

Conscience has been even more effectively banished from twentieth and twenty first century philosophy than *phronesis*; or at least it has been replaced with something like 'strongest preference', 'fondest wish', 'best hunch', or 'sincerity' (often still called 'conscience' out of fondness, or perhaps awe). Yet conscience in the traditional sense of shared moral knowledge (*con-scientia*) is a fundamental requirement of good living – a moral lynchpin for achieving happiness. To apply conscience is to bring one's perceptions, thoughts, and wishes regarding a certain situation together with relevant moral principles so as to judge what, concretely, one should do (or should have done). Without conscience, *phronesis* is inadequate for a good life, for in following conscience we are explicitly seeking to integrate life-planning with principles of moral decision-making; something that is difficult, and that troubles most people profoundly when they fail at it.[25]

Finally, people who choose activities and so have goals will always wish to consider ultimate goals. The question of a good life will always raise the further questions: 'is this the *best* life?', and 'if it ends, what then?', 'why is this the best life?, and 'why do I have life at all?' The capacity of human beings to ponder such questions – the capacity for transcendence – is an irreducible component of a human life. The capacity is often exercised inadequately (superstitiously, ignorantly, emotionally, sentimentally and so on), but if it is abused or ignored altogether, then we are harmed. For spiritual reflection, transcendent questioning, is required to give lasting unity and a sense of destiny to all our other capacities; without it, we are unfulfilled. All cases of true human happiness – as opposed to people simply having a good time – are instances of persons who have dealt honestly with the pressing questions of transcendence and religion. Our capacity for transcendence, or super-nature, is part of our nature.

Again, these parts of our nature point to various basic goods: health, reasonableness, moral uprightness, and religion. These goods are typically achieved through certain correlating activities that directly realise our capacities: (physical and mental) healthcare, philosophising (formally, or informally), taking counsel, meditating, praying. Again too, none of these capacities is explained as consumerism explains them.

On my account, life is integrated functioning and wholeness: not just a matter of quality of conscious experience. *Phronesis* is planning a life wisely: not following the pre-written scripts of fashionable modern life-styles. Conscience is moral knowledge and its application: not personal choice and felt sincerity. Transcendence is encounter with a source of ultimate meaning that proposes solutions to life's questions: not worshipping an image of self that only causes additional questions. The basic goods we achieve through realising these capacities – health, reasonableness, uprightness, and religion – are so far from the 'profile' of commodities that even slick twenty-first century consumerism has to struggle to accommodate them. Despite anxious attempts to privatise or subjectivise these goods, they remain symbols of the parts of human experience that cannot be bought or sought for status or fashion. Thus we think of them as goods of integrity, centrepieces of human privacy, and the territory of our individual commitments and obligations.

The elements of this account of human nature then are: emotion, sense perception, language, will, imagination, intelligence, sociability, sexuality, life, *phronesis*, conscience, and transcendence (with their associated q-basic and basic goods). And finally, recreation, for I have left our capacity for recreation for separate discussion.

Human nature and recreation

Part of consumerist leisure's impact has been to entrench the view of persons as passive consumers of others' ideas, products, and services with little or no judgement or invention of their own. Since consumerist leisure generally equates leisure and recreation, people in consumerist societies often see recreation as a brief break between activities of production or consumption, or idle leisure activities that make very few demands on us, or consumption of leisure goods and services that particularly please us. Recreation as a natural human power – the capacity to take charge of our lives, to reform and revitalise ourselves – is very much an alien idea.

When people do think of 'recreation-as-empowerment' today, they probably think of it in religious or philosophical terms. Thus religious writers can describe experiences such as conversion, repentance, and reconciliation as receiving, or praying for, a 'new heart', 'new spirit', 'renewal in body and soul'. And philosophical writers describe or certainly used to describe people's 'philosophies of life' as their ways of living by wisdom and, where we fail here, correcting our thoughts and purifying our motives so as to live more fittingly or righteously in future.[26] But there is a human need for renewal that is not particular to any one religious tradition or tied to any specific philosophical school; and there is a basic human capacity for just such renewal.

Even the most ethical and reasonable of lives is not lived as if following a computer programme. No one first adopts commitments about family, work, religion, and friends, next prioritises these by their opportunities and tastes, and then simply proceeds to live as if life is the automatic roll-out of a pre-programmed life-plan. Of course, people sometimes (and particularly when prompted by some suffering or distress) revisit their plans, and question the coherence and compatibility of their plans with ultimate goals. But people also, without questioning the basic form of their lives, seek fresh understanding of, recommitment to, and renewed gratitude for the lives they are leading. And further, people need regular periods of forgetfulness of their major commitments and rest from implementing their plans.

Such rest and relaxation are common, perhaps daily occurrences. Recommitment and renewal are rarer, but still identifiable experiences. For example, someone becomes aware of the value and intense happiness of a specific relationship, realises that a project long worked on is actually coming together as he hoped, is suddenly conscious of his own health and strength, reaches a moment of clarity in a conscientious decision, experiences the integration and sense of blessedness that comes, uniquely, through religious encounter. Such rejuvenating experiences are marked by confirmation of the broad outlines of our lives, fresh allegiance to them, and thankfulness for the rich fulfilment that life brings to us.

If we were to research each of these experiences, I suspect they would consist overwhelmingly in restoring to the exercise of some of our capacities a share in the (q-basic and basic) goods produced by these capacities. Thus someone goes from day to day exercising his capacity for sociability but growing stale in his relationships, not enjoying the basic goods of love and friendship that accompany these (not delighting in the company of spouses, playing with children, making new friendships, sharing 'quality' time and so on). Or a student or scholar goes through the motions of another hard slog in the library but without the excitement and wonder that can come from meeting the truth and having one's perspective changed. Recreation here is the restoration to us of the natural human goods that accompany exercise of our basic capacities. In sharing more fully in these goods, our understanding of and commitment to the activities connected with our capacities is increased.

Where recreation, either as rest or renewal, is obtained, there may be benefit for each part of our nature. None of our capacities, after all, is unconnected and self-standing. Natural capacities are integrated into a complex life, and where, for example, there is *bodily* rest or renewal this is not just physical reconditioning, but also encouragement to persevere in my endeavours at work, take new heart in approaching difficulties in relationships, find fresh angles on some intellectual or moral problem I am pondering, and so on. Similarly, to experience relaxation or rejuvenation through *meditation* is not just to receive spiritual enlightenment and peace, but also to enjoy new intensity of perception and strength of will, to notice new dimensions of other people, enjoy release of physical tension, and so on. In recreation, then, the benefits of rest and renewal in one part of our lives can be extended throughout our lives more generally speaking.

Recreation ordinarily comes through leisure. Playful leisure typically offers rest, refreshment, and recovery; and reflective leisure is particularly effective in achieving new heart, vitality, and greater hope for the future. Leisure activities are rich in the benefits they bring: typically, they fulfil some part(s) of us immediately (as intellect, imagination, and emotion are fulfilled by the activity of writing); fulfil the capacity for recreation (as play and/or reflection); and achieve for us a share in goods linked to all these capacities. Thus whether leisure offers dramatic recreation (personal development and a fresh outlook through reflection) or only routine recreation (another fresh start through play), well-chosen leisure is important for life and happiness.

We need not, however, consciously pursue recreation while we sing, or socialise, or study. Indeed, our well-being is often best served by building up good leisure habits that serve recreation without conscious deliberation or the need for frequent choices on our part.

Virtue and happiness

Reflective leisure activities are demanding because reflection on human life is among the most abstract and non-empirical of activities. It is therefore greatly to our recreational advantage, and for our ultimate happiness, if leisure becomes habitual, so that good leisure activity is part of our natural response to having free-time and so that reflective leisure becomes a source of familiar pleasure to us. Becoming habituated in choices such as contemplation, study, and appreciation of beauty may seem a tall order for many people. But it is here that the connection with play once again becomes relevant. Huizinga's analysis showed the deep naturalness of play to us, and the ways in which so natural an activity is taken up into our major cultural activities and institutions. Because reflective leisure activities can be playful as well as reflective, it is actually far easier to become habituated in them than their reflective status may suggest.

People play without prompting, and our play habits are ready sources of spontaneous motivation and familiar pleasures. So where the reflective activity has been well integrated with our play lives, developing good habits of play will include natural and enjoyable performance of the reflective activity. Someone who often plays as she paints or prays may come to play, and so paint or pray, habitually, thereby producing regular quality recreation for herself.

Good play habits are traditionally known as *eutrapelia*. *Eutrapelia*, which means literally 'turning well' or dancing around appropriately, is the special virtue of play, discussed by both Aristotle and Aquinas. *Eutrapelia* is reasonable attitude towards playing and games: the *eutrapelos* avoids the extremes of clownish buffoonery on the one hand and pomposity or boorishness on the other.[27] Aquinas discusses the importance of this virtue in the *Summa* and the *Commentary on the Nicomachean Ethics*. It is 'a virtue of Greek *humanitas*, baptized in Christ.'[28] Aquinas discusses the need for leisure time away from hard work and routine activity, and the need for play that is not vulgar or grudging but which represents a 'happy turn of mind'.[29] Hugo Rahner writes that for Aquinas, the well-turning man possesses 'a kind of mobility of soul, by which a truly cultured person "turns" to lovely, bright, and relaxing things, without losing himself in them; it is, so to speak, a spiritual elegance of mind in which his seriousness and his moral character can be perceived.'[30]

This civilising ideal is a highly appropriate approach to integrating play and reflection as a habit. Where buffoonery or philistinism become habitual play-vices, there is little hope of play habits hosting reflective activities. But where we become habituated in play that is eutrapelic – that does not seek to draw attention to ourselves or to belittle others, but rather seeks appropriate relaxation from our labours and honest fun with our talents – this play can readily support reflective activities. It will also help to maintain these activities as leisure: as delightful and uplifting, not as effortful or burdensome.

Because leisure serves recreation and can form virtuous habits it has an important role in happiness. Happiness requires full and appropriate realisation of human capacities, and reasonable pursuit of the moral life – clearly, closely related ends, though the latter is not my subject in this book. As I have argued, realising the human capacity for recreation has significant effects on other parts of our nature; therefore, it will have significant effects on our happiness generally. Some would argue that leisure serves happiness simply by giving us a break, satisfying our personal pleasures, or providing amusement and distraction. But such instrumental views of leisure reduce it to the experiences of relaxation and fun that (can) accompany leisure where it is playful. Leisure's more substantial contribution to happiness is achieving recreation and making the dividends of this recreation available throughout our lives generally. Thus leisure serves happiness by assisting in the on-going work of fully realising important parts of ourselves and providing us with a share in the various goods natural to human fulfilment.

There are two additional benefits which leisure brings to our pursuit of happiness. The first is encouraging us to guide as many of our choices as possible by the ideal or 'final end' of activity that is its own fulfilment. People who practice reflective leisure will be very used to activities that are done for their own sakes, and so will be more open to a life that is fulfilled and complete in itself, not looking beyond itself or striving for other real or imagined benefits. A good life is not formed by conscious focus on developing parts of our nature, bit by bit, piecemeal: with such an approach to life, choices would tend to degenerate into an interest in the individual capacities themselves rather than an interest in human life and fulfilment. Rather, a good life is one lived for the final good of leading a truly happy life. And such an ideal will tend to be more coherent and more attractive to people who regularly take part in self-fulfilling leisure activities.

Secondly, a healthy leisure life includes reflection. And not only are the chances of happiness greatly increased if we regularly examine our lives and choices reflectively; additionally, the inclusion of serious reflection within a human life dramatically alters the quality of its happiness. Reflective people are more aware of the path towards happiness and of obstacles on that path, so they are more prone to cherish happiness and to seek it wisely.

Challenging consumerism

This account of leisure and recreation cannot be justified on consumerist assumptions; and those assumptions are almost universal in modern societies. If the account is situated within a theory of human nature such as the one offered here, however, its justification is clear: leisure, whether playful or reflective, enables recreation, and recreation is restoration and renewal of the person pointing him towards a happy life. This is not a theory of the person that can be held by anyone who accepts consumerist assumptions; for this theory explains the person in terms of potential for flourishing in multiple dimensions, whereas consumerism explains the person in terms of satisfaction through identification with products we unendingly consume and the lifestyle that accompanies this.

Nevertheless, we should consider accepting the theory derived from natural law and so rejecting consumerism and its account of leisure. Two main reasons for rejecting consumerism are that this would justify our acceptance of reflective leisure which would improve the quality of life for many busy, stressed people; and secondly, that consumerism rests upon an inadequate view of the human person as consumer of resources and seeker of status, a view promoted simply to sustain and to spread consumerism's total logic.

An alternative to the natural law theory and to consumerism is to abandon altogether institutions such as buying and owning. This 'opting out' of commerce, purchase, and ownership – whether as consumerist lifestyle, or more limited service of natural human capacities – is only possible as part of a total opting out of many other social institutions and practices. This idealistic approach is advocated by postmodernism, as it once was by earlier modernists. But it is hardly a solution, since we are obliged to take some part in important social institutions if we are to be sufficiently active, informed, and to enjoy sufficient social relationships within our modern democracies. That liberal democracy implies consumerism is one of the great lies; and accepting this lie causes some to infer from the need to reject consumerism the need to reject democracy, with the postmodern intellectual and moral chaos consequent upon that. Liberal democracy does, however, imply necessary consumption.

A better approach to commerce and to necessary consumption would begin by recognising the place of material goods and manufacture and trade and merchandising within our complex human life and nature. We consume to live – food most obviously, and then the materials out of which we construct our clothes, homes and other buildings, healthcare, work, study, artistic works, religious images. In other words, there is a range of material goods properly required for the fulfilment of each part of our nature and our enjoyment of the associated q-basic and basic goods. These material goods are amongst our basic needs: they are *needed* so that human nature can flourish and goods be enjoyed. In addition, for many generations, we have not just taken material goods but made them into more complex and more fulfilling goods. Thus if modern people are to rear children, live long and healthy lives, work productively, educate themselves suitably, and so on, manufacture must be adopted; and the most rational approach here will be extensive manufacture by some as their chosen work. In turn, manufacture makes trade possible, and in large societies, particularly those that have trade relations with other, foreign societies, trade means merchants and whole systems of commerce and exchange.

This much is obvious. Just as obvious is the historical development of different economic systems and the legal systems, political codes and treaties that accompany these. The difficulties arise when there is an economic system, bolstered by a social ideology and supporting legal and political norms, that does not treat material goods as valuable; that instead treats persons as material goods, and argues that the value of material goods is simply the speed and success with which they can pass through the hands of consuming persons, who are somehow thereby 'dignified' by ownership.

Believers in consumerism are quick to say they do not believe that brand name and designer goods and bluechip services have value in themselves: rather, these items identify the consumer as a certain 'sort' of person, someone of status. But in arguing this, they actually downgrade the real, material value material goods have to (embodied) persons; for they treat food and clothes and books and transport simply as signs of status, indicators of club-membership to other fellow-consumers. Also, the consumerist here treats the person as material; bizarrely, more material than the goods he consumes. The person is simply a swallower of the food (books, clothes, opportunities and so on) that is currently deemed appropriate: he is a channel through which approved products and services will pass before being discarded as waste products. On this view, we are required, neurotically, to purchase and to show off our purchase quickly, for soon the brand will be out of fashion: where something becomes very popularly fashionable, it is cause, in this system, of its own imminent descent in the fashion stakes.

This theory finds little role for reasonable selection of goods and services that help us to realise human capacities in ways that respect (all) such capacities, ourselves, other persons, and the various other surrounding demands of the moral life. Where special pleas are entered in consumerist society – for example, for a broad range of educational opportunities feeding the life of the mind, comprehensive health services that heal whole persons, support for large, well fed, and well housed families, provision of great art to every citizen, generously endowed programmes to remove every drop-out by providing free drug rehabilitation – they are either rejected or grudgingly given the funding left over after 'necessary' (economic) commitments have been provided for.

Strangely, no one likes to be called 'a consumerist'. People rebel at the idea that all there is to them is their consumption of fashion labels

and status symbols. Those who are most deeply or flamboyantly consumerist usually believe there is more to their 'successful' lives than
compulsive commerce. In other words, even in the face of perhaps the
most successful ideological total logic ever, people actually continue to
identify themselves by the basic human capacities – to claim that what
matters most is life and health, knowledge, family, friendship, nature
and art, the religious life. This is not hypocrisy. It suggests that it is
not impossible to reclaim a natural law understanding of the person,
not impossible to make people question consumerist total logic. But
why do people identify themselves in practice by their consumption of
goods and services while rejecting the judgement that that is their real
personal identity?

One possibility is that our extensive daily involvement in consumerism is only an epiphenomenon of our actual lives. We live, as we
must, in the real world: realising or failing to realise parts of our
nature, enjoying or hindering our share in real human goods; yet
our social, and perhaps to some extent our inner, lives are also played
out as a continuous drama in scenes of buying, acquiring, performing
the right activities, possessing and saying and doing the fashionably
uncontroversial, status-enhancing thing. This image of an epiphenomenal life, a doppelganger-like existence, may not be entirely metaphorical. We do tune in and out of social situations regularly and smoothly:
we may move often between engagement with real (real-ised) life and
ideological life. Thus when challenged seriously about their basic
beliefs and purposes and values, people respond by appeal to real
capacities and objective goods, in which of course we all believe; but
when permitted to continue engagement with 'ordinary' life with like-
minded consumers and no criticism of their motives, the same people
place high or highest value on possessions and a certain life-style. If
there is any truth in this, the presence of a TV in every home is highly
significant, since it allows us to play out simultaneously in our living
rooms real life and ideological life, life lived epiphenomenally, and not
just vicariously, through the screen.[31]

Perhaps epiphenomenal life mirrors our worry at the continual need
to prove our status, especially in a world which has officially abolished
status and made us all equals. We are unaccustomed to the idea that
status can be won by birth, brains, skills, personal nobility, virtue; so
we seek status through ephemera – fashions and social approval, which
by definition are constantly changing. But this is self-defeating. The
neurosis behind this perhaps suggests a belief that, despite our real
human status and dignity and the objective goods we enjoy, 'real life'

must be elsewhere, purchasable if I keep buying, since my own life seems so unreal, unimportant, and not what really matters.

Such anxiety has had a terrible effect on happiness in the modern world; and consumerist leisure has of course been parasitical on the anxiety, failed to provide recreation that might offer relief from the anxiety. Indeed, so bland has consumerist leisure become that the drop-outs in the streets now look more interesting, eccentric, individual, freer than the rest of us.

The fact that so many people resist the judgement that they are purely fashion-led, compulsive consumers suggests that the doppelganger scenario expresses some truth: people still care very much about real human life in which (necessarily) even the wildest consumer must take part. Nevertheless, many people appear satisfied with this schizophrenic life, at least until the experience of stress becomes crippling for them. Rejecting consumerism would be traumatic: it would mean making human nature, basic and q-basic human goods, and human fulfilment, the centrepieces of our social and personal lives; it would also mean restoring the relation between leisure and reflection that these two shared from antiquity down to the beginnings of the industrial age, and focusing once again on the importance of recreation for the person. This would take a seismic social shift, an almost unthinkable change in lifestyle for many, or even most.[32] And it would no doubt be castigated as 'elitist' or benighted or millenarian by many social commentators.

But the only other choices seem to be to maintain, until we can bear it no longer, the total logic of consumerism, as its empire continues to grow and our anxieties to increase; or to embrace the postmodern narrative, in which consumerism, natural law, and the other rejected philosophies of modernity are exchanged for, literally, nill, and reflection on meaning is diagnosed as self-deceit or power-trip.

To complete my case for rethinking our leisure, I will look at some major leisure activities and ask to what extent they are, or would benefit from becoming, playful or reflective. Finally, I consider the relation of leisure to our working lives, and to the performing arts.

4
Playing by the Book

If questioned about their leisure activities today, many would cite as their main choice watching TV or reading. Despite decades of egalitarian talk and theory, these still indicate a social division: whether or not they are frequent readers, most would consider reading to be respectable use of leisure time and TV watching to be very slightly shameful. Leisure TV seems to identify people as having ordinary interests, being unimaginative, even uncultured. This perception is interesting. People lament growing illiteracy, but still reading has not become tarnished or downgraded in the public eye; and certainly, the mass production and retail of books is one of the great commercial success stories of the twentieth century. Most people still value reading as an ability. It remains a key to social status as well as a central leisure activity – and big business.

Reading is well placed to serve as reflective leisure, most obviously as means to study, contemplation, artistic appreciation. It is also playful leisure: a major source of relaxation and entertainment from childhood and throughout life. Not all reading is leisure, of course. Yet if we do choose to read as leisure, reading can provide, for minimum effort, major opportunities for quiet reflection and enjoyable relaxation. Reflective leisure has something to say about the nature and motivation of our reading: reading can serve to develop knowledge, taste, appreciation, and can open up reflection on serious questions and the ways in which people have tried to answer these. Meanwhile, playful leisure suggests that reading should be aimed at recreation through relaxation and pleasure: it should not serve external ends such as titillation or snobbery.

St Paul urged the early Christian Thessalonians that they should 'study to be quiet.'[1] Part of reading's special value is the opportunity for peace that it offers. Readers may experience contemplative moments, calm appreciation of or reflection upon the world. They have the opportunity to think without urgency about the meaning of things and to admire others' efforts to capture this. The best reading both invigorates and refreshes, and does not exhaust.

Something as personal and as solitary as reading has a certain insulation from consumerist pressures. But even here the market challenges the ideal of reading as contemplative pleasure. Best-sellers and blockbusters push other works to the back of the shelves; philosophy sections are replaced by 'Body, Mind, and Spirit' shelves; book supermarkets spring up with offers of 'three for the price of two'. Consumerism sees reading as worth colonising, and yet the world of reading still has mysterious status in most (especially unlearned) people's eyes. If so, why are we so much less a reading culture than we were previously? Why do so few students read as a habit, willingly use libraries, and know about the world of books and about literature?

First, literacy is more common than literary understanding. Literacy is an important tool and a popular entertainment in modern societies. We all benefit from (most people) being able to read instructions, directions, forms, surveys, questionnaires, and so on. And individuals take great daily delight in newspapers, theme magazines, bestselling fiction, comic books, and other pleasure-building or time-passing literature. But it does not follow from this that people use their literacy to increase their range of interests, deepen their understanding of some topic to semi-specialist level, investigate relations between different works, seek out new types of writing.

We often assume that in earlier times a wider variety of better quality reading was consumed by a broader reading public. We think that issues of depth and substance were more commonly given serious literary treatment, and that this was more seriously received. If this is true, it suggests that though reading today is a source of mass leisure, it is not the source of quality recreation it once was. As consumerism has extended over our leisure time, reading as leisure has lost its reflective status.

The history behind the claim that reflective reading has declined could be described sociologically, statistically, politically, or philosophically. A philosophical treatment will focus on various dimensions of reading, on analysis of what reading is, and the forms of value reading possesses. By charting changes within these literary dimensions, we can highlight changes in the recreational potential of reading. Some of these changes do suggest that reflective reading has reduced status today: that it is often seen as irrelevant and elitist; and that where people do read for leisure they are generally happier with non-reflective, non-demanding reading that pleasantly passes the time.

A second reason for declining interest in reflective reading is the Net. It is too early to know if this phenomenon will last for very long; we often tend to think that hugely popular devices will last for aeons, but of course there is little evidence of this. Replaceability is a major feature of technology, which is, after all, just one more aspect of contemporary consumerism. The motor car has lasted a century; cinemas, radios, telephones, television, and so on slightly less; near obsolete items such as teletext and fax machines may well have lasted less than thirty years. If we cannot assess the Net's staying power yet, we can assess its present impact.

The Net's effects on reading have been dramatic. Most obviously, it gives access to huge amounts of data, entire libraries. Does this mean that it is good for the reading public; or do the technical difficulties of using the Net, its lack of discrimination and self-monitoring, its tendency to minimise thought, originality, and analysis and to fragment readers into self-selecting interest-groups mean that it is in fact bad for the reading public? What seems clear is that the Net has not served to increase the incidence and quality of reflection; the Net is not major equipment for lasting recreation.

My brief survey of some dimensions of reading suggests that in an age that is leisure-conscious but recreation-shy there are good reasons to press for more good reading. Habits of serious reading are good for play and for reflection. They can achieve personal recreation in the sense described in Chapter 3 because they allow us to play with important and fascinating ideas – and even whole worlds – outside of our strictly necessary ends and purposes.

Reading silently and reading aloud

To most people, reading suggests sitting comfortably with one's head in a book. In fact, reading silently developed slowly from a number of sources, including listening: following a read text in one's head. There are reasons to consider reading aloud and being listened to as the primary reading activity. In antiquity, reading generally did mean reading aloud, although by the time ancient authors came to write largescale works of reflective history and philosophy, silent reading by author and reader can be taken for granted.

Today, though reading aloud is important in certain cultures and contexts,[2] many of us are read to only as children – and this too may be dying out. Talking books, authorial readings, 'book at bedtime' radio shows, and Scripture readings are now minority tastes; as, in the age of email, is the reading out of letters around the breakfast table. Reading aloud in the household was of course a great nineteenth century diversion[3] (though one not universally appreciated, as in Lydia Bennett's impatient response to Mr Collins reading aloud from 'improving' material in *Pride and Prejudice*). In the more distant days of thriving monasteries, the reading aloud or chanting of sacred texts and foundational narratives and 'Rules' helped to hold the community together and initiate the young into the tradition. Later, scholastic education and the creation of the first universities depended upon the new notion of spoken lectures based on Scripture readings and theological exegesis (a generation ago people still spoke of 'reading' English at university).[4]

For the monks, being able to read became an important part of worship and spiritual life. In his famous Rule, St Benedict made reading, aloud and silently, essential to the life of a monastery. Monastic reading included the progressive recitation during meals of the 'martyrology', the lives of the saints. These readings had a central role to play in encouraging devotion and supporting the vocations of the brothers who listened communally and piously to tales of their distant ancestors in faith.

Reading aloud decreased with the growth of Protestant traditions with their emphasis on private reading and individual interpretation of Scripture. Since the Reformation, reading aloud has been popular mainly where family life is strong and leisure outside the family circle uncommon, for example, in country areas until recently or in family homes during wartime. But reading aloud remains a powerful symbol in a world that increasingly hates and fears silence and so welcomes noise – particularly noisy leisure. For reading aloud requires careful listening and following a narrative, and this introduces order and meaning into clatter.

Of course, most who read regularly will read silently, and for dedicated readers this is a life-sustaining pleasure; but it is not simply pleasure. Silent communing with a book is one way in which we can lose consciousness of outer and inner distractions. And it is also a way in which we can reflect on what matters, freed from the world of everyday needs and demands, and stimulated only by a book we have chosen for ourselves. In silent reading we inhabit a world that can introduce important new thoughts or clarify a moral universe. Thus reading can recreate, construct a new perspective. For this reason, though few can be alone doing *nothing* with pleasure, most can become entranced alone with a book.

A strong theme in recent philosophy has been the ways in which we construct a 'narrative self'. The idea here is that we have a factual or metaphysical self (the individual I am from my beginning to my end) and we also have a constructed self or self-identity, which alters through time and by choice.[5] This work of self-construction can outstrip our metaphysical 'given' self: thus I might take myself to be a good capitalist now, but still be aware of the closer affinity there is between the youthful socialist I was and my given, metaphysical self. When this happens, I may choose to realign my values (sacrifice my capitalist beliefs), or (stubbornly, weakly, or heroically) choose to remain as I am and live with a break in identity and possibly personality. Private reading helps to keep this process of construction/reconstruction of a self rational, more reflective, and the lives we make for ourselves livable; reading of one sort in particular helps here.

Many people keep diaries. These are not usually intended for publication or for posterity; and they are generally more than factual records. Some are purely autobiographical, others are prescriptive, exhortative, wishful, historical. A major part of writing diaries is clarification of truths about oneself and integration of these into some sort of sense. To write a coherent and honest diary is to critique and guide the self one is becoming: to construct self-narrative from a position of reflective authority. Reading back over a diary, as writers must to some extent in order to continue it coherently, we have perhaps the most intense form of silent reading, reading that is self-reflexive and self-reconstructive. Writing an honest diary is one of the most effective reflective leisure activities, because it is regular, disciplined involvement in recreation of the self. Therefore, silent reading of published diaries also has high recreational potential, through reflection thereby stimulated and through the author's example of how to 'read' one's own life.

Moral purpose of reading

Self-development is a Kantian idea which became very unpopular in the twentieth century, and which later in that century became very popular once again. Today, there are sections of self-help, self-improvement, and self-development books in every high street book store. The objects of these books, however, are often far from Kantian duties to improve ourselves morally and to cultivate significant gifts and talents so we can make a suitable social contribution.

Moral improvement is certainly an important goal of reading: people do seek to improve their minds, tastes, and ideas, from the early discipline of family and school reading, through the development of youthful taste and building up of a repertoire of preferred works, and on to higher studies and choices to extend our reading into new fields and challenges. Readers have responsibility to read well, arising from the general responsibility to take care of ourselves (physically, psychologically, emotionally, intellectually, spiritually and so on) and from the moral responsibility to prepare ourselves so as to make some social contribution. This means there are duties to be observed by all involved in the world of reading: good writers, publishers, suppliers, booksellers, libraries will all give consideration not just to public entertainment, but to the improvement of readers' minds and ideas, and the improvement of the reading culture generally. Today's books may often be a product for consumption, but writing is not, and therefore reading is subject to rights and responsibilities.

It is not many years since a *fatwah* or death sentence was passed upon the author Salman Rushdie for his *Satanic Verses*. Books inflame people – and not just readers: relatively few read *Satanic Verses* (until it became a *cause celebre*), though many felt themselves to be caught up in the controversy. Are there some things that should not be written, or read?

Reflective leisure may imply that anything is publishable, for anything can be means to reflection. But it is not obvious that lies or hate help people to reflect on the meaning of their lives and of our world. Some fictional writing is offensive, inflammatory, provocative, obscene, and in certain circumstances its publication is banned on that account. But law has often made special provision for material that should not appear even if it offends or misleads no one. For example, many states ban blasphemous literature, not on grounds of offence but because it attacks God or things consecrated to God.[6] Pluralists argue this gives an unwarranted status to religion. But deliberate attack on sacred things seeks to undermine the source of ultimate meaning and destiny for whole communities; it refuses to meet and debate faith on its own grounds. If there is a basic human capacity for transcendence, such attacks risk alienating people, and communities, from part of their own deep nature.

There are also duties of factual literature, arising principally from the relation between fact and truth-telling. One might think that the only issues here are those of accuracy and sincerity. But there is also the case of 'revisionists' who produce and circulate apparently serious and sincere studies of the holocaust or the treatment of Aborigines that argue against the mainstream views. If it does not profoundly offend or dangerously incite its readers, may such a work be published, or are there modern political orthodoxies that may not ever be questioned?

Revisionism is usually approached in one of the following ways: the truth here is so clearly otherwise and the assault on human dignity and solidarity made by the book so great that the book can have no sincere purpose except that of hurting, titillating, or causing mischief, so it should not be published. Or: freedom of the factual press and of the author are extremely important values, thus even (probably) erroneous views should be heard precisely so as to demonstrate allegiance to these values and to encourage debate and scrupulous regard for truth.

This is not a debate that specifically concerns leisure reading; nevertheless, my own sympathy is with restrictions on factual work that is profoundly dangerous or provocative and scandalous to the international specialist community (generally, academics) concerned. But since I do not believe that academic self-monitoring is especially reliable, I suggest that this position is only coherent if specialist consensus on the question – and also the very idea of specialist consensus – is *itself* open to question and debate by serious and qualified writers and readers. No one can, coherently, police the policemen but the very idea of police can be coherently questioned and criticised.

As part of reading's moral purpose, we can also ask why readers read what they do? We have different purposes in approaching different styles of writing: information, amusement, cultivation of taste, exposure to places and people beyond our daily range, confirmation of opinions, and so on. Whatever our purpose, behind all reading is the notion of trust. We trust different sorts of people for different sorts of reasons: writers we trust because of their expertise, skill, and industry. We trust their words because we think they are well qualified to write and have exerted themselves to write well.

With factual writing this trust is fragile and extremely important, for almost all of us rely heavily on factual writers for our knowledge and so our opinions. Where we are wary of trusting a writer, we can take exactly the same steps we take when suspicious of anyone: make background checks, consult others, reflect carefully, seek all relevant information, rely on the opinions of wiser and more experienced people or on any well-defined or emerging consensus. The basic sign of trusting someone is accepting his words, and since a book is an offering to us above all of words, it raises some of the very same trust issues as do human relationships.

The ethics of reading and writing will always ring alarm bells. Censorship – the spectre of the Index – still has the power to panic; but in an open, public culture freedom to publish cannot mean absence of principles. Books have a life beyond their authors and publishers because texts exist for readers; that public existence means that authors and publishers must take reasonable steps to ensure that once it leaves their hands, their work will communicate honestly and will respect all readers.

The virtues of the good reader are many. Perhaps temperance is the most important virtue here, but good reading also includes bibliophilia (love of books), healthy curiosity, good judgement, and taste. Where the public culture is a reading culture and one that is healthy, varied, constantly replenished, and respectful of literary excellence, including classic excellence, reading will support the reflective and the moral life. In other words, building up a good reading culture is a better method than censorship for safeguarding the quality of our reading.

Education

Books are not just for leisure; they are also the key to knowledge. Some disagree with this, holding that to treat reading as paramount in education, to give centrality to books, is fraught with difficulties. This claim often has two parts: first, that too much emphasis on reading ignores important modern discoveries about education and relevance; secondly, that making choices about what children should read is or may be coercive or even indoctrination.

On the first claim, book-centred learning seems to be the only education respectful of children's freedom. While attempting to 'win' the classroom for one particular political (or religious) creed is wrong, by teaching reading skills we do the only thing we can that is genuinely creed-neutral: give access to all creeds. Generally, well-read thinkers seem to do comparatively well in life. This is not to say that learning comes only through reading, or that teaching reading is the only legitimate aim of schools (Piaget's theories, and the whole area of aesthetic education – through art, play, nature, environment etc. – come to mind[7]). But reading is beneficial and relevant in all societies and cultures, and it is also the only way to equip people to assess other, non-literary methods of education for themselves.

On the second claim, it is true that indoctrination is wrong, but it does not follow that the only alternative is to leave children to make up their own minds about the importance of reading, or what to read, or any other matter. If we were all left to 'make up our own minds', none of us would ever have a mind to make up. Only the reception of some standards and principles – and those in a coherent, systematic order – gives us the wherewithal later to develop standards and principles of our own, including those by which we may well criticise the systems we were first taught. As in all areas of education, good teaching is not brain-washing as long as reasons are offered for all opinions suggested, and time and resources for critically pondering these reasons is made available.

But education is not only for school and university: a public culture of reading will almost certainly be a better educated culture. Even when reading matter is limited, poor quality, or uniform, readers have the chance to learn a sufficient repertoire of critical concepts to critique the narrow range of reading available. Bad reading is better than no reading because it keeps reading skills and critical skills alive and so can, eventually, inspire commentary and review.

A well educated state is obviously essential, not merely desirable; no supporting argument is needed for the good effects of education upon every sphere of moral, social, and political life. But good effects apart, there are strong educative reasons for promoting and celebrating reading. The most obvious of these is demonstrated by the existence of libraries. The greatest library in history was that of Alexandria, a symbol of human intellectual potential (and in its burning, of tragic loss) for all times. But the primary purpose of the library was not to store books or facilitate study but to hold before the eyes of the world all that man's unaided mind could grasp: 'the magnificent purpose of the library was to encapsulate the totality of human knowledge.'[8] It existed simply to declare how much of truth we had seen and how powerful the human mind is.

Education through reading includes moral education. There are serious philosophical questions concerning moral education. Socrates is the first in western tradition to ask whether moral excellence can be taught at all, and he is extremely doubtful.[9] Whatever the philosophical debate, it seems that the attempt to educate people morally would be very difficult without books. Quite uneducated people, who may be good, even saintly, can raise children perfectly, and often do so much better than their tertiary educated counterparts. But when they do, the education they give is still that of a book, or a reader, writer or disciple, of a book. Not even God whispered the rules for moral learning directly into people's ears: he or his devotees provided a book. Without the existence of a set text, the very notion of moral education – arguably, the very notion of 'morality' – may have occurred to no one.

When Socrates queries teaching morality he does so as a character in one of Plato's books: he wrote no books of his own. We regard Socrates as possessing extraordinary authority and status although, or perhaps because, he only exists in others' books, great books he himself helped to inspire. The founder of ethics is certainly more real to us as a character in Plato's unforgettable dialogues than he would be as a remote historical figure who once did some teaching.

Authority of books

Books and readers have always possessed authority. To those who do not or cannot read, books and readers are intimidating, and those who read reflectively are suspect: 'almost everywhere the community of readers has an ambiguous reputation that comes from its acquired authority and perceived power.'[10] Those outside that community believe, and sometimes with very good reason, in the special knowledge and expertise of those within. For some people, that belief limits the leisure potential of reading: books are too serious, heavy, meant for people with qualifications.

Of course, literate authority comes not just from the ability and willingness to read but from what is read and what is done with it. People who parade their reading are rightly ridiculed as snobs; and avid readers of pulp and slush fiction tend not to be admired for their dedication but ridiculed for their narrowness. Readers of classic fiction, specialist and academic writing, however, are generally respected, or envied, because they choose to encounter great minds and great thoughts and allow themselves to be changed by these. Paradoxically, the less that reading is appreciated, and perhaps the less that authority in general is understood and respected, the greater authority books and those who do read them will come to have.

There are deeper issues too of the authority of books. The ultimate case of author-authority is the Bible, and its own literary history – the history of the 'canons' of the Old and New Testaments – is a study in how literary authority can arise. In reading the Bible, so believers hold, we can trace through a text written over centuries the processes of the world's creation and redemption. In the case of the New Testament, Timothy Radcliffe argues that early Christian communities determined just which of the many beliefs circulating about Christ's legacy were authoritative by inventing on the occasion of each disputation a new sort of writing and thinking that clarified how the authentic tradition should proceed – writing letters in Paul's case ('to be baptised "into Christ" meant to belong to the most efficient postal system in the Empire'[11]), writing Gospels in the case of the first century Church, forming the canonical 'New Testament' by the third and fourth century Church. 'The Tradition cannot be preserved by conserving it, but only by some unanticipated and creative breakthrough that enables us to see what fidelity to the Tradition might entail.'[12]

Radcliffe's point is that when there is uncertainty about the constitutive beliefs of a tradition, the invention of new ways of writing and reading can establish what it means to belong. Thus, according to St Paul, to be Christian is to seek the sort of relationships letter writers have – friendships in which we communicate on equal terms – rather than the less equal or less respectful or more self-focussed forms of reflection that other religions are thought to encourage. In the decades after Paul's death the issue of preserving the radical teachings of Christ was resolved by creating a new form of literature ('gospel') in which a unique mixture of public record and scholarly interpretation is blended within a narrative. Later still, in the fourth century, what it meant to be Christian was established by creating a 'canon', not just a collection of writings but a symbol of communion and identity around which the many local churches could unite as one, universal Church.

For believers, the Bible's authority is grounded on the notion that the Incarnation was both preceded and succeeded by the writing of books in which God spoke directly to and through men and women ('the word of God'). But for non-believers too the Bible is authoritative. The unique history of its creation, publication, and reception throughout the world gives it great interest; and its authority is sealed by its claim that to spread its message effectively this book must be an honest meeting of readers of all cultures, however skeptical, united by their common interest in the great questions that the book addresses.

The case of the Bible suggests that with books of the greatest authority, authority does not come from a single 'authoritative' voice (Jesus himself wrote nothing; the first Pope, Peter, contributed only a very little; 'Homer' almost certainly names a collection of authors separated in time; Socrates speaks only as a character in Plato), but from readers' ability to recognise the authentic version and interpretation of the book when it appears, by remaining faithful to the book's narrative as they have so far received it. This takes wisdom and trust and courage, for in the early days of the life of a great book there is likely to be confusion, split allegiances, and the need for risk-taking, if people are to establish the book's overall coherence. But it is part of the unique authority books possess that millions of human beings (the 'peoples of the book') can base their lives on books, books whose content they believe to come from God, but whose form is settled by men.

The other great canon of western tradition is the secular canon of great literary classics, popularised by T. S. Eliot,[13] and controversially defended in recent times by Harold Bloom.[14] Nothing is more calculated to infuriate certain academics and teachers than the idea of a 'canon' of classic works sharing timeless qualities and possessing seminal status. Bloom argues that what makes his chosen authors and schools canonical is: 'strangeness, a mode of originality that either cannot be assimilated, or that so assimilates us that we cease to see it as strange.'[15] In other words, this is a secular version of creating a new form of writing that reveals how the tradition should be read. Canonical works startle, sometimes making us feel at home in strange worlds, sometimes making us feel strange in our familiar world. Their occurrence, like the breakthroughs in forming the religious canon, are unanticipated and, at least initially, more disturbing than comforting.

Bloom's notion of the western canon raises various questions, but he is surely right that there do exist literary works of undisputed authority and cross-cultural appeal; works that can stimulate any serious reader to reflection. He argues that Shakespeare is a unique instance of such genius: that whichever literary tradition we consider, Shakespeare is central; or perhaps that Shakespeare being central, there only *is* one western literary tradition.[16] This idea of universally great texts or authors that will persist as such however long our way of life lasts is often ridiculed; but should it be? Great works revolutionise traditions, and among these are some unique works that may alter even our idea of what it is to revolutionise; works that change our very conception of human life, and so change our individual selves.

Writing of such authority calls for readers of great reflective seriousness. Bloom believes that 'Shakespeare, as we like to forget, largely invented us.'[17] His idea is not just that Shakespeare was the most successful or most cross-cultural revolutioniser of drama, but that he changed the very way people conceive of their activities and lives: post Shakespeare, we conceive of ourselves as characters, self-conscious actors or agents in the drama that is the modern world. If Bloom is right that Shakespeare created self-consciousness and made the modern world a stage, then reading his plays is extraordinarily potent recreation. It is recapitulating for oneself the great 'renaissance' that in the seventeenth century Shakespeare achieved for the emerging world.

Power of books

The power of books is a subject for a long book. Books move us despite ourselves; books start and conclude political revolutions; they talk, pitilessly, of everything under the sun – including themselves; they can capture our minds so completely that with a list of literary categories in our heads we say we can read someone 'like a book'. Discussion of their power often focuses on the commercial phenomenon of the best-seller, or on the political role of books in creating social change. But the power of books includes their ability to enter into and remake our thinking. To explain this, we can consider books as different as the Bible, pornographic books, and books about books.

Despite years of announcing that 'ordinary people' want a bible that is easily understood, ordinary people continue to love the archaic language of the King James' Bible: other translations are used, but not loved. Part of this is that the King James' Version, like Shakespeare, provides us with many of our 'higher' thoughts; it also provides us with a universe, a vision of the world in an age that has not managed to produce a stable, alternative vision for almost five hundred years. This world view is difficult for us to lose, and impossible to ignore. We may not all believe in or value it but it tells a great part of the world's story, individual stories – and helps many to complete their own stories whenever they 'lose the plot'. And by 'tells our stories' I mean just that: the King James' often speaks for us; in a thousand situations and dilemmas we do not grapple for our own words, but discover the King James' Version organising our minds and arranging our speech.

Because of its status, it can feel strange for English speakers to recall that the King James' is a translation. Older English speakers translate other bibles into the King James' translation in their heads (just as German philosophers are said to think of Kant's texts in Kemp-Smith's famous English translation). Understanding the reasons for this is a question for the history and sociology of the Bible; but partly it is that the King James' is so true to the bible's deepest purpose: to be read. The bible is a theory (of creation, salvation and morality), a history, a devotional and liturgical text, a set of literary genres, and much more; but fundamentally it is the world's best read. I do not mean just that it is the best book in the world, but that not to read the bible is to fail to understand the power of books and the effect of reading. Books can cut through their own textual surfaces and persuade us that they are relating realities, rather than merely, fictitiously, creating 'realities'. The power of books means that they can subvert themselves, making it appear that it is the universe depicted that is real and the book merely a fictitious creation.

Our minds are constructed, then, to read books with the power to persuade us not just of their stories, but of the worlds that the stories relate – worlds in which the book may be relatively powerless. Fiction can do this, but there is the complication that writer and reader then cooperate in willing the reader's imagination to make a major contribution to the fictitious world. The case is clearer and more remarkable with books which have the power *themselves* to introduce us to a new world: the Bible – and pornography. Despite sliding from the awe-inspiring to the vile, successful pornographic writing does show reading's power to take us beyond the book to a world in which the words do not feature but disappear.

Mention of pornography (literally, 'writing about prostitutes') usually brings images to mind. These tend to be graphic, often intended to shock as well as arouse, and often play on (explicit or implied) degradation for their pornographic effect. Pornographic images have power to enslave and corrupt even very good men and women. The power of pornographic writing, however, seems harder to explain: how can words enslave and corrupt as effectively as the images from which the words are at a remove and which, presumably, they attempt to summon?

The answer is that porn books rely on the power of words to transport our minds to a world that could not be further from that of books and words – one of speechless gratification, communication without interpretation, and the complete cooperation of characters. In most fictional writing, characters do not respond to each other as the reader would ideally choose but rather demonstrate imaginative and surprising sorts of relationships and tensions that give the book its power, autonomy, and dramatic character. In porn fiction the characters do exactly what the reader wants; the best porn has no surprises – beyond the initial thrilling surprise of discovering that one is going to get exactly what one knows and wants. Hence, the porn writer probably knows his readers better than any other writer. He knows which arrangements of words and ideas will definitely 'work', and his skill lies in serving precisely what is wanted: not stimulating new wants and thoughts but stimulating continually and addictively the same want. Thus porn is an example of consumerist leisure at its purest.

Like the King James' Version, pornographic books have the power to disappear. As soon as they 'appear', as soon as we become conscious of the book, or think this is 'just' a world created by a book – whether the Biblical masterpiece or a piece of trash – engagement lessens. We soon become again just a reader, our critical faculties at work, our reading now disturbed by questions about the rationality and morality of sex (or religion), our interest declining.

This strange power of books to vanish is itself the object of some books: there are books about the power of books. Books that take other books as their theme tend to be rarefied; unsurprisingly they can be bafflingly reflexive. The greatest of these include Dante's *Divine Comedy*, where Beatrice 'makes Virgil redundant, not because theology is replacing poetry, but because Dante's *Comedy* now wholly replaces Virgil's *Aeneid*';[18] Chaucer's *Canterbury Tales*, which studies and transforms the full range of England's literary genres; Milton's *Paradise Lost*, which attempts a 'Third Testament' using the structures of Virgil's *Aeneid*; Jane Austen's *Northanger Abbey*, elegantly and humorously demolishing the shock-horror tradition of gothic fiction; and James Joyce's *Ulysses* in which, miraculously, even Homer manages to disappear in Joyce's sublime journey through the history of a modern human day. There is one modern example of a book with the power itself to disappear in favour of the book(s) it relates – Umberto Eco's *The Name of the Rose*.

Eco's work is a novel about books, ultimately about a lost section of Aristotle' *Poetics*, his treatise on great books. But it is also about: a great mediæval monastery devoted to the protection and preservation of books; the book of the *Apocalypse* around which a dreadful series of murders is planned; the book of the *Gospels* and its view of poverty around which the theological interest of the novel centres; the book of *Genesis* on which the novel's chapters are based; and the *Book of Hours*, the devotional text dividing up the day, around which the development of each chapter of the novel proceeds. Within these learned circles of writing and reading Eco's twentieth century novel truly vanishes leaving us with a world built purely upon the power of (other) books – their very real power to make men murder, order a society, dominate politics and, ultimately, to divide and unite the different peoples of the world. In Eco, the power of the book re-orders and re-creates the whole world, even though the book in which we read of this – the twentieth century book – sacrifices itself for other classic books in telling its story.

Reading the world

It matters that books structure our private and public worlds, guide us morally, educate us, and have authority and power over us. If these effects were to vanish, we would have to develop other ways of structuring our minds and our relationships: to alter our views of morality and moral pedagogy, and of pedagogy generally; to acquire other symbols of authority and other ways of recognising and controlling power. Books are familiar; we have tried and tested ways of digging gold from them and defending ourselves, and others weaker than ourselves, against them. Reading has served us well and, both individually and collectively, we have good structures for controlling what is published, who reads it, and what they do with it. A 'new' view of minds, relationships, morality, education, authority, and power would raise new dangers without immediate and guaranteed means of coping with them.

To preserve this world, it is not enough to teach children 'how to read' in the sense of teaching them their letters: reading should also be taught as play and as reflective activity, as time away from utilitarian ends. We can teach this by encouraging people to love reading time and the whole world of books; to investigate its variety and traditions, to keep up with currents in contemporary fiction, and to develop critical standards. This is no easy task. Already, so James Schall writes, 'the real poverty in our society is intellectual. Students attend universities, listen to Professors, and come away intellectually poor, even when the university buildings and grounds are well-ordered and charming.'[19]

Ordinary folk too will lose out here. Everyone needs truth and beauty – we all seek it daily and take what we can get of it when modern culture reduces our opportunities for great learning and art. Trash fiction may be better than no fiction just because it keeps the skill of reading alive; but there is serious danger of sentimentalism replacing truth on many readers' wish-lists, and only a revival of the reading culture can stop that.[20] To make leisure time literate again will not be easy in consumerist society. Reading is time away from buying; second hand book stores are anathema (unless retailers have already worked out that they will increase first hand book buying). Where people read to recreate, they read for life: they literally seek refreshment and rejuvenation of their lives. To choose to spend leisure time in activity that is fact-gathering, world-building, imagination-stimulating, and emotion-clarifying will surely have beneficial effects on all parts of our nature.

Perhaps we in consumerist culture should focus not on the world of *books* but on the *world* of books. For the whole world can be read as a book, though only by people who revere books and reading. The medievals were more practiced in reading the world iconographically. They believed that the world and all it contains has deep symbolic meaning: everything we encounter means something else; and with skill, practice, and love of interpreting signs we can read the world and grasp our place within it. Such familiarity with symbols breaks down the barrier between learning from the 'real' world and from books. In our scientific and post-scientific world most people no longer read symbolically: we have abandoned complex symbolism, and consumer goods distract us from deeper issues of meaning. But reading books reflectively will train in symbol, and will also teach the ability to question ideologies and religions, including consumerism. Sadly, however, a new enemy of reflective reading has now appeared.

The Net

It all began well; and everyone agrees that it is very useful and great fun; but what has the internet done for reading? Some of the problems of this technological attempt to build a new Alexandria are now well known, and increasingly well discussed.[21] Yet for many, discussion of internet vices still amounts to no more than restrictions on porn sites and invasion of privacy issues. But there are more serious problems. For example, while academics tackle new strategies for dealing with a variety of forms of academic plagiarism, parents, employers and the public generally have to deal with the fact the Net has no critical standards. Rather, like Edinburgh's famous Fringe Festival, anyone who registers can appear. Thus there is rubbish, corruption, and deception among the electronic riches. Those who rely on the net for a large part of their information or as a work resource have to supply their own external criticism; the monster is too large to be self-monitoring. And those who just log on for a pleasant hour risk encountering something that will transform their lives – and which may be false, misleading, or plain dangerous. Since standards of external criticism will come from the very sources which the Net's existence is now threatening, there is a real problem.[22]

The main vice of the net is curiosity: the 'lust of the eyes'.[23] Augustine speaks in the *Confessions* of 'a kind of empty longing and curiosity which aims not at taking pleasure in the flesh but at acquiring experience through the flesh.' Gilbert Meilander comments on this: 'Augustine does not write that all learning and science are merely vice; he says that sometimes we practice vice and dignify it with the honourable names of learning and science.'[24] Just what is the vice? It is sometimes taken to mean seeking useless knowledge but this is not so: whatever 'useless knowledge' actually means, there is no good reason to think seeking it is always wrong. Instead *curiositas* for Augustine is where 'our desire to know is only a greedy longing for a new kind of experience'.[25] The vice here consists in a thirst for empty novelty, intemperate desire to gratify our tastes or extend our tastes just because of what this will feel like. There are things that it would be wrong to try to know because the *motive* for knowing them could not be a good one.

Clear formulation of the relevant distinction here came with Aquinas.[26] All knowledge is good but we must also consider the knower, his motives, and the effects of knowledge upon him and others. Like everything else, knowledge should serve virtue and ultimate happiness. Thus we all require the virtue of *studiositas* to form and guide the natural human desire to know so that it is genuine human good that is being served when we seek knowledge. We should avoid knowledge-seeking motivated by malice or self-hatred: we should shun the vice of *curiositas*, which corrupts our desire to know by directing it towards harmful ends. It in fact undermines truth and enquiry, making them serve other ends.

There are many such harmful ends; one of these is idling, which is the major Net vice: we look for one item, get diverted to another, think of a third, and soon enter a pathway of someone else's choosing. Time disappears, the Net exercises its hypnotic – possibly, addictive – magic and before we know it, time that could have been spent on more important matters has been squandered on the *experience* of seeking and knowing. Due to this, work, other duties, or relationships may be ignored or sacrificed; and increasingly leisure too – time that could be spent reading! – is lost in the hard work of surfing, learning more about the Net, and devoting oneself to the technology. What was presented as a labour saving device has become a time wasting, labour-intensive device. The Net has taken over, and its power does not even offer us the pleasure and instruction of entering a new world, because its successful use relies on us never resting but always moving on, being introduced via the next screen to yet another new world. This is man the consumer at his least autonomous: lured into chasing worlds.

There is a general message in the intemperance of the internet for the way we live now. The orthodoxy of today's world is that we all shun the unfashionable virtue of temperance; but things are more complex. A society in which status is determined by consumer wealth and adherence to glamorous lifestyle will fixate on the appearance of the body: the ultimate consumer indulgence is designing one's own body as a commodity that will gain access to the right lifestyle. This fixation has risen steadily with the growth in consumerist leisure, for this growth suggests we have spare time for our 'duty' to remake ourselves physically so as to return better prepared for participation in the world of consumption. Diets, gyms, self-help books, yoga and meditation, physical therapies and procedures, and image counsellors are available everywhere. As people struggle against the many weaknesses of flesh in order to fit the desired social image, our major intemperance is fast becoming over-reliance on the *apparatus* of temperance. The implements and procedures of the old Scottish 'temperance hotels' are as nothing compared to face lifts, body tucks, high-fat diets, sensory deprivation tanks, and so on.

The driven quality of these regimens is not to be compared with genuine temperance. Temperate people are not passionate about temperance: they are passionate about health. Internet use encourages a different disorder – not abstinence and self-punishment, but application and self-indulgence. As people are driven by their desire to consume themselves and achieve a certain bodily appearance, they can be driven too by desire to consume knowledge and so achieve – ? But that is the point: internet intemperance does not even have a (disordered) goal: this *curiositas* is the perfect consumer image of the desire to keep on consuming just because the possibility is there.

In addition to intemperance, the Net feeds upon the vice of impatience. In the world of the Net everything is expected to be at our fingertips: libraries whose resources people in the great days of writing and reading could not imagine; instant access to commerce, government, education, general knowledge, gambling, sex, other people's private lives and secrets. There is a patience about books. Whether we are reading for leisure or the hard slog of study in the library, both are slow, both grow, as we do, through perseverance. Thus many people who love the Net still return to books for leisure – return to real books: ebooks have had little impact, and the failure of Stephen King's recent attempt to serialise, a la Dickens, via the Net is telling. The Net is slow, cumbersome, uncomfortable, unreliable, and tiring to use; books were designed, centuries before the concept was born, with our 'ergonomic health' in mind. The Net does not make us impatient with books, but with the Net.

All of this has had a major impact on reflection and respect for contemplative life in our communities, including our universities. Contemplation, as Aristotle believed, is the highest leisure and the hardest slog. Books have been wonderfully effective at assisting contemplation and developing the reflection both of trained thinkers and ordinary folk. Books have helped people to enter other worlds and then to return to their own world, thinking more deeply about it and their place within it. Books demand time and leisure; they exercise the critical mind and they build it up, so making the leisure they demand a joy. The Net on the other hand involves restlessly moving from screen to screen and site to site. It does not demand thought. Indeed, if we stop to think, we are already ceasing to be Net users; just as if we stop to talk, we are on the path to abandoning the mobile phone.

With our encouragement of the Net we have replaced contemplation with constant, low-grade activity: reflective leisure is replaced by action on screen. And all of this is terrible hubris. It is hubris – interestingly, the very hubris of Eden – to believe that all knowledge can be catalogued, possessed, and accessed at will; to think that we can replace reading books – an activity crafted over millenia – with an activity only a couple of decades old. And hubris too to place screens in every home so that places of rest and leisure are subtly invaded by the great tool and stressful activity of the modern workplace.[27]

5
Playing Abroad

In *Ego and Soul* John Carroll describes tourism as the greatest and most successful lie of western, consumerist culture.[1] It is not meant as a compliment. Tourists wander the world in search of the adventure and glamour promised by purveyors of holidays. They believe they are set for authentic encounters with other places and peoples and see their trip as their major exercise of freedom in the year – freedom of choice, freedom from home, freedom from familiar responsibilities.

In fact, Carroll argues, they are duped. They and the tourist industry collaborate in a sophisticated hoax in which tourists persuade themselves they are heroic and happy while in fact clinging to the few traces of the everyday which the holiday package allows them. What little enjoyment they get comes from petty domestic and bureaucratic crises, rather than the wonderful things and alien customs the brochure promised.

If Carroll is right, tourism is the greatest achievement of consumerist leisure: tourists believe they are leaving consumerist routine at home for a fortnight, and in fact they have simply purchased the opportunity to continue the same routine elsewhere, since consumerism's empire is global and its logic total. Yet travel has been a means of refreshment and of serious recreation and stimulation for centuries. It would seem travel is an honourable means to reflective activities such as contemplation, spiritual discovery, appreciation of beauty and artistry, and enjoyment of new relationships. Reflection generally benefits from a change of scene and opportunity to discover new perspectives; so if tourism is simply more accessible travel, its growth is to be welcomed. The question is: *is* mass tourism the opening up of travel, or is it simply another (the worst?) application of consumerist leisure?

Hard work of tourism

'Travel', Carroll reminds us, is from travail, meaning work and suffering, cause of stress. Travel is hard work. Certainly, even the best packaged tour involves effort and a strain – often disliked by the modern tourist, who really looks forward to a pleasant room, a hot shower, and someone else doing all the work at the end of the day. The tourist shirks real work both in preparation for the holiday and during it: 'receptive to the dream, he is swindled into believing it can be bought & consumed, rather than earned. He is deceived too in believing that his work ends with the saving up to afford it.'[2]

Carroll sees little to redeem tourism. Even postcards, presents, and photographs are 'in part an act of aggression against those at home, designed to stimulate their envy....after all, it was the envy of others who had already gone, stimulated by stories and glamorous advertisements that sent these tourists in the first place.'[3] Tourists cannot stand still and think, contemplate, or see but must be constantly moving – and moving according to rules and patterns governed by the laws of holiday consumption and 'the industry'. The only redemption for tourism is that its 'victims' do go on a journey, do subject themselves to the great strain of the ordeals that modern tourism involves, and so show initiative, guts, and a certain hope. Carroll's message: 'travel, as spiritual testing, is an art, and has to be worked at, in the mode of vocation. We are reminded yet again that the Calvinist cultural form of work is the royal road to meaning in the modern West.'[4]

Much of this rings true. I share Carroll's anti-consumerism, but I think his pessimism unbalances his very necessary critique of tourism. Leisure travel is a precious resource, and where tourism secures this for greater numbers, it is welcome; and where it secures this not just as relaxation or entertainment but as reflective activity, it is doubly welcome. The question is whether tourism does effectively secure leisure travel and reflective travel, or whether it diminishes or replaces it. I will address this concern by considering some purposes and conundrums of modern travel, and by looking at the relation of travel to tourism, holidays, holydays, and pilgrimages. I also make some suggestions about the 'phenomenology' of travel – why the experience of travel matters so much, and how it matters.

Some purposes of travel

(1) Discovery

All travel needs a goal; otherwise we are just wandering. Some travel consists in a journey focussed on a clear purpose; other travel may be focussed on the clarification of just what our real purpose is; and travel can be a series of mini-journeys, each arrival the attainment of one small part of a greater purpose. Just which purposes guide the typical traveller today?

Part at least of the motivation is the desire for novelty: new thoughts, feelings, and opportunities; this may be why tourist packages, which tend to be highly predictable, are not the best travel. For centuries people have walked in calm enjoyment, or grim determination, past renowned sights in order to acquire new ideas or be moved in new ways, exposed to new possibilities of living and behaving. In today's world this thirst for knowledge and understanding is no less real, often more real.[5]

Discovery travel, travel for knowledge and experiences, can be excellent recreation. One problem, however, is that travel means temporary residence, thus during our stay there are only certain thoughts we can have and certain depths to which we can be moved, since we must also eat, sleep, rest, and arrange our onward journeys.[6] But perhaps what matters is not the new experiences in situ but the effects on our later reflection and feeling which travel experiences cause: not so much the uplifting and enjoyable experience itself, but its effect on our future happiness and development? When I gaze at a beautiful seascape on holiday I often try to commit it to memory. Should I instead simply enjoy the colours and sounds right now; or am I right to attempt to record them for future revisiting and on-going beneficial effects? Should I try to concentrate on storing the thoughts and memories which the seascape evokes, or should I just stop thinking and enter a meditative state?

Asking this question is pondering leisure travel as self-improvement: travel to broaden our horizons and make us better informed, wiser, more tolerant, in the future. Is the best recreation future-oriented or heightening the quality of present experience? These need not be alternatives: enjoying present leisure is experiencing freedom from work and daily cares; and the more we can do this – the more playful and reflective we make ourselves – the better the quality of our future thought and choices. It is rather like having children: every moment of their development is precious to parents as it happens, but it is precious too because it is the gradual revelation of what their futures will be like. With travel experiences, it is the quality of present enjoyment that matters, but this quality is part-determined by our estimation of the experience's positive effect on our futures.

Discovery travel can be courageous and open-minded, recalling the amateur explorers and pioneers of previous times; it can also be driven by a less admirable curiosity that raises issues of sincerity of motive and cultural sensitivity. To travel in order to find out about people requires a great deal of thought. People cannot be studied as anthropological specimens – not even by anthropologists. An encounter with strangers in their land has to show politeness and respect, but even that is not enough: sensitive travel begins with receiving welcome of the hosts; without this it is exploitative.

In a speech at the Catholic Church's Sixth World Congress on the Pastoral Care of Tourism in 2004, Archbishop Raul Gonsalves, of Goa and Damao, India, spoke of 'the host countries who have had the sad experience of not only not enjoying the many benefits expected to improve their human living conditions but, on the contrary, of being deprived of their natural resources and made victims of deceit and exploitation when tourism is seen and capitalized on as an industry and commercial venture for market forces.' Where travel is consumerist tourism, people in developing areas are vulnerable – not just to obvious forms of exploitation, but to more subtle coercion and deception always built into any encounter between the well-off and the dependent. Avoiding exploitation requires a welcome given by those who know the visitors' identity and motives, and that welcome being honoured by travelers.

Respect for persons is not the only condition of ethically sensitive discovery travel. Respect for customs matters too, as does respect for cultures, religions, and particular social groups. This notion has become fashionable as lip-service paid to different ways of life, which then pays off our moral dues and allows us to go on largely as before. This politicised 'respect for multiculturalism' can become patronising where the better-off person rejects any thought of changing his lifestyle and attempting to live together with very different people.

What is required here varies with the visitor's own reasonable limitations of time and interest, but genuine respect will involve at least a minimal attempt to understand customs and their contexts: resentfully covering bare limbs in a Catholic church is not enough to show respect for local ways. Respect is not just basic tolerance that advertises itself by a willingness to act for a day as if one *were* a Spanish Catholic, Polish Jew, or Indonesian Muslim. Respectful discovery travel means a commitment to learn and understand, and so to admit the possibility of being changed by other people and customs. It involves taking people *that* seriously. Perhaps above all, respect for cultures is openness to learning (if possible) or recognising (at least) the host language – the key to all culture. Tourists who travel in such a spirit of ethical discovery are not the passive consumers and digital camera-clickers Carroll describes.

(2) Recovery

More passive is the sort of travel that aims at recovery. Those who travel for only a few weeks of the year often cite rest, relaxation, and recovery from work as a prime purpose of their investment of precious leave time and income. Of course, there is work and effort involved in recovery travel and the preparation for it, but even this can be a pleasurable change from daily work and can have a significant rejuvenating effect: 'a change is as good as a rest'. Undoubtedly, much of the success of a modern holiday is judged in terms of absence of tension, deadlines, and unwished for expenditure of energy, with maximisation of rest, indulgence of long-dreamt of hobbies and interests, and return to a simpler, more 'natural' style of life. Is travel for the sake of recovery vulnerable to the anti-consumerist critique?

For most people, there are other at least equally important methods of recovery: regular sleep and exercise, meditation and healthy living, personal relationships, sports and arts. But the forms of jadedness these address are different from those addressed by travel. Travel addresses the sense of being trapped in the daily grind, surrounded by things and people whose value we cannot see because of busyness and tiredness. A reasonable response to this is to choose a holiday which combines a break from the familiar, an interesting or challenging environment, and better opportunities for rest, sleep, exercise, reading, and so on than one normally has at home.

This may seem the least adventurous of holidays, but it can actually involve significant challenge. Recovery can aid rest and sleep without simply *being* rest and sleep: it can come through extreme sports or living without modern amenities. Successful travel for recovery may well be travel for discovery too; it may require that therapy be part of the vacation's goal. But we should be wary of luxury: the jaded palate does not easily recover by having Sauternes and *foie gras* passed over it: it may require a reasonable abstinence, unfamiliar taste sensations, or a mouth-wash. Recovery from deprivation may respond to self-indulgence for a period, but sheer luxury is unlikely to make for a recuperative or unforgettable holiday.

Recovering and relaxing are certainly strongly advertised themes of modern tourism. And if Alain be Botton is right,[7] they have been a purpose and theme of holidaymaking at least since Wordsworth made recovery an acceptable goal of travel. Are tourists here deceived by the myth of 'packaged' holidays? Are cruises and beach holidays a con-trick in which the 'victim' struggles with, and becomes increasingly intimidated by, demanding people and surroundings in order to persuade himself he has had a few days of genuine rest and restoration?

Not necessarily. Leaving home temporarily, and arranging for our needs while away, is effortsome, but the days on the mountain or beach can be the most restful of the year – and of course, rest may be greater the more effort required to achieve it. It is not true that tourist travel only ever *seems* to be restful and to induce relaxation, or that rested tourists are always deceived or self-deceived. Despite my memories of packing and flight delays, and of the traumas of daily existence – despite the fact that I have 'brought myself along too' – I can still feel real contentment and note genuine recovery in visiting a place where everyone expects me only to rest in the way I have chosen. This need not be some bizarre, superficial consumerist attempt to purchase rest; it can be an intelligent choice earlier in the year not to become over-stressed later in the year but to head towards a short period of escape from care and pressure.

(3) Activity

Over-work and unemployment produce different forms of inactivity. As technology grows, there is down-sizing, and as a result, people of work age become unemployed and spend inactive and depressing hours with the TV – while their former colleagues are over-worked and spend long hours in the office with the computer. Inactivity due to unemployment, or inactivity due to the pressures of work, means activity is becoming as crucial to modern people as rest. The modern work-station is now a focus of millions of lives, bursting with busyness, limiting physical and mental functioning and activity. Thus it is as necessary for the busy executive as for the longterm unemployed to be sent whitewater rafting or on bush camps.

Human beings are naturally active – and active throughout a range of activities, given the complexity of our nature. Some at least of these activities should pose regular challenges. Routines are necessary, but they are destructive if followed as worthwhile ends in themselves. To travel with the goal of activity need not be to buy into an exploitative and deceptive consumerist system: it may be to take wise steps to abandon the enforced inactivity of work or unemployment (both commercially determined states) and to make choices for oneself that strengthen body and mind and help alleviate the sense of boredom or fatigue.

Adventure and themed travel holidays abound; sadly, generally for the wealthy: people take time off to go mountaineering, sailing, enjoy bush treks; and more sedately, go on opera tours, wine tours, improve your German, Asian cookery, architecture skills tours, and so on. Meanwhile, some strive heroically for funding to take groups of young unemployed and deprived for adventure and skills-improving holidays in the countryside.

If activity is to be a worthy goal of travel, it has to be well chosen. In a chapter on leisure, Jonathan Margolis explains the concept of the 'yuppie trek': young professionals leave their desks in London on a Friday evening, fly to South America, climb a peak in the Andes, and are back at work, near breakdown point, of course, by eight-thirty on Monday morning.[8] This sort of chest-beating is probably not what is needed to correct the inactivity of modern work. The adrenalin rush apart, part of the purpose of activity travel is the enjoyment of travel and of the destination itself. Indeed, part of the value of Carroll's critique is that the process of journeying is itself so often instrumentalised in tourism. There is a particular danger in activity travel that the actual travel will be judged mere means to the end of staged activity; something hastily to be got over, or extravagantly to be pursued with the distractions of expensive champagne and movies in the air. Perhaps the best activity travel is where people begin new activities the moment they lace up their walking boots and leave the front door.

People not used to traveling may be thrilled (or disturbed) by journeying outside the territories and boundaries that define the familiar, and by the speed of travel. This is not a function only of the jet plane: leaving the parish boundary and catching a coach-and-four was probably even more unsettling and thrilling to our forebears because of their infrequency. Travel literature, including the flourishing sub-genre of travel guides and planners, is a significant aid in keeping the actual experience of travel an exciting aspect of a holiday. Unfortunately, modern travel is often expensive and ordinary – economy class on a long-haul flight does not long remain a thrill – and these days, also a danger. Air travel and airports are major consumerist icons, but with imagination, travel can be more leisurely and active. 'Traveling holi-days' (barges, sailing, rail trips, cycling and so on), though only a frac-tion of the tourist industry, are far from Carroll's rightful targets and involve as much *travail* as the travel of previous centuries.

(4) Therapy

Activity travel is largely, though not exclusively, remedial travel. However, it is not therapeutic: therapy is intervention which addresses some dysfunction and would not otherwise be required; activity is natural, the expression of healthy functioning. Therapy too is a legit-imate and non-trivial purpose of travel. Since Roman days people have travelled to take the cure: mineral waters, diet, exercise, tranquility, and a generally healthy regime. At its fashionable height in the eight-eenth and early nineteenth centuries, Bath as Jane Austen knew it was the object of travel that blended vacation and cure in a way very acceptable to the affluent and elegant sufferers. Spa towns have always suffered from their self-presentation as combination luxury resorts/ health camps: those who can afford such 'alternative' healthcare tend to appreciate the spartan qualities only for a few hours a day, to be fol-lowed by large cakes and comfortable bedrooms. But this should not detract from the genuine importance of travel as and for therapy.

Travel as therapy became something of an icon in the 1960s. Several generations of all ages have now set off into the deserts and jungles, towards Uluru or Tibet or Patagonia, seeking healing or balm for the soul. This is a genuine sort of travel for therapy, often associated with specific popular cults and movements (hippies, Buddhists, greenies, New Age and so on). It is catered for today, somewhat ironically, by the tourist industry, but its aim could not be further from con-sumerism. It defines itself as 'anti' ('drop-out', 'alternative') those things for which consumerist society stands. It would be wrong to say that simply by being marketed alternative therapies have become non-therapeutic, and are dragged deep within the consumerist net. The authentic end of therapy can be retained with at least some purity, though this will take considerable integrity and effort.

Other travel as therapy is more traditional: the simple exercise and fresh air of walking, pony trekking, seaside holidays; or the lift to the spirits that comes by journeying to something unique and awesome either in nature or in art. Many therapies would be artificial or second best if practiced from home: they work because of the stimulation of leaving home, moving and arriving at the health-focussed destination. There is also traveling for therapy: leaving familiar places and people and taking a journey to cure body, mind, perspective. Journeys are an ancient spiritual medicine. On the night when millions gathered around TV screens to be 'there' when man walked on the moon, something deep and atavistic stirred in people.

Travel for therapy today may include the services of counsellors and psychologists, as well as dieticians, physiotherapists, and other therapists. It may also involve clergymen or others involved with religion; part of the obligation of a monastic house, after all, is to offer hospitality and care to the *hospes* or guests who still visit this very special form of hosp-ital. There is no clear demarcation between the care of souls and the cure of bodies; monastic foods and (especially) drinks, sanctuary, silence, contemplation, prayer, meditation are all undergoing renewal and increased popularity for people seeking more effective therapies than those the twentieth century provided. What is clear is that none of this can be dismissed as mere deluded commercialism. Travel with the goal of therapy is an important part of our history and culture and is enjoying a revival, thanks in part to modern tourism.

(5) Luxury

The last purpose of travel is uniquely vulnerable to Carroll's critique. There is a style of traveller – and here 'tourist' may sound more natural – who simply travels for and in luxury. This can range from false luxury at the lower end of the economic spectrum, to ocean liners, de luxe trains, and hotels chosen simply as vehicles to sensuous enjoyment and pampering. Here – rather as in a tramcar restaurant – travel is actually not necessary to the luxury provided but is harnessed, quixotically, to luxury in order to increase the exotic indulgence aimed at.

A little luxury hurts no one; but to travel simply to indulge oneself, at heights to which everyday life never rises, is to do what is worthless, may well unsettle, and does not serve to return us more contented to our daily lives. The consumer myth of spending so as to be or join the jet-setting movie star, super-model, or playboy millionaire reaches its nadir here. Here, the supreme icons of consumerist lifestyle are coyly and deceptively packaged as 'exclusive' and 'life-changing' for greedy consumers by a greedy industry.

To be anti-luxury as a goal of travel is not to be a kill-joy. After a day spent in discovery, recovery, activity, or therapy a little luxury is perfectly appropriate: fine food and wine, attentive service, splendid views – the brief fantasy of living a quite different life (as opposed to the other four purposes which prepare us for our *own* lives). But to travel purely for luxury, or to travel *in* luxury as the main purpose of one's holiday, has no recreative value: nothing is learned for renewing one's *own* life.

Especially harmful at the lower end of luxury are the ideas of a 'resort' and a 'package'. 'Resort' – whatever the reality – conjures up visions of a compound we enter, leaving behind the expectations and restraints of the normal world and surrendering to the attentions of those entirely dedicated to making us feel elite and spoilt. The resort is a playground in which we convince ourselves that we are where we belong, that we are different from those outside, and that something of importance in our lives is taking place – something we have been, wrongly, deprived of until now. In fact, the resort is the concept of 'hospitality as commerce'.[9] We are not elite, we do not belong, and nothing important is happening here; this is travel as sharp-clawed consumerism and the idyll is vacuous and self-deceptive. Whole towns can be given over to compounds of luxury ('resort towns'), so that the town itself basically becomes a mega-resort, a 'paradise' for surfers or whomever. Economies can be built around this and these will often scar otherwise beautiful country and can bring out, in those inside and those outside, shameful emotions.

The 'package' holiday is a more openly sordid proposition. The original idea – that for ease and economic advantage the various necessary elements of a trip can be packaged together, offered at discounted rate, and prepared by a specialist – suggested the possibility of the high-life for fourteen days to lower income families in the 1960s. With the whole package taken care of, there is nothing to do but soak up the sun, luxuriate in freedom from decision-making, and use up pocket money on cocktails and souvenirs.

Nowadays, like so much from that strange decade, the package holiday increasingly suggests low-life, cheapness, and squalor; the evidence of this is visible in the package-ghettoes of Mediterranean countries. Nevertheless, it is still marketed as economy with a dash of luxury for the money-conscious. As such, it is frequently deceptive: tales of tourist disappointment, sickness, and danger are legion; while packages with truly satisfied customers (for example, 18–30 holidays) may aim very low indeed. Resorts and packages can add a touch of glamour to tired lives, but only a touch. They promote an easy access to a conception of luxury and are thin on leisure; instead, they confirm the everyday – including the everyday fantasies people have of resorts and packages.

Is luxury bad for people? Usually, yes; and it is generally to the detriment of true leisure. It does not allow people to restore exhausted minds, or to gain lasting recreation. It encourages people to believe they are who they are not, or encourages them to identify with the worst parts of themselves. It breeds and is fuelled by envy and dissatisfaction, two leading consumer instincts. It works only where the real truth is kept at bay, caricatured, or creatively reinterpreted. It is a highpoint of the great consumerist deception, promising the ultimate deference from others, exquisite sensations, absolute consumer sovereignty, confirmation of social status, insulation from reality, and above all, the idea that life will be different from now on. It is unworthy of the activity and experience of travel, irrelevant to personal recreation and development, and where tourism has promoted it, tourism, as Carroll argues, has done travel a disservice.

Four conundrums of travel

When we travel for leisure, one of the topics we might reflect on is travel itself. The philosophy of travel barely exists. To begin a reflection on the topic travelers could start by musing on some basic conundrums.

The first conundrum concerns travel as relaxation. If one purpose of leisure travel is to relax, travellers require a certain ease in body and mind; but the very novelties of the travel situation – both journey and destination – mean that travellers are busily occupied taking in, coping with, understanding, and recording the experience. It seems we sometimes need the unfamiliar in order to relax, but its very unfamiliarity means we cannot readily relax. This conundrum has its counterpart in practical experience. How often do people return from holiday claiming 'I need a rest now to recover from all that'? Workers cherish their periods of leave and almost universally long for those times in which they can afford to travel and relax; but even happy holidays involve significant mental stimulation and physical effort.

The second conundrum is the one we met above. If leisure travel is to succeed, it must have a lasting effect and this means our actual travel experiences must be intense and intensely enjoyed. But to enjoy present experiences intensely may be to compromise their potential to benefit us in the future; while, likewise, preparing now for future benefits from our travel may undermine the intensity of present experiences. The practical counterpart of this is the debate between the near-pathological photographer or video enthusiast and the person wishing to absorb himself quietly in his chosen, temporary environment. Perhaps many individuals feel a conflict within themselves between these two aims when on holiday; perhaps too for some people, considering this puzzle and working out a practical solution to it is a mark of the trip's success.

A third conundrum concerns security. The motivation to travel is always bound up with exposing oneself to the unexpected or uncertain, but modern travellers are often people at their most nervous and security-conscious. The conundrum is that good travel must be flexible and open to adventure; however, good preparation for travel involves taking steps to limit uncertainties and to prepare for the unexpected. Naturally, we try to strike a reasonable balance here, but the problem is the criterion of reasonableness in planning a trip is precisely eliminating sources of danger, fear, and insecurity, and without these the motivation to travel is much reduced!

Practically, we meet this conundrum often in the inanities of travel agents and the holidays they put together. They boast of maintaining all the comforts of home while leaving open the possibilities of risky romance, physical danger, implication in local ways of life and potential hardships. In so far as they replicate home (comfort, privacy, healthcare, physical security, communications and so on), packaged holidays insulate us in all sorts of ways from danger, and in fact no agent can take the legal and commercial risk of leaving us in any significant danger at all. Travellers are trapped between the inclination to break out and be bold and the domestic habits by which they define an acceptable level of comfort and security in daily life.

A final conundrum concerns authenticity and the contribution of the traveller to his travel destination. We like to travel to places and cultures with a life and existence of their own; however, simply by being present there, and present as a paying traveller, we change what we visit, accepting its toleration of ourselves and of the institutions of travel and the culture we represent as normal. We crave the authentic, but the truth is that in a globalised world there is no place that is truly alien to us; in that sense, there is really nowhere to travel to any longer. This is a specific application of the general political problem of multiculturalism: we want to endorse and visit other cultures but to do so as part of *our* (multiculturalist) outlook.

And if our experience of other cultures is ambiguous, host cultures are generally ambivalent about tourists; both dependent and resentful, and sometimes patronising (for example, the British treatment of visiting Americans, or Australian treatment of Japanese). Travel once gained in richness and excitement from the discrepancy of visitors placed in an alien world; mass tourism, and the general framework of consumerism that it represents, has now altered many of these foreign worlds, and indeed made many of them no longer foreign.

These conundrums suggest that leisure travel will involve paradox and puzzle. Attempting to travel 'for its own sake' requires a practical response to questions of novelty, immediacy, security, authenticity; otherwise, we are diverted from leisure by anxieties for ourselves or our hosts. These anxieties certainly do not make for quiet reflection, but in a reflective leisure holiday pondering them will be part of solving them and will increase the recreation of our travel.

Travel or tourism?

It is common – if rather cheap – to imply a real distinction between travel and tourism: to claim that the two are distinct activities, defined by different purposes and goals, and with different standards of success and excellence. I suspect there is no real distinction to be made here. Though sometimes useful, such a distinction is usually great snobbery. However, focussing on some aspects of modern tourism will allow us to ask how it compares with the more reflective leisure which non-tourist travel, allegedly, provides.

In comparison with travel in the grand, eighteenth century sense, it can seem that tourists are flippant and superficial. Concern about this was the basis of Pope John Paul II's critique in the 2001 World Tourism Day address. The Pope believes that real travel should open us up to other ways of living and thinking so as to discourage us from being selfishly bound up with ourselves; by contrast, mass tourism offers only 'superficial exoticism' and caters to a consumerist 'thirst for thrills'. The Pope also calls for holiday-makers seeking a richer experience not to be satisfied with a packaged 'reconstructed ethnicity', but to pursue cultural and aesthetic encounters intelligently. Above all: 'let no one succumb to the temptation of making free time a period of rest from values'; good leisure is cause of reflection and support of ethical values.

The Pope clearly has a point. Tourist packages can be mind-numbing, and even more adventurous, non-packaged holidays may be unfulfilling: 'a danger of travel is that we see things at the wrong time, before we have had a chance to build up the necessary receptivity and when new information is as useless and fugitive as necklace beads without a connecting chain.'[10] But still, tourism today has developed beyond Butlins holiday camps at home and cheap beer and sex abroad. People who for whatever reason (linguistic, cultural, intellectual, age, health, fear, busyness and so on) cannot organise short, quality holidays for themselves can now be well served by a huge range of quality tour operators. Of course, we have to pick and choose, but many people now visit the Pope's own city on an unforgettable trip made possible by the services and resources of modern tourism. Tourism need not be a diabolic force – though individual tour operators can be. With right motivation and respect for self and others, tourists can make a significant, and not only economic, contribution to the regions they visit, as well as to their own lives.[11]

Tourism can be leisure travel, even reflective leisure. In fact, it is not actually clear what *non-tourist* leisure travel is. The first 'tourists' toured the ancient empires; later tourists explored the shrines of Europe for the good of their souls; until by the early eighteenth century the soul was left to languish and aesthetics and exotic delight (the 'Grand Tour') took over. We often dignify this older tourism as 'travel', and not tourism. Is this because it involves expeditions or adventures? Longer stays? Absorption in, and by, other cultures?[12] What the claim seems to come down to is this: real travellers are more discerning in their choices, undertake proper research, and are willing to put up with discomfort so as not to be treated 'like a tourist'; all of which requires a certain independence and intelligence. Meantime, mere tourists seek more immediate gratification, thus undertake less research and preparation, have less interest in coming to grips with alien peoples and places, and expect their home comforts. But is there evidence of these differences?

It would be scurrilous to describe people as undiscerning just because they have less money or less time to spend on a holiday. The experience of a brief trip, well chosen and sensitively executed, can be a thrill greater than a long holiday, and certainly more than simple gratification. I once travelled to Toledo (from Australia!) for a long weekend and still recall the intensity of the encounter with the old city, the El Greco masterpieces, the moon over the *meseta*, and my earnest wish to get the most from the one gentle afternoon in the gardens at Aranjuez. And wonderful travel experiences need not – and perhaps should not – cost the earth. People who have been to Lourdes, even as curious tourists, return with a very different view of mass travel, and inexpensive souvenirs, than those who deride it all as spiritual tourism and commercial tat. The chip shops and discos of the Costa del Sol of Spain and the Gold Coast of Australia are not pretty, but most tourists would *agree* with this judgement; and for many of those who would not, chips and dancing by the beach may be a reasonable way to spend days away from inner cities and dull jobs and routines.

The point about research is also false, for nowadays, with so much riding on the all-important choice of where to go, there is a plethora of books, travel supplements, internet sites, and tourist information services. Ordinary folk may well spend more time choosing and preparing for what they really want than people only interested in conforming to the latest fashionable destination or politically correct venue; after all, poorer people stand to lose more if they get their holiday choice wrong. As for enduring discomfort, there is little merit in sitting cross-legged in a dusty Hindu temple after traveling business-class from London Heathrow, or before checking into the local Hilton in New Delhi. Economy class (travel, food, accommodation, treatment by locals and so on) is a far likelier source of discomfort than the attractively authentic and eco-sensitive cabins and tents of self-appointed non-tourists.

Independence and intelligence are also alleged grounds of a real distinction. But the phrase an 'independent traveller' has little meaning in a world in which there is little left to explore and not much to conquer. Tourists do get their hands dirty. Meeting the locals may happen more effectively at a cheap, popular bar than on the quasi-anthropological safaris of 'real' travellers. And tourism need not be a brain-dead option. Those who went on the grand tour with little real understanding of the lands they visited and often the most idle and extravagant of motives may have contributed as much to the negative image of 'tourism' as today's rampaging package tourists (Elizabeth Bennet in Pride and Prejudice certainly thinks they did[13]). And today's student backpackers are certainly excellent advertisement for intelligent and discriminating cheap travel. In all cases, it is abuse of reason and intelligence that condemns travel, not its mass appeal and economic value.

There are delicate personal judgements of how far individuals can set aside their own comforts before they cease to be able to appreciate new peoples and places properly: by trial and effort we establish our own balances of temporary self-deprivation and real enjoyment of the travel experience. What is clear is that a good leisure tourist can do this as well as a self-styled non-tourist traveller. Indeed, the greater importance to him of his holiday may make him more motivated to get the most from it, and that 'most' may include reflection as well as play.

As we will probably continue to use the tourism-travel distinction, it is important to emphasise that far from craving beer, sand, sun, and sex, most of today's tourists are craving a greater authenticity. This may be a rediscovery of their own identities, or of the quality of their personal relationships; or a return to inner peace through time and activities that are more healthy, natural, and less superficial. In short, tourism itself has become much more reflective in the past two decades. Tourists may not always be challenged to go beyond themselves in the way the Pope hopes for, but in the twenty first century mass tourism has moved further towards an activity undertaken for its own sake and not for selfish gratification or status enhancement.

Where we do find it useful still to distinguish tourism from travel, it matters that we avoid doing so ignorantly, or insultingly. I have regularly encountered thoughtless and ill-informed comments about Japanese tourists in Australia. These visitors in fact can usually take only very brief holidays, hence the rush; they travel in groups for good practical and cultural reasons; and if they tend to play follow the leader, this is preferable to exposing themselves to unfriendly looks and comments from locals. They take many photos because of the wish to share the visit with those less fortunate, including the elderly, at home; and they shop extravagantly because of their custom of giving generous presents to large numbers of family, friends, and colleagues. They are sometimes singled out as the purest instance of superficial-tourist-syndrome but their fidelity to their own cultural standards and customs even in the face of others' ridicule is exceptional, and we can be sure the pre-trip preparation and post-trip consolidation are extensive. There is no real distinction between travel and tourism in today's world; and if the distinction is relied upon at all, it should be made carefully.

Holidaymaking and holydaymaking

All holidays were once holy-days. When the rhythms of an established faith marked the year, a second cycle of work and leisure underpinned the lives of workers – a cycle distinct from our secular cycle of weekdays, weekends, and seasons. On this cycle, there are 'ordinary' days on which people work, fast periods during which they work with extra burdens, and feast days during which they rest with extra rights and special obligations. Earlier western societies valued feasts or holy-days not just for the leisure they offered but for the different obligations they conferred and required: on the annual quarter-days rents and debts were due; on the major holydays special obligations of employers to employees were observed and normal obligations suspended (time off work, present giving, merrymaking); working children could leave their workplaces for the day and travel to their families; Christians were obliged to attend mass; local justice broke out into mercy, and acts of greater than usual charity were performed.

This rather exposes our modern holiday-making. Modern holidays are often very much about individual pleasure and the exercise of free choice and personal autonomy; even when the purpose of the holiday is a good one, the means adopted to it can be self-focussed or thoughtless of others. People tend to travel either with a heightened sense of privacy, or in a special group. In contrast, holyday-making in which a whole community joins in a day off, each with responsibilities to discharge and to benefit from, is clearly preferable in terms of integration of people and fairness in the distribution of leisure opportunities.

One major difference is that holydays were usually stay-at-home or return-to-home days, whereas holidays usually involve traveling away from home. But if we could reclaim something of the idea of vacation as communal and justly distributed, it might encourage us to think more about the seriousness of holidays and what we should do with holiday time, either at home or when traveling. In particular, we might revise some of our attitudes towards the individualism and expense of holidays.

The concept of holyday is no longer available to assist the mainstream in reclaiming these ideas, but an alternative might be the concept of festivity. Festivity and festivals – from the aesthetically highbrow to the local 'pink lamb and purple shiraz' version – are springing up in most fair-sized towns. They can carry some of the legacy of holydays, though admittedly, most have been instituted, adopted, or adapted by canny tourist authorities and commercial interests.

Josef Pieper suggests that 'a festival can arise only out of the foundation of a life whose ordinary shape is given by the working day.'[14] Festivals are breaks from work. But they are more than that; they are not simply avoidance of work: they involve the celebration by working people of their own selves, their communities, and the things and values they hold dear. To take part in a festival is to sacrifice time, and the money that could be made from work, just for the sake of enjoying and affirming who we are, how we live, and what we believe in. So festivals truly so-called are the opposite of commerce and money-making; festival givers and goers declare 'normally, we would be lavish on this scale only to gain money or personal advantage; but today, we do so purely as a thanksgiving for all we are, have, and believe.'

This would be foolishness if it were not done within some long-established tradition, philosophy of life, or system of religious belief. Sacrifice and thanksgiving are celebrations not of egotism – even of communal egotism – but of the traditions and contexts that shape us and our world: 'there are worldly, but there is no purely profane, festivals... A festival without gods is a non-concept, is inconceivable.'[15] Thus we cannot create a festival just from nothing, legislate it into being; it is always a recognition of something already ethical (even spiritual) about us and our way of life. Hence, the widespread ridicule met by authorities such as the Birmingham City Council in England which decided to replace Christmas with 'winterval', believing they could retain the meaning and emotion of the Christian festival but without the tradition which they did not approve.

A little conceptual work on the communality and inclusiveness of genuine festivals might help to provide a critique of our own avalanche of popular festivals, some of which are no more than (local or national) money-making schemes trading on the natural human love of celebration. If we can establish a critique of festival and festivity, we may also have something with which to address our modern practices of holidaymaking, which can indeed seem wanting in terms of fairness for all, a sense of obligation, and the building up of communities. Perhaps western people have something important to learn from Japanese and other holiday-makers here.

Pilgrimage

Traveling to sacred places pre-dates Christianity; if we are now in a post-Christian world, it post-dates it too, for pilgrimages such as Santiago de Compostela have experienced a revival. Of course, today's pilgrims are often in search of a goal that sounds very different from that of traditional religion; but in fact it often is not so. New Age and other contemporary spiritualities share with mainstream pilgrimage the aim of travel for the sake of a metaphysical commitment, and belief in certain qualities or experiences uniquely attached to the shrine or other pilgrim goal, and to the travel activity itself. Among contemporary pilgrimages popular today are eco-travel and travel to the shrines of indigenous cultures. In these cases what we have is very much the notion of sacred travel (something which sits particularly awkwardly with consumerism: 'religious tourism'!). Since sacred traveling is still very much in the culture, it is doubly important to prevent it from becoming infected by consumerist considerations: there is no such thing as 'pilgrimage holidays'.

Part of what we value about pilgrimage sites is that we believe they retain their sacred qualities in advance of our arrival and after our departure. We would not so highly regard them if their effect was a result only of their interaction with our individual personalities and needs; we believe their sacred qualities are available to us precisely because they are not specially tailored to us – that rather, we must make an effort to tailor ourselves to them. We see this aspect of pilgrim sites in their resilience and appeal down the centuries, the fact that they inspire and uplift people from vastly different social worlds and times, and absorb the dedication of the pilgrim generations into the shrine's meaning and appeal.

There are two features of pilgrimage worth emphasising. The first is that pilgrimage does not belong to the rarefied world of high ritual and sacred liturgy; people do not 'qualify' for pilgrimage. It is an activity of ordinary people, distinguished only by the extraordinariness of the ends at which they aim. In the greatest of all recorded pilgrimages, that of *The Canterbury Tales*, it is a real cross-section of people that takes part in the mess, ambiguity, bawdiness, hilarity, and piety of a journey that is marked as much by realism and irreverence about human nature as by the hope of heaven and the expiation of guilt.

Despite their transcendental goal, pilgrims' behaviour is often very earthy indeed. The pilgrim mind-set does not distinguish cleanly between the secular and the sacred, but finds God and holiness in the midst of physical challenges, party-going, and love-making. Indeed, a criticism of contemporary, including secular, versions of pilgrimage is that they are often too sanitised and poe-faced compared to their mediæval originals.[16] Pilgrims do have a certain immunity from normal expectations and obligations: even today something of their sacred mission and holy status clings to them as they pass by on their way to Compostela or Guadalupe or Rome. But at the same time, their progress should be a progress of men and women like us; it is sinners who need to travel to shrines.

The second important feature of pilgrimage is the way in which pilgrims are changed by their travel. There is no stay-home pilgrimage: pilgrimage means leaving your home, your community, your comforts, and your expectations and heading off for unsettling and dramatic experiences. It also means leaving your everyday time-scale and entering God's and the pilgrimage's time. All travellers have unusual experiences of time and keep to unfamiliar clocks (staying up late, losing track of time, crossing the date-line, jet-lag, feeling the time pass quickly, or slowly and so on). Pilgrims experience yet more radical temporal dislocation. Their journey is marked not in miles and days, but by prayers and devotions, nights spent at interim religious sites, recitation of the 'holy hours', spiritual preparation for the climax of the shrine.

The pilgrim journey is not purely a means to some end beyond itself: it is itself part of the process by which people uncover the true ends of their lives, including the end of their pilgrimage. It is travel at its most reflective: travel that is pure self-reflection. Alasdair MacIntyre describes the mediæval notion of a quest and its importance for us today: 'It is in the course of the quest and only through encountering and coping with the various particular harms, dangers, temptations and distractions which provide any quest with its episodes and incidents that the goal of the quest is finally to be understood.'[17] The point of the journey only becomes clear by making the journey and learning to cope with the joys and troubles the journey poses, including challenges to our original notion of what the journey was all about.

The geographical, social, and temporal dislocations of pilgrimage have many positive roles. They are unsettling; but their point is not to change people by giving them sore heads and making them irritable, but rather, to lead people stage by stage to renounce normal, 'worldly' concern for externals and to embrace the profound effects the journey can have. To enter seriously upon a pilgrimage is to accept the difficulties of travel as deeply meaningful, ways of freeing ourselves from everyday life and concerns so as to grasp the point of our lives. Pilgrimage is the form of travel in which people are most transparent to, and patient with, travel's demands – not just to get the most out of traveling, but to achieve a new understanding of themselves and their world, which will change them for ever and guide their return home.

Experience of travel

Philosophers have often used the image of a journey to explain the experience of leading a human life. In Judeo-Christian tradition the chosen/saved are constantly on literal or metaphorical journeys (through desert or through confusion); in classical antiquity journeys of conquest, honour, and expiation are threaded through the foundational (epic and tragic) narratives. Like a journey, life has uncertainties and certainties, demands preparation and planning but also openness to setback and the unforseen. Life also has a destination – for some an absurd, nihilist end, but an end nonetheless.

Part of the travel experience is encountering unusual patterns so as to test and train ourselves for what may arise when we return home, to family, and to work; part of the experience too is that particular journeys we make confirm and celebrate different stages of our lives. Thus retired people often get their second wind for travel, young people take a year-off, newly-weds set off on honeymoon. The experience of leisure travel then can be recreative in all sorts of ways; an encounter with our life's horizons.

Travel experience also revives our sense of nostalgia: travel literature capitalises on sentimental attachments to healthy, natural environments (Tuscany, Provence, Swiss mountains, Scottish Highlands and so on), idylls (Oxford, Florence, Siena and so on), the unspoilt (tropical beaches, antarctic wastes and so on), the past (Knossos, Vienna, Bath and so on). Part of temporarily leaving our communities and lives behind is a search for the never-never world of youthful dreams and aspirations which our busy lifestyles do not let us satisfy. These dreams and hopes are real and for most of us they cannot be satisfied in the everyday; so it is important we reach some satisfaction through experiences such as travel. For, however partial, this demi-satisfaction can be sufficient to allow us to return home and continue.

Connected to this too is the desire for utopia. Utopia is different from nostalgia: it is not a powerful sentiment but the object of a passionate belief. People believe in ways of life better than the present, and in the possibility, however unlikely, of our finding or creating them. When we travel, part of what we seek may be utopias that others have established, or possibilities for our own utopias, or a new concept of utopia that makes normal life more bearable or meaningful. Often on holiday, there is the powerful conviction that '*this* is it!': this is where and how I want to live. The conviction (fortunately) rarely out-lives the holiday, but it may answer effectively to the sense of utopia: recognising it without fulfilling it; making it possible to live our everyday lives without either the full realisation of utopia, or its full abandonment.

After good travel we are never quite the same. At the simplest level, our memories are now different and some of our beliefs will be altered. Occasionally, especially after extended travel, people find themselves unable to fit back into home and normality. Often too, however, an attempt to live permanently in the travel destination will prove impossible, despite many, many bestselling books to the contrary. Settling in a place where one has spent a happy holiday can be as disillusioning as sharing a house with a friend: there are daily reminders that what one is doing is self-contradictory to holiday – and despite protesting that the object is 'change of lifestyle', permanent holiday is in fact what people who move to Tuscany or Provence are generally after. Of course, it is not self-contradictory to *travel* all the time, but leisure-migrants are usually not after constant travel but a highly specific (and much improved) location and an end to all imminent traveling.

Inevitably, different nationalities, ages, and groups have different travel habits and customs and this affects their travel experiences. People do not always react well to others' differences: I have mentioned that ridicule of others' holiday customs is a problem. But enjoyment of these differences is a great part of youth travel and the backpacker experience. In fact, the mix of perspectives and ideas here is fertile enough to make more affluent but more insulated tourists eavesdropping groups of backpackers in the café feel envious. This suggests that older and wealthier people have something to learn from new travelers here. Where once young men crossed continents in thousands for war and conquest, they generally travel now in peace and with open minds and in search of a more reflective leisure; and this can only have good effects on that generation as it ages.

Photography, video photography, and now the ease of digital photography, is another issue profoundly affecting the modern experience of travel. For some, the real experience of the Taj Mahal is unavailable to those who are more concerned with adding to the world's stock of images: 'the camera blurs the distinction between looking and noticing, between seeing and possessing; it may give us the option of true knowledge but it may unwittingly make the effort of acquiring it seem superfluous.'[18] But again, for certain cultures and individuals, creating, cataloguing, and then sharing images is an important part of sensitive, well-informed traveling. For those who think this way, photographing and planning to share the image and memories is part-constitutive of the experience of the Taj Mahal.

Other less useful parts of the travel experience include the growing perception among people that there is a necessity to travel, even where the urge is missing; that they are obliged to travel for holidays, as they are to own their own home, or drive a car. This is a consumerist victory: to bring travel inside the network of external ends and status pressures; to cancel out its leisure status as play, or reflection. Through advertising, this view is sustained and exploited by the tourist industry – the campaign sometimes beginning in mid-winter. Related to this is the repetitive approach to traveling where providers are guaranteed annual bookings by the same people. People often feel the call to return to the same spot: our holidays are precious and we cannot afford to get it wrong; we need the reassurance that our choice will be successful; so we choose conservatively, which suits the tourist industry perfectly. For some people this is ideal, the guarantee of satisfaction is more important than openness to novelty or risk. We vary after all, in our relative needs for security – and uncertainty – and for some, holiday travel is there to provide the safe and secure experiences in which the remainder of the year may be deficient. But repeat holidays, if sometimes good for play, may be bad for reflection. Reading a favourite novel over and over is fine if we did not get the message the first time, but not if it is a substitute for moving on. Repetition does not generally support recreation.

There are good reasons – economic, health-related, responsibilities at home – why some people should not travel. It is unlikely, however, that most people today can enjoy life over many years without traveling at all; unlikely too that we can adequately satisfy our interests in discovery, recovery, activity, and therapy without undertaking some travel from time to time. We have developed as creatures of the hearth, and of the trail. We do not set off for fight or food as we used to. But leisure travel now answers some of the cravings necessity bred in us in the past, including the desire to travel so as to dream and ponder. I suggest that the development of modern tourism has been useful here in directing the travel urge towards playful leisure, and even reflective leisure, for great numbers of people – people who might otherwise suffer from enforced domesticity. Tourism can challenge consumerism, but people who travel need to prepare well if they are to avoid holidays that identify free time with consuming a different range of products and services, taunt with promise of temporary status-enhancement, and tempt with luxuries.

6
Playing in Tune

The film *Shawkshank Redemption* is set in a tough 1940s prison in which inmates are treated as if they are sub-human and so become more and more brutal. In one scene, the central character breaks into the warden's office, turns the microphone towards a turntable, and plays over the prison's loudspeaker system a soaring soprano duet from Mozart's *Marriage of Figaro*. As the voices rise through the prison halls and yards, prisoners everywhere come to a standstill and gaze upwards, their faces transfigured by the power of the music. The message is plain: music frees the human soul; music turns our minds from suffering and routine and stress and towards the sublime.[1] Listening to music is a truly contemplative activity: activity that fills people with joy and provides new meaning.

Music can do this, and so, naturally, music can be reflective leisure, as well as play; yet a classic work on music listing its functions (emotional expression, aesthetic enjoyment, entertainment, communication, symbolic representation, physical response, social conformity and so on) does not even mention leisure.[2] And for millions of people, music is simply noise to be consumed, mood-enhancing sounds with obvious and welcome messages about romance, sex, or politics attached; stress-increasing rather than stress-breaking. Is the instrumentalisation of music purely an effect of the consumerist age? And how damaging to the contemplative ideal is music's present commodification?

Classical music

The case of classical music (what to call it? 'Classic' includes established pop and rock; 'serious' is insulting to ethnic, folk, jazz, and world; 'good' is offensive to nearly everyone; 'classical' is unsatisfactory yet common) is complicated – though perhaps less so than that of popular music. The latter is organised as a hugely successful international commodity. As music, it is generally very simple indeed; but unlike the simple music of previous ages, contemporary popular music makes grand claims for itself. To hundreds of millions, it *is* music, and classical music just an incomprehensible minority taste. Thirteenth-century market-place music would never have claimed to *be* music, to be anything other than simple music-making only distantly related to real music. By comparison, pop is organised, marketed, and has a high opinion of itself; though rarely challenging and designed to be soon disposed of and replaced, it is massively popular and product of a notoriously ruthless 'music business'. It is of enormous cultural significance today. Around its edges, and perhaps in the hands of experimental practitioners, it can offer some material for aesthetic appreciation, material for reflection. Yet mass production, fashionably short lifespan, and concern for a mass audience – for a 'hit': setting a record, however briefly, in the popular buying stakes – declares it to be strictly for consumption only.

It is only relatively recently that classical music has been conceived of *as* music. For most of its history it has been thought of and enjoyed not in musical terms but as the revelation of some metaphysical or cosmological order that can be described musically but also pondered intellectually.[3] Formerly, music mattered not primarily as music: aesthetic appreciation of music is only a couple of centuries old (roughly, from around the time of Mozart); from antiquity, through the early middle ages and up to the Renaissance, music was regarded as a normal means of examining the natural (and supernatural) order of things, an opportunity for enjoyable contemplation, study, and reflection on the secrets of life. Of course music was also thought of as 'the use of instruments to make music' (*musica instrumentalis*), but for Boethius in his great treatise on *Fundamentals of Music* which stood for centuries as the *quasi*-official guide to music, music-making is the least worthy area of music: it is subordinate to *musica humana*, which revealed the organisation of the human being, and decidedly inferior to *musica mundane*, which revealed the organisation of the universe.[4] Thus the modern idea of listening to music as music, listening attentively to details of score and performance, is recent, and well worth contrasting with more established ideas of reflection through music on the nature of the world and on our nature.

Our modern emphasis on performers is also an innovation. For most of history, people writing about music would have meant by 'musician' those who meditate on music, whether they wrote it, studied it, played it, or listened; executants, or performers, would have been rather lowly, their activities worth little attention from someone with a serious interest in music. Naturally, musical performance standards and the listening experience, were of secondary importance to people concerned to discover the meaning of life, patterns of cosmic order, the inner secrets of the universe. In fact, to such 'musicians', it does not particularly matter whether music is actually performed or not.[5]

This conception of the musician seems to have persisted until the seventeenth century, when music, by then largely demystified due to the scientific revolution and the birth of acoustical science, began to pass from the theorists and contemplatives into the hands of the leisured classes who now wanted to listen to, or play, the music – no doubt, sometimes for aesthetic reasons, and sometimes for reasons of (non-reflective) play.

The most important change here occurs mid-way through the eighteenth century. At this period, people began to write about and listen to music purely aesthetically, in terms of its emotional expression, power, and musical meaning; a canon of classics began to form, and executants were now admired and regarded as worthy of the title of musician. Composers too began to develop a more visible role as 'artists': they took it upon themselves to explain their music; thus listeners are now people who want to know about the *music*, people soaking up knowledge from musical technicians. By the mid-twentieth century, composers would not have the option of explaining what they are doing: they would *need* to do this, as classical music responded to the bland unimaginativeness of pop by becoming more and more zanily imaginative itself. A composer not explaining himself today by talks or writing would be considered bad mannered, elitist, disrespectful of his audience – unless, as Part, Rautavaara, and MacMillan do, he has already made a clear effort to speak in the language the audience knows best. Thus by the twenty first century, listeners are dependent on expert guidance and illumination from music professionals; ordinary listeners are no longer themselves 'musicians', able to contemplate the world and their lives through the structures of music.

The eighteenth century development of a musical canon looks to 'classic' works and recycles them in new versions and new, ever more polished performances. Audiences begin to expect compositions to reflect – not on timeless truths but on this 'traditional' canon.[6] From this, develops the classical-music tradition of the nineteenth century, still with us, in which new works are only tolerated if it is obvious they are reflecting, or reflecting upon, well established works.

The present commercialisation of classical music grows out of realisation of the popularity and familiarity (and so exploitability) of the canon by the marketers of the recording industry. But it was also helped by some fascinating experimentation early last century in making classical music utilitarian. These experiments began with fairly harmless attempts to evacuate music of intrinsic meaning and to treat it as utilitarian object. For example, Erik Satie wrote mind-numbingly simple music in the hope that people would treat his compositions like furniture – background, occasionally useful, comfortable, inherently meaningless.[7] This is the origin of 'background' music, ultimately muzak, the aural accompaniment to shopping-mall culture. Satie's often bizarre instructions to performers mock the performers, himself, listeners, and above all critics who take this whole business too seriously.

The Italian futurists Luigi Russolo and Filippo Marinetti asked questions about the relations of noise, sound, and music. Treating music as the 'liberation of sound' and arguing that traditional forms could no longer satisfy the public's auditory hunger, they built noise-emitting machines designed to bring noise of all different types within the ambit of musical performance. The actual work of music is itself here dethroned, its sacrosanct pretensions exposed; this is the forerunner of John Cage's work, including the infamous 4'33, in which the audience sits in silence forced to make 'music' from the arbitrary sounds they hear. Meantime, in the 1920s and 30s (for example, in works by Paul Hindemith and Kurt Weill), there developed an identifiable type of utility-music. *Gebrauchsmusik* was designed to be social useful, relevant, simple to perform. This development, however, rapidly deteriorated into the discredited propaganda tool of those repressive societies for which music, like all else, was treated as means to brainwash and to implement political ideology.

By the time of *Gebrauchsmusik*, classical music had become unpopular with the great majority of people, or popular only if packaged and useful for some external end (usually nationalism or ambience). As the century progressed, what is popular becomes whatever is popular: as with clothes, it is popular success that determines what will be popularly listened to. Today, popularity is the sole basis on which huge numbers of people make their musical choices (for pop). This situation is partly an outcome of the history of classical music itself – since the early eighteenth century, the connection with contemplation and philosophy has diminished, and classical music has not managed either to beat pop at the popularity game or to supply itself with an alternative purpose. In the later twentieth century, some classical music did attempt popularity again (usually by bizarre novelties, social 'relevance', or regurgitating pastiches of traditional musical forms), but most has simply become weirder and weirder, almost wallowing in its inaccessibility, lack of popular success and of clear purpose. Classical music does not 'need' to compete with pop, in the sense of winning numbers. But in the absence of any alternative purpose, it must restore the reflective function to people who enjoy music; and for this to occur, some breakthrough is necessary.

The breakthrough is not on the horizon. Music for consumption has won not only the numbers, but also the expulsion of reflection. This is partly because pop is extremely good at what it does, but mostly because a powerful economic and social system supports music-for-consumption, be it pop or classical. As a reaction against this, all that contemporary classical music has managed to come up with is to become absurdly complicated, as if snubbing its nose like a fretful child at the extreme simplicity of pop and the commercialisation of music generally. This has won it few new friends. Meanwhile, the reflective lives of dedicated concert-goers are routinely disregarded by composers and, apart from the small number of specialists who dedicate themselves to working out what contemporary music is about, performers and listeners now sit in opposing camps and judge one another.

Of course, reflective listening does survive. There are thousands of descendants of the contemplative listeners of former centuries. But most now attend repeat performances of the canon instead of new works; or, more likely, sit at home watching perfect recreations of perfect performances of the canon on their DVDs, which can hardly feed the reflective life adequately. Also, no one is quite sure if this audience will replicate itself in sufficient numbers devoted to ever more technically assured performances of a static repertory, or whether it should.[8]

Can music today provide the recreation of the person that philosophers from Plato and Aristotle, to Augustine and Boethius, and on to Schopenhauer thought it could? We get the music we deserve, and a long-term fragmented society does not deserve a coherent musical life and vision. Yet within the two broad categories of classical and pop, leisure, reflection, and recreation can still occur – and not only within the territory most commonly identified as 'classical'.

Dance music

In the great Gothic Cathedral of Seville the lucky visitor can occasionally see the strange sight of groups of young boys in sixes (*los seises*) dancing in sombre formation before the altar. Dancing in church is now rarely seen[9] (though a sort of liturgical ballet has become popular in some western religious orders), except in Seville, where many years ago Papal permission was reluctantly given for the boys to continue the custom until the garments they wear – now meticulously restored each year – finally fall apart. The philosopher Heidigger once wistfully complained that most of us have forgotten how to laugh and dance before the altar of God: where dancing is dissociated from deep questions of exploring and expressing life's meaning – where it is secularised and reduced either to complete informality, or to courtship displays – our grasp of transcendence and so our self-knowledge suffer – and so does our dancing! Where formal dancing survives at all today it is often severed from serious context and so is self-conscious, even precious. Thus ballets, ballrooms, and barndances are alien rituals to most of us who dance only as occasional party-goers, or reluctant guests at weddings.[10]

Where formal dancing does flourish today it is because a style of music has become archaic and is now venerated and enjoyed partly for that very reason. Successful dance music is anachronistic: no one pretends that even the best ballet scores and performances provide the shattering and ever new experiences of a mighty symphony or opera, or that tango and waltz rhythms fulfil the same highly contemporary functions as night club beat or celtic folk fiddles. In successful formal dancing, the music is not of course the sole end or focus of the activity; nevertheless, it is a contributor to a total experience that is rooted in nostalgia. Dance music helps to carry us to a more glamorous past, a past at least part of whose remoteness and appeal is more glamorous past in that dance played a much more significant role.

Where formal dance provides meaning to its devotees it is not because of the power of the music (listening to recorded dance music is always less rewarding than recorded opera), but because of the power of dance awakened by music. Just what is this power and what is its effect?

Its first element is obviously the body. Dance is the most extrovert of physical activities, the closest (most) people come to making love or waging war in public. Unlike some other forms of dancing, formal dance means *trying* to dance in such a way that all eyes are fixed on the performer. Dancers make themselves stand out and do so – if they are good – by a forgetfulness of the body that allows them to perform manoeuvres no one but a formal dancer would think of making today. When they do this, their dancing can have the quality of an offering, a making over of themselves to the audience or perhaps to the spirit of the dance. This means that as well as extrovert physicality, dancers are also capable of a degree of sacrifice, even self-sacrifice, and not just of representation. Where dancers express profound thoughts and feelings, and not mere virtuosity, the sacrifice of their dancing may be to something less tangible but more real than an audience: to art, history, God; hence, the boys of Seville, and the hopes of Heidigger for a more complete, sensual, and uninhibited Christianity.

Another aspect of the power of dance is its maintenance of a patch of formality amid the determination of the modern world to abandon both order and mystery. Modern people are extremely inhibited compared with their ancestors of almost every period. Paradoxically, a partial cure for this is greater love of and participation in formality. Where there are formal codes, clear customs, and shared practices it is easier to 'let oneself go', since there are declared boundaries within which we can be confident not to be mocked or attacked, and so able to become self-forgetful and openly expressive. Good dancers can achieve this. Thus the spirit or *daimon* of dance can serve leisure, and even contemplation, by reclaiming territory that is formal and stylised, as well as demonstrative and extravagant.

A third part of dance's potential is its continuity with activities and customs which sociology and anthropology confirm to be of high significance. All people and all peoples dance. From childhood games to celebrations of victory or the rituals of religion, dancing to music is important to people. Where a culture develops formal dance and dance music these will have continuities with the psychologies, memories, celebrations, and leisure activities of dominant individuals and groups. Formal dancing therefore helps dancers to integrate with the wider customs and practices of the community and its leaders. We can see the influence of this in the West still: adopting the trappings of ballroom dancing (gowns and tails, suited dance bands, formal sequences of dances, bows, curtsies and polite applause, and so on) are still *the* way in which ordinary people celebrate special events; the daughters of society's leaders until very recently were presented at Court after a series of 'coming out' dances; the Queen Mother concluded her very public hundredth birthday celebrations with a trip to the Royal Ballet; new US Presidents attend a series of inaugural balls, and so on.

Formal dance places the human body and its graceful potential before an age that is ever more body-conscious, but body-denying and grace-denying. It does this in a way that is more extrovert and much more extravagant than sport. Formal dance integrates formality and studied technique with self-forgetfulness and the expression of strong and deep emotions. It is one clear way in which nostalgia is good for us.

Opera

We get the music (architecture, universities, politics and so on) we deserve.[11] In recent times operatic performance has never been so popular, yet contributions to the genre have never been so few or so unpopular: practically no opera of the last fifty years will be listened to except by specialists, or those interested in discovering what happened to opera in the late twentieth century; just as non-specialists who pay to see heaps of bricks are interested in art – but not in its life-transforming potential, only in what has happened to it. Perhaps part of what our society deserves musically is the death of opera. But if it is dying, then opera's unprecedented popularity must be due either to consumerist love of (any) extravagance, or to nostalgia.

Perhaps opera is a substitute for the decline of religious practice, liturgy, and public magnificence. If this is so, then opera will in time come to acquire the anachronistic position now enjoyed by formal dance: ballet and opera are already frequently performed on the same stage and financed by the same administration; yet if opera becomes an anachronism, we have broken faith with opera, whereas ballet performances *should* be anachronistic. Just what is it we have lost by losing opera as a contemporary, living art, and why have we lost it?

The temptation is to explain opera in terms of music and drama, but music and drama were only ever half the story. Opera takes the ability of some people to sing very well after training, and asks them to perform in a large theatre, balancing their performance with that of a symphony orchestra. We should therefore think of opera's power first and foremost in terms of the power of singing and of singers.[12]

Western societies were seduced for three hundred years by trained singing from the stage, and by the great singers. Few would have disagreed that when this force was unleashed something very fine and aesthetically important was taking place, something it would be unthinkable to criticise politically as 'elitist' or 'irrelevant'. Of course, in terms of direct utility opera is sheerly wasteful; but people were formerly too well read to think that direct utility was the purpose of music, celebration, or leisure activity. Today, impressarios sometimes disastrously intervene to invent a direct utility value for opera or to make singers use microphones in front of numbers similar to pop concerts (Three Tenors, Three Irish Tenors, Three Sopranos, Montserrat Caballe advertising the Barcelona Olympics with Freddy Mercury). But the gulf between this and opera is great: amplified great hits and crossover classics gets few people along to performances of Mozart.

If not utility, which are the values of opera? Opera takes core, 'forbidden' parts of human personality – most commonly, sex, power, and injustice – and allows us to think and feel about them in ways that are usually prohibited. Since the days of the first opera performances, composers have been expert at getting around censors: opera *libretti* are craftily constructed to look like edifying or amusing tales, when in fact we are confronted with the power of singing and singers to make the shameful appear beautiful. And all of this dangerous business takes place in the most public of settings: often before monarchs and prelates, millionaires and *papparazzi*. Opera is most definitely not for young children, or the timid.[13]

Opera has always possessd a whiff of the immoral; something that cannot be said about oratorio, symphony music, chamber music or lieder. *Castrati* were perhaps acceptable in Church, but add a few wigs and men playing women, women playing men, and men who sound like women playing men, and some delightful feelings can be enjoyed in the dark. Critics and marketing men enthuse today over attractive and slim (!) sopranos, as if opera were formerly the territory of fat, unattractive women; but this says more about our ignorance of what seems desirable in different periods than about some sea-change in opera. Desirability is built into our response to singing, especially to sopranos and soprano singing. The modern diva is a new sexual incarnation in a line that stretches from Callas to Melba, back to Pasta and Viardot-Garcia, and then breaks up, ambiguously, with the mutilated and androgenous artists of the baroque period. Tenors meanwhile, are symbols of virility, traceable back into early tenor history. Enrico Caruso had the genius and resources to blend the delicacy of traditional Italian art-song with the full-chested bellow of post-Wagnerian *verismo* or realism; thus he made modern, sensitive-but-exciting tenors possible. But before Caruso, audiences, including Queen Victoria, swooned over De Reszke, as ladies previously had lost consciousness at the performances of Mario and Rubini.

Opera is well adapted to the presentation of aspects of sex and sensuality that are normally matters for public reticence. Operatic stories, costumes, acting, and emotions are crafted so as to be over-the-top. Sensual pleasure is found too in the very sound of trained singing that combines power with the vulnerable, open vowels of the preferred operatic languages (basically, languages other than English). Stratospheric, high notes are physically thrilling; middle register singing is rich and satisfying. Pop cannot make sex thrilling in this way: you cannot bring out of the closet and reveal what has never been in it.

As well as sex, opera glories in power. Everyone loves stories of the old autocratic divas – Patti, Melba, Albani – terrifying impressarios and reducing royalty to fawning slaves; or more modern divas like Caballe or Sutherland cancelling, apparently wilfully, and plunging thousands into despair. In the 1950s the impressarios Bing at New York's Met and Ghiringelli at Milan's La Scala were international public figures, auto-cratic, famous, loved or loathed by whole nations. The appointment of a Director at Vienna's famous Staatsoper is still an event that can divide the nation; in Milan the annual ritual of opening night is a focus for political discontent and popular protest; the antics of star conductors such as Kleiber, Muti, Barenboim, and Maazel are reported as national (at least) events; and audiences in any capital city will still include a share of local power brokers, even on a routine night.

The operatic stage deals with power in various ways – by putting song into the mouths of powerless and pitiful characters, and by making the powerful expose their inner thoughts through musical monologues. Too strong a focus on star singers in the consumerist age has overlooked the endless maids and messengers of opera who are insignificant but made eternal through their music. A good ensemble team values the *comprimarii* singers, whom Donizetti thought fit to include with the stars in the famous sestet from *Lucia di Lamermoor* and Mozart employed to build up the incomparable finale to *Marriage of Figaro's* second act. An indifferent (to my mind) modern recording of *Aida* under Abbado has the stellar international cast go through its familiar paces but brings the listener to a halt only with the minute of song of the expert *comprimario* Piero de Palma as the Messenger from the Ethiopian front. Opera can reverse power relations; and empower the listener: the thrill of eavesdropping on Otello's monologue, or Boris's, or King Philip's, or on a hundred aristocratic soprano arias poured out stage left, is partly the thrill of access to the inner worlds of the rich and famous that are normally closed to us.

We often talk of the power of singing. But this refers not only to singing's ability to move us but also its ability to make power beautiful. Few people have the power of a singer with an audience in his hand; and where this power seduces and converts, it makes us aware of what people can do with power and what can be done to us. It is so too with injustice. The operatic world is filled with the rhetoric of injustice: its very existence depends on the sheer luck of someone who has a peculiar throat and gets a break. Those who make it are surrounded by those who do not (especially the chorus), and who inevitably feel they too could do well, and that the thing is all so unfair. The salaries involved at the very top end are thought to be unjust by just about everyone. Many argue the expense of producing opera is unjust; to some, the existence and level of subsidies seems iniquitous.

The extravagance and irrationality that Dr Johnson perceived in opera is the result of singing and singers who specialise in the extreme, including thoughts and acts we normally despise or ignore. The sex, power, and politics of opera is good for us in the way all catharsis is: it allows us to contemplate (reasonably) safely the fairly appalling clothed in wonderful colours, and then to return to daily life, with its rather drab colours, more thoughtful about these matters. Ironically, the more holy or morally pure opera tries to be, the more unsettling it is, since it inevitably stirs up dangerous thoughts and passions within the context of its treatment of religion and morality. Thus in Wagner's *Parsifal* – opera's most elevated experience – we find the power of pagan magic and the sultriness of temptation at the very heart of a story and score imbued with sacred qualities.

By concentrating on sex, power, and politics – particularly in staging – opera in some companies comes close to, or even sells out to, consumerism: ten popular operas endlessly repeated; status-enhancement catered for; advertising that emphasises not meaning or beauty but thrills and spills. This suggests that to maintain opera as reflective leisure, it is the music – playing and singing – that must be placed first. And this suggests why today we may have lost opera as a contemporary, popular art: there is simply not enough great classical music being composed to keep opera live. The two greatest sopranos of the twentieth century help to illustrate the decline of opera as a living cultural influence.

Maria Callas was surrounded wherever she went by powerful men and confirmation of her own stellar power. Her name is linked with sexual intrigues, and with the alleged injustices of her treatment of others. She is associated with law suits, brittleness, and concern for immense fees and star billing. Yet with her, opera is gloriously alive. She revitalised a forgotten early nineteenth century repertoire, but, strangely, had no interest in contemporary opera or in works composed for her. Her successor, Joan Sutherland, showed the ordinary decency and easy-going friendliness of her native Australia. Her feet are planted on the ground; she enjoys a happy marriage; and rather than injustice, she is known for tolerance, fairness, and modesty. Yet for all the glories of her singing, we already look back on her career as something of an anachronism; an attempt to bring *bel canto* display out of the museum, not as cutting-edge theatre in Callas's style, but just as a miraculously beautiful song. Yet Sutherland had no more interest in contemporary work than Callas and has inspired no major composers.

The danger, then, is that even at its greatest, opera will become nostalgia, since classical music is insufficiently robust to support it as a genre. But its potential for promoting reflection on difficult and controversial areas of human life and ethics should offer sufficient stimulation to good composers. Certainly, personal and social recreation is what is at stake in the masterworks of Handel, Mozart, and Wagner.

Music and the sacred

In the Christian story, ordinary human expectations concerning the gravitas of God and religion are time and again subverted: for example, by the humour of Jesus' preaching; the levitas of King David dancing and singing naked before the Ark of the Covenant, to the horror of his wife; Jesus and the disciples picking corn on the Sabbath precisely to demonstrate that the Sabbath must not become just another day of gravitas. The sheer fun and joy of the life of God and the saints is often communicated in musical terms. When painters and writers think of heaven, they have in mind heavenly choirs and orchestras (who thinks of heaven as silent?). God and the angels tumble playfully together, as in the famous Byzantine icon of the Trinity dancing, or the *Transparente* of Toledo Cathedral, or Fra Angelico's musical and dancing angels. Hell, by comparison, is sheer noise: disorder and cacophony.

Philosophers have often suspected a connection between music and the sacred. Honorius of Auton describes the sweet 'celestial' music of the heavenly spheres as they move; music beyond our hearing, just as there are frequencies registered by bats but not by us.[14] Aquinas supports chants and hymns (he wrote some beautiful ones) in the worship of God – but argues against musical instruments in church, believing they can sir up pagan feelings and distract people from higher things.[15] Modern thinkers are more coy about the relations of music to the transcendent and eternal – with one shining exception. Schopenhauer gives cosmic centrality to music in his vast theory of the world as 'will and representation'.[16] In Schopenhauer's richly extravagant writings the core of reality is will, discoverable in all phenomena, whether inanimate, animate, or intelligent. Intelligent life exists in constant battle with will, which it must seek to dominate if it is not to become pure victim. Domination, however, is complex: how do we dominate will except by an assertion of will, in which case, whose is the victory?

Instead, Schopenhauer suggests we should concentrate more on stilling the will, quietening the impulse to strive and progress that we find deep inside ourselves. This self-quietening can be achieved either ethically through the sort of conduct that displaces will and accepts in tranquility the renunciation of egoism (and ultimately of the world), or aesthetically through the sort of contemplation in which the conscious self and its individual concerns are lost and the universal 'Ideas' behind things made apparent.

The most effective escape from the meaninglessness of will is music. Whereas other arts express universal Ideas, music expresses the force of will directly. If reality is will and music its direct expression, then to appreciate music is to look at reality directly and to be made profoundly aware of the inner meaning of things. Listening seriously to music is a special sort of integration, for here (one manifestation of) will encounters will-as-world directly, an experience both tranquilising and terrifying.

Few people accept Schopenhauer's views, but the idea of music expressing some deep reality and calming the will when seriously attended to is common and important. Music certainly does calm will, emotion, heartbeat, thus it allows for contemplation and reflection. And in the hands of sacred composers, it can form, or inform, prayer and worship directly; it can also express the religious emotions of joy, hope, and ecstasy, as in the *Sanctus* of the Verdi *Requiem*, the soprano's *Ihr habt nun Traurigkeit* from Brahms' *German Requiem*, or the *Kyrie* from Palestrina's *Missa Papae Marcelli*.

Religious believers and their traditions are never without music, whether the booming of organs or tinkling of prayer bells in the breeze. Music is not just handy in religion for expressing and promoting religious sentiments: it is deeply revealing about the human person and our spirituality. Who can imagine the Last Judgement taking place in silence; or the Blessed meeting God with a polite handshake and entering quietly into his Kingdom? Human beings exist in worlds of sound, and where they picture a perfect and communal existence for themselves, that noise has to be ordered into music.

Icon makers do not manufacture pictures of divine realities, but rather pray through their work so that the icons they make embody the holy truths they reveal. Composers and performers of sacred music should pray and reflect too as they work, for this same reason. But late nineteenth century practice was to include sacred music in concert packages, with remaining connections to religion only those that occur in individual listeners' minds. And twentieth century consumerist society affected religious music in many ways: if we compare trends in contemporary hymns and the mawkish lyrics of feel-good faith with the rhythms of plain-chant which attempted to voice something of the rhythm of 'God's time', or Baroque mass settings and cantatas which brought something of God's power and majesty and the narrative music of the Scriptures to men and women in a fairly chaotic age, the result is condemnation of most contemporary efforts. Again, we get the music we deserve. A culture that does not take religion seriously (far less practise it) and rejects the spiritual life as a private indulgence will not seek music that seriously embodies the sacred. It will then miss out on one of the most sublime experiences of reflective leisure.

Folk and ethnic music

There are reasons for treating these types of music together. Each claims to represent something larger than the performer; not transcendent values in this case, but 'we, the people' in the case of folk and 'culture under threat' in the case of ethnic music. In both cases the notion of performance seems a misnomer. We are dealing with the expression of feelings deeply important to people and the preservation of traditional ways of life. Folk and ethnic music play a vital role in helping people to recognise and understand their identities, histories, and traditions. Integrating ordinary people with one another and with their pasts is the very important task of music as diverse as warrior songs, lullabies, native instrument music, epic ballads, folk dances, and laments.

Folk music has not taken kindly to the modern, recorded age. Music designed to give voice to ordinary people's thoughts and hopes is made redundant or trivialised where the people already have voice; especially if that voice is part of a multi-million dollar enterprise. The issue is a complex one: how far can the disenfranchised remain so when they are a major social 'cause' and a healthy business proposition? It is debatable whether anyone is helped by the popularisation and commercialisation of their own social exclusion or misfortune. Speaking musically, when the music of the poor of Havana or the Irish moors or the Australian deserts is popular and deeply enjoyable to so many, has the authentic voice been taken away, or has it actually been extended, and heeded; and if it has been heeded, does that now mean the music has become inauthentic, merely nostalgic? Perhaps, if the music brings about important changes and its original audience is satisfied, popularity may be worthwhile. Where it does not achieve this, however, I suspect people and traditions that become 'pop' are exploited or sentimentalised.

With ethnic music we meet one of the great sacred monsters of the age: who would dare fail to pay homage to the importance of cultures under threat or to the multicultural dream? People are not always clear what they mean by 'culture' – usually something like a way of life that helps to make existence meaningful to large numbers of people with a shared set of goals, principles, and norms. Promotion of the intersection of these cultures – inter-culturalism – is almost uniquely cherished today as a (almost the) basic moral and political principle. The hoped-for result of that intersection – multiculturalism – is one of the utopias which countries such as the USA and Australia believe in their optimistic moods they have already reached.

This, actually very ancient, commitment to universal brotherly living is vulnerable to the criticism that it is universalist and imperialist: it is a Western philosophical idea, and one not universally welcomed by other cultures. Perhaps inevitably, then, these aspirations tip over into cultural relativism, which recognises (and 'respects') incommensurable value systems in each identifiable culture. This means that music that is very important in the life of a culture may be classed together with trivial or manufactured music that is simply jumping on the multicultural bandwagon – which is disrespectful to music that is genuinely integrative of cultures and supportive of meaningful ways of life.

Music is linked to culture in ways that repay close study: music reflects, sustains, may even enact culture (thus pop and rock movements trace our western history from existentialism to deconstructed nihilism). It is false to say that this relationship is not about leisure: genuine folk and ethnic music is music that sustains play and reflection on lives, activities, philosophies, and faiths. It is important that the real needs of peripheral and sub-cultures for identity, integration, and reflection through music are not lost, swamped, or exploited by the musical mainstream; and it is hard to ensure this given the mass music industry that propels and defines that mainstream.

Recorded music

The first record to achieve major commercial success was Enrico Caruso's 1907 version of *Vesti la giubba*, a recording that has never left the catalogues. Caruso's sobs changed the world of music practically overnight, a change which makes Al Jolson's giving birth to the talkies small beer indeed. With recording a viable, popular success, it became possible for ordinary people to enjoy music and to do so without reliance on the vagaries of performances and performers. The very best that musicians could do had been preserved; the best technological resources were used, the recordings mass-produced and made available to the public at a reasonable price.

For a time, recorded music supported and increased the popularity of the classics. In the first decade of the twentieth century, popular music was still classical music (not all of it, of course, and not exclusively, but much of it). Twenty years later the relationship between popularity and classics changed – to significant extent because of developments in the recording business. Quality but non-classical popular music (music hall, music theatre, light music, musicals) held sway for a time, but by the mid 1950s mass-appeal pop dominated performance schedules, radio programmes, and recording catalogues. Of course, quality popular music existed, and still does; but the extraordinary success of recording, and the consumerist boom generally, carried lower quality, accessible pop into every home – or at least every home in which a teenager lived.

Meanwhile, classical music too developed its relationship with the new recording industry. At first this situation proved very healthy for the classics: public knowledge of the repertoire grew and appreciation of excellence in music was extended to those living far (geographically and socially) from concert halls. But recording has also contributed to the diminishment of the classics. Business mergers and takeovers have meant tamer repertoire, which in turn has effects on orchestral programming and public support for new and challenging works.[17] The very existence and popularity of superb recorded performances, most often assembled in segments, alters what we understand to be performance. For many people, these simulated accounts are the reality; the local symphony a poor imitation.

The recording industry has made a significant contribution to what people choose to do in their free time. CDs and now DVDs are cheap, even if generally sold at inflated prices, reliable, brief enough for most attention spans, collectable, and most important of all, they are private. People listen to CDs in the privacy of their homes or through mini head-sets while they jog, commute, or shop; thus private listening infiltrates social and active life. But the question is: has recording served music, or has it diminished the power and value of music by focussing too much on accompanying consumer activities? Does music that is sold on privately-owned CDs and played on 'personal' stereos still serve contemplation and insight; or are its higher ends now forgotten as people buy seventy minute musical fixes of the works (and performers) which the industry giants believe have best chance of selling well?

Night-clubbing or the symphony?

The distinction between classical and popular music is fast within most people's minds. But any attempt to justify it faces difficulties: how to do full justice to each without cheapening either? How do we deal with borderline cases? How can we – and should we? – minimise the influence of our personal tastes, prejudices, and idiosyncrasies upon the judgements we make about music? And is a two term distinction simply too weak, or too general, to provide insight into contemporary music-making?[18]

We cannot discuss classical music without some attempt to explain it, even if the attempt is merely a working model and not a definition. 'Popular music' is an even more troublesome designation. Is pop just whatever is most popular (would Beethoven be pop if we had a revolution in public taste?), or is it a qualitative, and not a purely quantitative, description? And if qualitative, just what is the qualitative point being made?

People are generally happiest with a sociological justification of the classic/popular distinction: classic (or popular) music is the sort listened to by *these* groups of people (or the majority of these people), for these sorts of reasons, in the context of these sorts of activities, and so on. A philosophical justification would be different. First, it will acknowledge musicological criteria for distinguishing the two, and also for distinguishing good from trivial pop (and classical) music. But this is not sufficient, for excluded pop composers might reply 'yes, but we are not interested in musicology's criteria or its conception of quality.' To deal with this difficulty an adequate philosophical treatment of the distinction must begin with reflection on the nature and purpose of the two forms of music, and some analysis of how each fares in terms of a conception of the more general ends of music. I cannot produce an account of music, but some of the differences are clear between what is usually played in the night club and encountered in symphony hall.

People often begin this topic with a strong defence of the autonomy of both forms of music: each has its own goals and values, and neither should impose its standards on the other.[19] But one problem with this approach is that it can mean people are unable, or at least less willing, to criticise popular music (criticism of classical music rarely presents a problem: lovers of classical music expect and encourage musical, and wider cultural, criticism). For this reason, I prefer to begin by asking what pop music is, how it works, and how it stands to music generally.[20]

Pop lovers believe in and respond to what is immediately appealing in music: simple melodies, no complex intervals, simple lyrics, strong rhythmic beat.[21] The music should attract quickly and simply, without making demands: if it is over-demanding, it is unsuccessful pop. From the perspective of reflective leisure, it is hardly a good thing that music *comes to you* in this way. By contrast, classical music makes heavy demands, and it is precisely by everyone involved in the performance applying themselves to answer these demands that the rewards of the music come. Put simply, the rewards of the classics are a result of what *we* bring to the music: what we *do* to it. Classics lovers quickly come to realise that their appreciation and enjoyment deepens the less passive they are, the more willing they are to encounter the unfamiliar, study it, ponder it, contrast it, explore it, take up an active position on it. So people who take classical music seriously learn to inform their listening by understanding the cultural and historical background, building some technical musical knowledge, being willing to postpone immediate gratification and easy access in order to cultivate taste and gain aesthetic and intellectual rewards.

With most pop music we rarely need to do anything at all. Pop does it all; it comes to us, packaged and familiar. Hence, there are fewer opportunities for developing insight, learning, understanding, and seeking depth. Correspondingly, classical music expects its devotees to be highly active: if people who attend string quartet recitals are not active before, during, and after the performance, they will be bored and mystified.

Musicologically, we meet much less development within individual pop pieces, pop creative outputs, or pop genres taken as a whole. Instead, there are fairly similar variations on simple themes. This helps to explain why bands last such a short time: it is not simply consumerist desire for ever-changing personalities and appearances, but also the fact that in terms of the music they offer there is often little difference between one band and another. Since they are all doing much the same thing, there is no *musical* reason to prefer one to the other. At its worst, this can mean critical standards are reduced to personal crushes on lead singers; perfectly fine in consumerist terms, senseless in terms of human recreation.

Contemporary classical music can also be criticised here, but from the opposite extreme: whereas contemporary pop makes no demands, much contemporary classical makes *unlimited* demands on the listener. With many classical composers today we can take nothing for granted. The abolition of musical form in most compositions of the past fifty years means that audiences are often disoriented and the only people who can truly appreciate the music are those in the elite group that has undertaken serious study of the music's content and intent. If pop binds together enormous global audiences, and contemporary classics unites tiny, specialist groups, Schubert and Richard Strauss have the potential to integrate vast international audiences who are willing to be active in their listening and happy to learn slowly and for life.

The breakdown of form in classics and the rigid adherence to a simple form in pop both seem to me the result of a more general breakdown of form in culture. Societies in confusion or fragmentation can provide no consensus on cultural frames or forms: social life becomes mere bureaucratic management, working through the implications of economic imperatives. In this environment, our music, and many of our other institutions too, will reflect our confusion. The majority of people stick to a safe, familiar pop formula; while those who are more reflective seek form among the fragments wherever they can find it.

Of course this is not to do anything like full justice to the phenomenon of pop, and pop lovers will emphasise its many alleged benefits:

pop gives voice to people, entertains, provides an escape, and expresses a cultural environment suitable to modern, urbanised populations. But these points are all debatable.[22]

First, there is a sense in which pop muffles or reduces voices rather than expressing them.[23] Successful pop consists almost solely in songs. The songs are brief, the poetry weak, and the themes limited – a heavily disproportionate number concern teenage relationships. The dominance of this mode plays some part in fortifying, and so limiting, teen concerns and horizons – and keeping older listeners 'teenage' – rather than simply speaking up for people.

Secondly, it is hard to understand in what sense mainstream pop can be truly entertaining; most older adults can rarely put up with it for more than a few minutes, which is in fact the attention span it caters to. It is as if we need the lyrics and the voices and, in particular, the personalities and appearances behind them because so banal is the musical structure, we could not otherwise think there is any real purpose to it. Pop has to be sung (by stars) to justify itself. It also needs its regular diet of Number One hits. Without a doubt, whipping up excitement in terms of commercial achievement helps to make up for a certain lack of musical distinction. 'Entertainment' is never perhaps a vital goal, but together with relaxation it is one part of playful leisure; repeated doses of repetitive pop, however, are not particularly entertaining. In fact, it risks gradual dulling of the capacity for real fun and even, occasionally, causing depression (part of pop's message is the great seriousness with which it takes itself and its teen-sex themes).

Thirdly, pop is only a limited escape. Modern societies are huge consumerist systems and pop music can offer only very little escape since it conforms so carefully to the pattern and logic of consumption. The music is created with a view to selling vast numbers of recordings, and to a lesser extent concert tickets: it takes the form of short, three minute songs, with lyrics reduced in scope and range of references so that those who represent the bulk of the market can 'relate' to them; performers and songs are replaceable; and the music never really attacks 'the system', since the pop business, its customers, and their preferences are heavily dependent on the consumer system. If the western world is riddled with problems of consumerism – including consumption of harmful drugs, commodification of the body, and commercialisation of sex – escape from these is not to be found in pop music.

Fourthly, pop does express a culture and create a cultural environment, but we should be aware of what this means. Because of the numbers and resources involved, pop has great power: 'the question we should be asking is not what does popular music reveal about "the people" but how does it *construct* them...Youth music is socially important not because it reflects youth experience...but because it defines for us what "youthfulness" is.'[24] Because it constructs or creates people, pop gives an identity and so helps to bridge private and public worlds, makes feelings seem stronger, organises experience, and so on.[25] But all of this is at the level of satisfaction of desires, and expressing the frustration of preferences: pop does not recreate people in the sense of renewing important human capacities and restoring natural human goods to our exercise and enjoyment of these capacities.

Of course, if pop defines people in terms of satisfaction/frustration of preferences, it is deeply useful to consumerist society. But is it good for those whom it creates in its image? Pop listening, like sports watching, does construct identity, confer allegiance, set up dependencies. But sports rarely carry the powerful subliminal messages of pop. For every boy who wants to grow up to cheat or intimidate at sport, thousands grow up who want to follow the patterns of sex and consumption preached by pop.

Of course, there are numerous forms of non-classical music other than pop; but pop and classical define themselves by their mutual relation, and it is pop, through its identity with consumerism, that is the main opponent to reflective musical leisure. Classical music has devalued its own tradition since the eighteenth century, and its dalliance with consumerism has not helped. But I think that the present bleak patch, like all aesthetic bleak patches, will be temporary. If people at some point in the future want to reclaim the sort of cosmic and contemplative importance music was once believed to possess, one priority will be to write – and play and sing – about the consumerist stranglehold over music and leisure. But for today, we have allowed music to become 'the perfumed balm to tranquilise and lubricate a system geared to profits.'[26]

Because of how we see our world, we see music as a product to buy and sell, and to use to promote the buying and selling of other things, including concert tickets. Where music is commercialised in this way, musical success is judged in terms of immediate sales numbers; and then music naturally adapts to this sort of expectation and demand. Neither the classical nor the popular tradition benefits from this. Perhaps what is needed now is a standard of popularity independent of the market: a standard that might serve as a benchmark for new, popular classical music. In the meantime, some inroads can be made on the dominant system by re-thinking the role of the arts as reflective leisure in modern societies (Chapter 9). But there is little point in this until we consider just how much time modern people have, and how much they should have, for reflective leisure. What, in other words, is the appropriate balance of work and leisure in the twenty first century?

7
Playing by the Rules

Sport and philosophy are our major legacies from ancient Greece. This is not a coincidence: we take brains and muscle apart at our peril. Even today, the Olympics Movement website includes at the top of its homepage a list of the philosophers who attended the original Olympic Games. This is the basis of sports' claim to support human excellence and happiness: sport arises from within a philosophical culture and gives its adherents – whether participants or spectators – opportunities for reflection on features of life that are otherwise difficult to reflect upon. Sport is an important addition to contemplation, artistry, appreciation, socialising, worship, and the other reflective leisure activities. But it is also the leisure activity that is most naturally understood as playing: if an activity is sport, it is always 'people playing'.

Or at least, this is one view of sport. But how does it relate to the crude, often commercialised, and increasingly brutal field sports played by so-called elite sportspeople before audiences of braying spectators today? How does it relate to the raw activity of doing whatever you can get away with so as to win? I am writing in the week preceding the Athens Olympics. Practically every news bulletin contains stories of almost-paranoid levels of dope testing, athletes taking doping authorities to national courts, allegations over cheating, fury and recriminations over individuals missing out on Olympics places; plus the usual winter stories of on-pitch football violence, off-pitch thuggery and sexual assault allegations, and on-court and off-court self-indulgence and prima donna-ism by tennis stars in sports most popular soap-opera. In the same week, the Vatican has announced the establishment of a new department 'Church and Sport' with the stated aim of re-injecting fundamental values of fairness, ethics, transparency, and legality into sports.

Modern sport looks shabby; its primary values are those of assertiveness, acquisitiveness, reward, and status. Modern professional sport is now very well integrated with consumerist aspirations. Players in bright jerseys advertise rich corporations; major games are crafted around TV schedules that are crafted around lucrative twenty second commercial advertising spots; the rewards for successful individuals in terms of sponsorships, promotions, earnings, and lifestyle are enormous.

With this background, what can be done to save sport from commerce and for leisure? How can sport be reclaimed for fulfilling play and deep reflection? Can it be stopped from adding to, rather than decreasing, twenty first century stress levels? One approach to these questions is that of Heather Reid, in *The Philosophical Athlete*.[1] For Reid, sportspeople at all levels can learn about life in and from their sporting experience. Key values of self-discovery, responsibility, respect, and citizenship are not just an ideal to be taught to college sports players: they are ideas the players will themselves encounter, wrestle with, and develop if they are playing their sport well – that is, in freedom from external questions such as money, fame, sex, and status. Reid encourages us to exercise in ways that open up our minds reflectively to who and what we are. She shows how exercising and playing sport can reveal that, for example, body-mind dualism is false; that, however briefly, we can enjoy moments of genuine freedom; that faced with knowledge of our limitations we can finally grasp what life means. She shows too how learning and loving your sport can develop a sense of respect for ourselves, others, and for sport; and how participation in sport helps people to understand some of our most cherished social values, such as liberty, equality, and fairness.

Reid's book is written so as to engage sports enthusiasts and it certainly indicates one way in which people serious about sport can be serious: they can be philosophical athletes. But people can also be 'good at sport' *without* playing philosophically. There are benefits in the philosophical approach according to Reid; but it is not conceptually required to be philosophical in order to be a sportsperson.

Another approach to reclaiming sport is to recall that all sport is not professional sport, far less elite sport. Most sport is play.[2] Most children play games, and when the children go off to school most will take part in larger scale, more organised games. Sports abilities and enthusiasms tend to develop either through clubs or physical education classes. And after school days, this sporting activity continues for an (admittedly, dwindling) number of people; and continues for many more as spectating. Huge numbers of people take part in sport for no rewards other than playful leisure and fitness, in good spirits, and in healthy balance with other parts of their nature. This tradition of sport as play offers important leisure opportunities, and these can be enhanced when play is combined with competitions. In amateur sport, the competitive element can significantly increase the playfulness. Individuals and teams who compete against each other need not compromise their play by seeking some external benefit ('winning'), but can seek simply to be the best on the day at playing the game. Amateur competition simply means playing together with other sports lovers as well as you possibly can.

So sport can be philosophical and sport can survive as play in amateur hands: two ways in which sport defeats consumerism. But what about professional sport? Can this still be done for play, or reflection, today? Or does the massive commercial and televised empire built around elite sports mean that sport has now lost its links with the classical ideal and so is no longer immune to consumerism's total logic?

Fitness, winning, and character

According to Jan Boxill, the 'paradigm form' of sport is voluntary, rule-governed, physically challenging, and competitive.[3] I think this is probably what most people who reflect on professional sport think. But surely it misses too much of importance. Boxill says it is only a model; but it could be a model of modern business life, politics, military, or whatever. It is of course a perfect sports model for a contractualist society, a society whose key activities and values are determined by contract and consensus (a model of 'liberal sports'). For that reason, it will be alien to real amateurs, but will probably gain ascendancy as we move through the ranks of professionals towards the elite, the national representatives, and international superstars. Boxill's model does, however, rightly bring to prominence one element that few writers on the topic treat: physical challenge. Sport is about building, and skillfully employing, physical fitness.

There are of course various indicators of fitness, and different systems for ranking those indicators. My concern is not with how most accurately to assess fitness, but with just why fitness matters in sport. Fitness is a property of the body, but fitness in sport is not just a matter of exercising hard. Fitness has meaning: the fitness of sportspeople reveals not just the body functioning well, even superlatively well, but the body exposed as mortal even when it is at its peak.[4] Many forms of human activity can demonstrate excellence (choral singing, scholarship, parliamentary debate, military manoeuvres); but no activity better announces our common limitations and shared vulnerability than sport: even at their peak, we watch elite athletes make a titanic effort and then suffer and struggle to recover straight afterwards, and we can *imagine* how they feel. For this reason, sport must include losers: the message cannot be 'everyone is a winner; no one gets hurt: we are all gods.'[5] Someone has to exhibit frailty combined with the reality of setback: sport teaches that even when strong and successful, there is the possibility of hurt, and the inevitability of death. That is also why (unintended) physical hurt is a rightful part of sport: it makes us look at things, however briefly, from the viewpoint of the loser, the viewpoint of the mortal sufferer – something consumer society and consumers are more and more reluctant to do.

The focus of sportspersons' frailty is of course the body – toned up to full fitness and power, and yet still easily hurt and damaged, still a potential loser. Because sportspeople identify strongly with their sport, they know minutely the movements and experiences of their bodies – hence, the great danger of identity problems when a career ends: 'being a hero was exciting; now, I am just a body'. Good sports training will teach the power and beauty of the body exercising for no external end or reward, and the limitations of the body: it will not only teach how to win, or preach a deceptive message of 'transcending' bodily limitations. It ought also to teach thoughtfulness and the meaning of the sporting activity: after all, if great players demonstrate mortality to all of us, they should also demonstrate this to themselves. Sportsmen and women are not naturally 'stupid and strong'. They will improve if aware of the meaning of what they do. Rodin's *The Thinker* is an athlete, but that is not the reason he is more beautiful to look at than the average philosophy professor: he is beautiful because he is an athlete reflecting on life.

Winning is important to sport, not just to sportspeople. Demonstrating the beauty and fragility of the human frame would be solely aesthetic if it were not for sportspeople also attempting to play their sport as best as they can and so attempting to win. Of course, this ideal has become badly misunderstood, thanks in no small part to consumerist need (and greed) for the rewards at stake. Sportsmen and women are presented as living advertisements for consumption of sports equipment, cars, lifestyle, and so on; and the more they win at sport, the more they can win in endorsements, so the identification of winning at sport with being a leader and model in consumerist society is confirmed. In the *nike* era, the idea of ethical victory becomes a quaint, pre-consumerist ideal.

But winning is not just about beating other people ('beating' should tell us that this alone is hardly admirable).[6] Winning can only matter for one reason: because the winner is thereby 'best on field', the competitor who has played the sport best. It cannot matter for prizes, rewards, and endorsements: for these are sought and admired either for extra-sport reasons, or because they are taken as evidence that someone *is* best on field. Heather Reid writes, 'our conception of a winner runs much deeper than the ability to fulfil the analytic definition of victory in sport.' The existence of notions like' moral victory', 'personal victory', being 'cheated of a victory' tell us victory is not a simple, first-over-the-line matter.[7] For example, we do not award victory to people who have crossed the line by cheating; and even when they have crossed the line in a clean race, it is sometimes still a complex matter to determine who is the real victor. And this is to say that competitive sport is actually a contest – not just seeking to win but deserving to win.[8]

Such a notion of winning will seem remote to some people in professionalised, commercialised sport. Basically, they may say, why does it matter? There is no answer to this from within consumer culture. The only response is to recall a different way of living and to cite the presence and role of sport within it. Sport, and in particular athletics, once spoke of mankind's striving for perfection.[9] Sport in ancient predecessor-cultures was marked by personal excellence; strong and reliable character that could then be called upon in state emergency or social need; the willingness to leave comforts and train so as to develop physical gifts; and the celebration of sporting excellence in public rituals dedicated to the gods and uniting athletics with the arts. Much of this is – rightly – history; but personal excellence, character, self-perfection, and celebration are elements of the concept of sport which we have inherited, and they do suggest an activity of higher value and interest than the version of professional sport acted out today for the sake of numerous commercial interests.

Excellence or virtue usually suggests moral virtue to us. But to the Greeks, virtue was also physical, and intellectual. The great symbols of intellectual and physical excellence are philosophy and the Olympic Games, institutions high in their respective virtues still. The great tragedy is that the role of *moral* excellence in philosophy and sport is so much more obscure than it once was, thus a link between the physical and the intellectual has gone. Thus in sport, courage often becomes fierceness and fearlessness – actually vices associated with courage; justice is often limited to partiality for one's teammates, or team, or country; moderation has collapsed, with greed to win and the popularity even of illegal substances as a means to win. And wisdom? The rare and reflective sportsperson certainly does exist – but he is rare indeed.

Yet in sports training and rhetoric, virtue is still evident: few would say 'none of this matters: it's just about winning.' Everyone would endorse respect to players and officials, courtesy and gratitude to spectators, taking defeat well, being generous in winning. So there seems to be a certain self-deception (no worse, surely?) off-field and on-field: as if the pressure of the few minutes of play when the result is in doubt is so extreme and demanding that players assume they can, briefly, forget about virtue if only they can get this one result on the board. An ex- professional footballer friend tells me that he often loved training more than playing – because it *was* playing, whereas the Sunday game in the stadium had become performing: the need to win just this one more victory.

Character and self-perfection too can be misunderstood in sport. In a sports ethics book aimed at practitioners Russell Gough recalls that after being kicked hard between the legs in a tae kwon do class he was ordered to stand up and continue by his coach. He sees this as exercising courage in the face of adversity, building character.[10] Perhaps such an act might lead to the virtue of courage, but only indirectly and not as the rightful end of the act; enduring a beating about the head by your father can toughen you up, but that is not because standing upright through a beating is the natural path to courage – and the one administering the beating is certainly well outside the logic of the virtue, whatever his intended aim. Good character is not steely determination, or refusal to submit. It is commitment to ends intrinsic to those activities we choose to undertake; unwillingness to settle for other ends or to betray these ends. As for self-perfection, the activities we do choose to perform will make for self-perfection if they exercise basic capacities and do so in a reasonable and conscientious way. Concern with perfecting oneself sounds, unavoidably, like a dated boy scout's aim today. But there is also a strong perception that modern life and habits leave many parts of out potential latent and untapped. 'Self-perfection' simple means bringing into reasonable and balanced activity all natural capacities necessary for our well-being.

But perhaps public celebration is the aspect of sport that has suffered most in the contemporary world. Today, genuine public spaces have vanished – generally, to be replaced by shopping malls, leisure centres, and entry-by-ticket super-stadiums, open to those who pay and with those with no money to spare excluded. What actually happens on great public sports occasions today and what connection do these occasions have with the great civic and religious festivals of the people who first established our sporting classifications and concepts?

Sport and religion

In both countries in which I have lived sport, especially football, is often described as 'a religion'. In Scotland, sectarian memories still rise to the surface during important clashes between leading teams; in Australia, national holidays, general elections, and school holidays are planned around a complex network of finals competitions of the various football codes and a horse race. The one stirs up something dark and tribal connected with religion; the other adopts an entertainment view of sport but tries to adapt it to the mass support base built nostalgically around the old suburbs and parishes. The Australian experience here is bland; the Scottish violent. Neither makes a proud contribution to public celebration. For someone who does not like football, the day of the big game means exclusion: nothing is offered to the non-connoisseur; there is no equivalent of the symphony orchestra's advertising for new subscribers – because the football team does not need to advertise: it has enough fans to make its millions. Nothing could be further from the spirit of religion or genuine public celebration. Of course, modern sport shares some elements of religion (and art, and friendship, and education and so on), but that does not qualify it for the role which the Greeks created: thanksgiving to our gods, celebration of our faith, expression of our hope, and reminder of our mortality.

Nevertheless, perhaps the minimalist celebrations offered at major sporting contests are as close to religion and festival as most people can get today. John Carroll writes: 'sport...is a secular means for tapping transcendental sources or powers, reviving some fleeting contact with the sacred, testing whether the gods are on your side or not. In the process it teaches lessons, not directly through language, indirectly through experience, of the existence of a metaphysical order and of the workings of some of its laws. As such it is pioneering the way modern societies seem to like their religion.'[11]

Certainly, vast sporting occasions have national and international significance, and it is difficult to explain why this is so except as 'fleeting contact with the sacred'. These contests produce intense, if brief, emotions in many people. Perhaps this is indeed a glimpse of something transcendent, something so vast in conception and significant in meaning that it can unite great crowds of people briefly in a sort of *pietas* for the remnants of the gods to be found lurking in the venerated game or the idolised team. Sport may be religion today; religion-lite – like the short, emotional though shallow, experiences of non-church goers who attend weddings or funerals in church. But our sport lacks the profundity of festival or liturgy. To grasp this, we need only reflect that drastically reducing the numbers of spectators affects the meaningfulness of the sporting occasion (if no one cares, there is no occasion); but this is not the case for genuine religious celebrations, in which only atmosphere but not meaning is adversely affected by declining numbers.

Can the connection between sport and living celebrations that maintain and uplift cultures be recovered? I suggest not without the recovery of public religion (which is barely imaginable) or nationalist sporting ideologies (which will not be desirable for many years, after the experiences of Nazi Germany and Soviet Russia). Sport as national celebration capable of renewing a culture and genuinely uniting its diverse peoples is over, perhaps for ever. Olympic opening ceremonies are now high points of entertainment and showmanship: no one even says a prayer. For non-partisan public celebration today there is only the large-scale, public-funded arts festival.

The connection between sport and religion may now be trivial, but sport is still a stimulus to ethical thought, behaviour, and rhetoric for many people. The existence of sports ethics as a sub-discipline of applied philosophy and the wide public interest in players ethics and ethical violations witnesses to this. 'Fair play', 'personal best', 'code of honour', 'role model', 'keeping to the rules', 'gracious in victory', 'dignified in defeat' – these are ethical notions that 'live' for people today (like the notions of 'accountability' and 'transparency' in contemporary business and politics). They mean something to ordinary folk, for better or worse, as the philosopher's apparatus of consequences, virtues, and norms does not. This may, again, be ethics-lite, but at least it is some public contact with ethics; and after all, the living ethics which binds a culture over space and time is one of the key criteria of a religion and so a place-holder for the future.

Doping

In a widely read book John Hoberman catalogues and analyses the medical damage caused to professional athletes by their training and their drug use.[12] He argues that we should see this history as part of the history of applied medical research into human biology: sport as biological experimentation upon the human organism, sometimes coerced and manipulated, sometimes voluntary. He suggests that the tradition and ideal of 'sportsmanship' has now almost vanished under the 'performance principle' which encourages, and even requires, experimentation upon athletes. Individuals, nations, and other interested parties are gripped by the idea of increasing performance levels to hitherto unimaginable heights. Thus we should understand doping not as simple cheating but as an 'ideology of uninhibited performance', something that grows out of the logic of contemporary sport itself.[13]

However appalling people find this, the difficulty in preventing doping now is that stimulating people beyond the normal metabolic state is common in all areas of life. Thus it may seem not only unfair but also puzzling that we are scandalised by it in sport. Hoberman suggests that if we do not worry so much about doping of violinists, then anger at sports doping must indicate something of the intensity of our wish for untainted corporeal display. Personally, I think I *would* worry just as much about elite orchestral doping; in fact, because music is not competitive, it seems even worse to me (there is not even *that* excuse). But it is probably true that untainted athleticism remains an ideal for great numbers of people, since almost all try some sport sometime and try to maintain some fitness, while fewer people persevere at music, writing, public speaking, and so on.

There are three main forms of doping worry: worry about harm done to subjects, worry about violating the high ideals of the activity itself, and worry about cheating. In sport, since it is competitive activity, cheating is a major worry: a contest presumes that everyone begins from a level playing field, a position of rough equality. As Hoberman has well argued, physical damage to subjects is also now a serious concern in sport. Worry about betraying the ends of sport itself, however, is less clear. We can compare it with modern music. Synthesisers and electric guitars do make music: just not very good or original music; for it does not originate with, and is not controlled in the same way by, the musician; similarly, doped athletes do play sport: just not very good sport; since it does not originate with them and is not fully controlled by them. Doping does not betray sport so much as degrades it: it is an artificial, 'pop' version of the real thing. Perhaps then the logical solution would be to hold an alternative Doping Olympics, admitting monitored use of drugs up to a certain level of self-damage, but excluding cheating, and targeting those spectators more interested in the thrill of seeing what humans can do under induced conditions than learning about human courage, perseverance, excellence, and mortality.

Such a suggestion would not be accepted by Claudio Tamburrini, who argues – and without tongue in cheek – that the ban should be lifted altogether and substance-using sportspeople allowed to compete side-by-side with others, using whatever resources they can obtain to boost their performance.[14] The suggestion would horrify authorities. But, as Hoberman has argued, we presently ban, inconsistently, certain substances while allowing various other enhancers. We try to uphold various distinctions but there are no sharp lines here: only an evolving list of forbidden narcotics which is, in effect, a socially relative creation. Hoberman is particularly concerned that while banning certain drugs, we allow the use of sports psychologists: not professionals who make scientific study of the elements of performance, but scientists who seek to influence athletes' minds and personalities so they can do what their bodies cannot or should not attempt: 'despite its scientific appearance, the aim of elite sports psychology is to abolish thought itself'; to seek 'a robot possessed of an inhuman force of will.'[15]

Serious scruples about doping should also mean taking a good hard look at the sports psychology phenomenon, and more generally at the motivation and programmes behind elite national academies of sports training. Is Hoberman right that the performance principle is their ultimate guide and that the 'legitimate' means to following the principle are unregulated and often seriously worrying? If so, adherence to socially relative lists of banned substances and increasingly fanatic media responses to caught users appears tokenistic.

Hoberman feels sure the unhealthy obsession with performance will in time lead to genetic engineering. The authors of a recent Report by the US President's Council on Bioethics agree.[16] These distinguished bioethicists devote a whole chapter to biotechnology, self-enhacement, and sport, arguing that sport is an activity in which excellence is widely admired, through which we are invited to deeper reflection on our bodily nature, and in which we have made effort to preserve dignity and excellence from cheating.

Commenting first on high quality sports equipment, the authors argue 'our gear (like all our technology) not only improves the way we do things. In the process, it often changes the very things that we do.'[17] For example, because of the equipment, modern tennis is a different game from the past sport (as is modern warfare). But we can distinguish tools that allow us to perform in new ways from 'interventions that work by changing us directly'.[18] These latter include self-directed activity and training, and direct biological interventions in the person. Activity and training improve performance by utilising the very powers in which performance consists: you run better by repeatedly using, and so increasing, your capacity to run. If, however, we use steroids or biotechnology to improve performance, we do so by means other than the powers we demonstrate in performance. Thus 'we paradoxically make improvements to our performance less intelligible, in the sense of being less connected to our own self-conscious activity and exertion.'[19]

The Report's point is precisely that doping, and more extreme genetic intervention, means alienating the sportsperson from his own activity: 'from the athlete's perspective, he improves as if by "magic"…he has the advantage of the mastery of modern biology, but he risks a partial alienation from his own doings, as his identity increasingly takes shape at the "molecular" rather than the experiential level.' Alienated human activity is activity at the furthest remove from reflective activity.[20] Here, activity is a mystery to the agent rather than a revelation; something to be observed rather than a source of personal reflection. Thus it is of very low recreational potential.

Thus fears of alienation – historically, the great curse of the consumerist nations – are dramatically highlighted by the plight of the modern athlete. Machine Man is not named for the machinery built into his body (the '6 Million Dollar Man'), but in recognition that he no longer experiences himself fully as human. In the powerful image with which the Report concludes its investigation into sport, modern athletes become spectators: detached from the performances that issue from their biologically modified bodies.

Spectating

Spectating is, of course, the way in which most sports enthusiasts today 'take part'. Thus in countries like the US or Australia intense interest in sport exists along with high levels of inactivity and alarming rates of child and young adult obesity. A habit of merely spectating would have worried Plato, who thought all children should take part in sports to develop strength and skill, social cooperation, and strategic thinking (the terms in which concerned Health Ministers still tend to speak today). Spectating is perhaps the strangest phenomenon of sport. The word suggests detachment, coolness; but people who choose to spectate sport are usually very involved and passionate. They are, however, physically apart from this physical contest, and they may be uninterested in physical involvement. And this is why spectating sport is puzzling: of all human activities sport is the one most concerned with the body and fitness, yet the spectating phenomenon dissociates the sports enthusiast from his own bodily life and often comes at the cost of his fitness. This is very largely the fault of TV which increases the sports audience at the expense of sport.[21] Of course people can place sensible limits on spectating; but season tickets and TV schedules are targeted at people's regular leisure time, encouraging them to spend more and more of their leisure time in this way and not in training.

Why are there such huge numbers of sports spectators? People seem to identify sport as much more real to them than other highly trained human activities. They find an identity, a home almost, in following 'their' team or becoming gripped by the antics of their star player. There is no reason why people could not also feel this for the local ballet company or brass band or museum; and some do, but they seem not to identify with such intensity and in such numbers. And this is not a class issue: cricket, golf, rugby, tennis, basketball, and many other sports cut across socio-economic groups in their appeal. Rather, the significant fact is our interest in human bodily performances: people are deeply attracted to watching competing human beings. This may formerly have involved giving thanks to the gods for what we can do and who we are; but today, the players are the gods, and it is the players whom the spectators hail and thank at the close of play. The focus now is on elite human performance and physical endurance, and even when dissociated from more existential questions, this is still enough to enthuse huge numbers.

As well as physical skill and power, people also want to know and admire the athletes as people. Thus spectators are extremely upset at or fascinated by sex scandals of young footballers, sports cheats, drug allegations, and so on. We want star players to be heroes, but we love them being fallible, and we enjoy the right to judge and forgive them when they fall: 'It is in fact no secret that athletes suffer, and it may be that the public expects them to suffer for their fame and their fortunes.'[22] We invest young sportspeople with moral qualities – perhaps far in excess of the standards we expect from ourselves – and we accept, or even require, their tragic downfall when they are unable to handle the pressures placed upon them. Perhaps in this tragic guise something of ancient Greece does persist.

This whole approach can also of course be questioned. Torbjorn Tannsjo argues that our admiration for sports heroes is fascist: 'our enthusiasm springs from the very core of fascist ideology: admiration for strength and contempt for weakness.'[23] He argues we need to lose our present interest in sport if we are to grow as moral agents. And he is quite right – *if* what spectators do enthuse about is strength and if they are taught to develop a contempt for weakness, then this is a serious setback to mature moral agency. But it is possible to admire sport as an activity done for its own sake, and to see the game as an opportunity to learn something about human nature, limitations, even humility from the willingness of both sides to lose in public.

Just as there are dangers of power-fetish for supporters, there are dangers of victimisation for players. Where sports and players are regarded as commodities, the players are turned into bodies, and then the bodies into objects; and today, that often means commercialised or sexualised objects. We should guard against 'the danger of turning our would-be heroes into slaves, persons who exist only to entertain us and meet our standards and whose freedom to pursue human excellence has been shackled by the need to perform – and conform – for our amusement and applause.'[24] Sport has traditionally had a concern for human nobility; with the idea of activities performed because they are a fine thing for humans to do, ennobling and dignifying, symbols of the greatness of the human spirit. It is in this sense that people who merit the title of 'athlete' perform: they 'perform' in the sense of giving to the best of their ability, not in the sense of performing tricks to amuse us. Concern with popularity, looks and sex appeal, earnings and endorsements, even breaking records, can enslave the athlete, turning him or her into the object of non-sporting interest, commercial speculation, erotic fascination (consider the fact that no one even *questions* the rightness or wrongness of nude athletes calendars). Commodified athletes take us back into the Arena, where human dignity and nobility are pulled apart – whether by wild animals or commercial pressures – and people take delight in the (profoundly alienating) spectacle of bodies turned into objects. In such a world, public celebration becomes ritual slaughter in one sense or another of the young and healthy; and many people think that is fine since if people are so highly paid, they cannot be victims.

Can there be elite sport without spectators? Probably, yes. Can it exist without anyone recording and reporting the score, without anyone other than the players having any interest in the contest? That would be a farce. Elite sport is a public performance, and especially now when it is rarely done for its own sake but for entertainment, earnings, or national interests, it requires a sizeable audience to function. It can indeed be a civilising and educative experience to spectate great sport; but that requires a willingness to celebrate the human person stretching to his limits and to reflect on what this tells us about ourselves and human life.

Violence

The ancient world provides two great models of people gathered together to spend their leisure hours spectating other people: the Greek stadium and the Roman Arena. In both, citizens participated in the great cycle of state religion and celebrated the public achievements of the gods and men. In the stadium, the beauty and potential of the human body was celebrated; in the Arena, bodies were torn to bits by men, beasts, and machines. In each, human frailty is marked and witnessed; but in the Arena this happens through violence against those at a disadvantage. Some modern day sport and sports spectators perpetuate the Arena, though we like to pretend that is 'just history'.

Sport is physical; though sporting behaviour may be found in other less physical games and parts of life too. Many sports codes include extreme, and painful, physical contact within the rules of the code. Sometimes extreme contact is only legally accepted because it is permitted by a legally accepted sports code; sometimes it will be contact that violates that code; and sometimes it will be contact so serious that it also violates the law. Obviously, there is a difference between violent contact necessary or at least foreseeable in the game, and contact that is intentionally violent. Attempts to hurt or harm as a *means* of winning are taken more seriously by all sports professionals than attempts to win that accept as necessary the possibility of hurt or harm if we are to play this particular sport well at all.

Wherever such extreme contact sports are permitted and strong violent contact does regularly occur, a little of the Arena persists; though throwing or driving a ball with speed and accuracy raises fewer controversial issues than attempting to knock someone down or throwing a punch at their head or internal organs. Many people attend willing, and sometimes even eager, to see violence. Some spectators, and even commentators, spectate violence with the indifference (and for a minority no doubt, the cruelty) of their Roman ancestors. Of course, when the violent contact is intentional and spectated by an indifferent or approving public this raises highly serious moral problems – and when the violence breaks the code of the sport or the law of the land or when it is regular with a particular player, then the scale of the moral problem increases. Some will argue that you just cannot have men (in particular) playing at this level a fast contact sport without frequent, intentional violent contact. Perhaps this is so, but then it might be necessary to question the existence of the sport, the code, the training, the speed, the understanding of the players, and so on.

Where the crowd (or the commentator) actually thirsts for, encourages, enjoys, or jokes about this violence, there is cruelty, brutality, and desensitisation to malice. The self-reflexive damage spectators cause to themselves by their own brutality or indifference is sufficient reason for questioning a sport such as boxing, where law and code permit intentional violence as the means of winning. Here, the physical harm is clear and controversial; more damaging, however, and damaging even if helmets and full body armour is worn, is the moral harm done to the triumphant boxer, promoters, and spectators.

Where officials detect that the code has been broken, a serious approach to leisure will demand strong penalties, for the point of the code is to give people some security from attack and damage so they can live much more physically than we do in daily life. Violating the code is therefore a serious offence in itself, apart from the physical damage caused in an attack. Penalties are often symbolic; but they should be stiff: professional sportspeople are given much and much should be expected; a couple of Saturdays off or losing the equivalent of a couple of days salary (or couple of hours endorsement money) is pitiful and does nothing to raise the profile of sport as recreation, or to connect sportspeople with the high ideals and honour of their predecessors. Since there *is* professionalism in sport, this professionalism should work to resurrect something of that ancient sporting culture and not to promote sport as a guaranteed money-making career option for very fit people.

Where violence is extreme, litigation does sometimes, though rarely, take place, though criminal prosecution hardly ever.[25] There are various reasons for the rarity of legal process here: extreme passion whipped up in front of a screaming crowd may be exculpating; the violence, though intentional, flares down quickly, and there may be personal apology and a continuing relationship among the players concerned; and there is an undoubted public feeling that 'it's different in a game.' For some, the violent profile and history of certain star players is a central part of their appeal and following, and the idea of a player suing a big kicker or hitter would seem outrageous, namby-pamby, not 'sporting' behaviour. These attitudes mean that a message goes out that violence is necessary, violence is part of the game, and violence sells: even news readers will laugh and jokingly wince at watching someone 'kill', 'bruise', 'destroy'.

Consumerism of the body has extended to regular consumerism of bodily violence in certain team sports. One message sent out is that this is 'awesome', admirable, all part of the 'tradition of the game' to encourage a man built like a tank to build intentional harm into his normal approach to 'play'. A more sobering message is that it is normal for people to fill up their spare time entertaining themselves by watching all this. Of course, the people involved may not consider it to be violence: it is a blokey thing; 'they don't *mean* it as violence' (just as wife-beaters don't); they can sort it out in the locker room afterwards; we are just loyal sports fans supporting the manly traditions of a noble game.

Football codes certainly can give some meaning to some people's lives (which is a different thing from allowing people to reflect on the meaning of their lives). But we should not overlook the negative effects of a whole media empire (and to some extent, a political ideology) built around extreme contact sports which advertise themselves, and are reported by, images and descriptions of sheer physical aggression, brutality, and raw power. There was nothing to be said for destroying people's bodies in the Arena, even with the religious and civic rationales of the Romans; and there is certainly nothing to be said for it now, even with the consent of the victims.

Education and character

It is a commonplace that sport builds character. By this people often mean steeliness, manliness, grit, determination; and to a lesser extent, nobility, fairness, uprightness, integrity. In other words, it is one, or perhaps a blend of two, particular types of character that sport builds. The blended view (strength + goodness) grows out of what John Heeley identifies as the Victorian/Edwardian view of 'rational recreation': the idea that 'people's leisure can be supervised so as to foster good habits and counter anti-social ones.'[26] Rational recreation was aimed mainly at the working class, whom their betters wished to instill with honour, courage, unselfishness, and leadership (as opposed to the moral dangers lurking for those who spent their free time in pubs, music halls, and brothels, and not museums, libraries, and swimming baths). But similar 'moral-engineering' is also reflected in the training which the upper and upper-middle classes gave to their sons about to set out to the empire, the army, the home civil service, or just the administration of the family estates.

Such a conscientious view of leisure – which Heeley thinks is still with us – gives prominence to sports, and especially to team games. The thought here is that cricket, rugby, and other such games involve cooperation and trust, acceptance of leadership, refusal to let others down, a spirit of service and sacrifice, and the virtues necessary for a certain conception of citizenship.

There are two things worth saying about this character-building. First, this notion of 'character' is not in any simple way that of the traditional virtues, the (roughly, four) states of rational balance that are habitual responses to emotions, relationships, and one's own goals and principles. Victorian 'character' does indeed find room for courage, fairness, moderation, and good sense; but all of these are subordinate to an ideal of inflexible principles, sense of rectitude, diminishment of passion, and a sheer absence of playfulness. In other words, the muscular Christianity of the empire favoured the singular and Stoic notion of 'virtue' and not the Aristotelian and plural 'virtues'. This one-dimensional view of character adapts certain other virtues to itself but has little room for *eutrapelia*: it sacrifices playfulness for dutiful striving to win, and win fairly.

The second thing to be said is that building strong character includes opening people's eyes to the goals intrinsic to worthwhile activities; and it is not clear that sport achieves this in any special way. The great test here would be whether the upright sportsman functions well and with good character in other areas of life: but much talk of sport cultivating social ideals and duties avoids taking a serious look at how the sportsperson behaves at home, in social life, at work, in church. And much of this talk also takes for granted that a correlation between someone who *is* of good character and plays sports means that it is the sport that develops the character; but unless empirically tested, it may simply be that sport does not undermine the good character.

In some people, no doubt, sport does create self-respect, cooperation, respect for rules. Where it does so, this is because sport is the sort of activity Alasdair MacIntyre has identified as a practice: an activity with ends and goods intrinsic to itself which can be realised by excellent engagement with the activity.[27] But there are many other practices that can achieve good character – or achieve it more effectively (for example, raising a family, running a youth group, volunteer service, backpacking and so on); and sport is not a practice that can achieve character for everyone. Indeed, as Anthony Skillen argues, at this particular time, unless we can take violence and aggressive competitiveness out of sport, there may be little morally elevating or educational about it.[28]

But when we do succeed in detaching sport from commercialisation, sport still has potent educational effect in one direction: reflecting on our common human frailty is an important means to contemplating human life and it is best served by sport. It should not be too difficult for interested individuals to reclaim sport from consumerism and for reflection on mortality. For sport is the way in which most people admire human beings pushing themselves to the limits so as to excel, and it is not far from this admiration to pondering what it means that we have limits, can excel – and will, eventually, fail. This is something an athlete can teach even when losing – whereas failure of a star violinist is just an embarrassment.

Nationalism

Individual nations have a great deal invested in sport: investments in schools, public health, mass leisure, and in contests with national and international significance. Major international sporting occasions are now budgetary commitments as serious as building a new battle fleet, and the return received on this investment is national prestige: the nation's standing is more affected by how it stages the competition than how well its athletes perform. Prizes and prize money are irrelevant: the occasion exists to focus on individual personalities and their achievements, to unify and give expression to national sentiments, and to facilitate international competition.

It is of immense importance not just to sporting authorities but to governments that major contests are clean and that play is fair. This idea of fair play is not just about playing by the rules but honouring the rules, the game, its past traditions, present adherents, and all who have invested in it or care about it. This sense of honour manifests itself in commitment to certain values: in particular, playing one's best for one's country, and accepting that the result is indeterminate until close to the end of play. Violations of this honour-code are treated as very serious national occurrences, with even political authorities expressing outrage and dismay. Offences here go beyond mere cheating, which is dirty, mean, contemptible: un-fair play at national level is judged to be betrayal, letting the nation down, one of the few absolute and serious moral norms the majority today will acknowledge.

But this whole idea of national importance of sport and sport as activity of national significance can be questioned. Paul Gomberg argues that in today's world, patriotism is always deadly. Nationalism in sport contributes to mobilising populations for war or genocide and that is enough to condemn it.[29] This may sound extreme if read in a peaceful, comfortable land. But in war-torn territory the young men who fight, take part in deadly war games, cooperate so as to win, are the young men who grew strong playing games in these very terms and perhaps in this spirit; men whose team games rolled over into Basic Training. Armed services depend upon sports and physical fitness, and sports and physical fitness are achieved by activities that resemble armed activities – except there are no arms and (should be) no intent to wound. At some periods of history we could associate sport and patriotism in the same sentence with little fear; today, perhaps, we are more cautious.

Yet sport is so woven into national life that separating it from national aspirations and national identity would hardly be possible. William Morgan argues that though we cannot ignore the signs of the degradation of sport – they are everywhere – sport is so integrated with society we cannot afford to underrate it: social rehabilitation will require the rehabilitation of sport.[30] There is no question of de-politicising sport or of de-sporting the nation; it is a matter of re-conceiving the autonomy of the two in appropriate relation to each other. At the moment, elite sport is an expression of national pride, superiority, quest for supremacy, and ability and willingness to resource sports training and provision. This context means that elite sport does not attract and recreate people as an activity performed for its own sake: it is a political phenomenon, an expression of national pride and priority. To renegotiate the terms of this relationship today would mean, for example, statements from national sports bodies that sport is far from the only valuable activity in the nation's life; that sport can allow people to contemplate human life, achievements, and frailties, and that this matters more than national victory or league tables; that a nation's pride is humbled by morally degrading treatment of any of its citizens or unethical conduct abroad, not by under-achieving at a leisure activity; that though funding for leisure is important and sport's budgets high because of the enormous public interest in physical challenge and excellence, this cannot be at the expense of music, libraries, theatre, and other leisure activities. It is hard to imagine such a renegotiation in a proud, sporting nation; though the examples of Germany and Italy, with their superb support for the arts and great sporting records ought to make other nations stop and think.

Sport has always suffered from stereotypes, and these sporting stereotypes often develop into dominant national stereotypes ('icons'). There are, however, many forms of leisure other than sport, and many other key, non-leisurely activities; and if the nation represents itself 'iconically' in only one way – and that the sporting way which the great majority *already* admires – then this limits thought and future and may feed consumerist habits (a single, physical, admired type is easy to market, reproduce, and go on selling). Heroes and heroines is a complex topic. Representing the nation by the image most people already recognise and admire – whether Princess Diana or Ian Thorpe – may not be the best way to celebrate what we are capable of.

The popularity of sport means there is a danger that, internationally and nationally, elite sport is currently limiting the national leisure life and also lending support to our consumerist habits. In the service of nationalism, and the corporate interests that now have such a complex relationship with nation states, our achievements in arts and sciences take second place to sports achievements. Reversing this does not mean giving up on sport or sporting excellence, but an enthusiastic and public endorsement – by sportspeople wherever possible – of our great thinkers, artists, and humanitarians would help.

Working-out and body image

A new phenomenon of sports in the 1980s was the dramatic increase in numbers of people using gyms, health clubs, jogging, playing squash, learning martial arts, dance-sports, and other forms of personal exercise and physical relaxation. Much of the time this has offered much-needed recreation, improved health, and fed good habits of reflection, meditation, and the general search for inner peace. After twenty five years, however, it is not so clear that working out is still developing in healthy ways – however much it may have served human health. The problem lies with one of the most extraordinary extensions of consumerism: the commodification of the body.

We find bodily commodification not only in 'recreational' sex, trade in body parts, slave trade, IVF, but also in TV shows 'selling' hospital dramas and operations, surprise-surprise cosmetic surgery shows, and in gym culture. Many gyms are full of ordinary men and women keeping fit and balancing daily exercise with a desk job. But there is also a use of gyms and the fitness infrastructure of modern leisure which is focussed not on fitness but on image, fashion, and sex. None of these is intrinsically bad, but nor are they intelligible ends of leisure or sport. The image of 'working out' – and the image achieved after the work-out – is an image sold as a desirable goal and a lifestyle foundation. It is something to be worked at and paid for. The image is sold as a fashionable means of making ourselves desirable: live this way, and you will have the sex appeal, youth, and body which currently you believe others enjoy and you miss out on.

The sheer energy and anxiety wasted on this dream is colossal. It is supported by whole industries of dieting, foods and drinks, the health venues themselves, gym 'professionals', equipment and clothing. And all this commerce in turn is supported by the anxieties, neuroses, and compulsions of those who do fashionable exercise to recover youth and looks. This has little if anything to do with sport, and is a glaring example of leisure at its most consumerised. Exercise and gymnastics as playful leisure, far less reflective leisure, are vanishing in this the least leisurely (the 'work-out') of today's recreational activities.

Consumerist logic has led inevitably to the commodification of one's own body; as it has meant the commodification of soul (as we see with New Age and self-help movements, bookshop sections on 'spirituality', televangelisation, and a whole range of quick-fix cures for the spirit). The purpose of good leisure is to stop the logic of commodification, to create private, free spaces into which consumerism cannot or cannot easily extend. The development of gym culture and body cults – as of soul cults – is an immensely disheartening sign that popular culture is less and less free, less and less playful and reflective.

Because sport has such enormous appeal, and because it focuses on the body with all its glories and setbacks, a real test-case for reflective leisure will be to encourage modern sport to become, at all levels, more playful and then, hopefully, more reflective. A sign of this would be if gym cults with their concern for body image and status and lifestyle ceased to dominate so many people's attitudes towards their free time. At the moment, gym culture reigns. Leisure looks to the tradition of sport as a noble path to a more reflective and playful culture; but leisure is not the basis of gym culture.

8
Work and Leisure

In his 'In Praise of Idleness' Bertrand Russell lists some of the projected benefits of his plan for all of us to have more leisure: artists and scientists will be able to pursue real research without irrelevant considerations of utility; professional people will be able to develop and use their skills fully and not just so as to make money; there will be greater joy of life throughout the various parts of society; there will be more freedom from nervousness and weariness, growth in public spiritedness, more kindness, less chance of war, and so on.[1] Russell suggests that the modern work/leisure balance is inappropriate. Our active energies are so taken up by work that when we do play, our leisure is generally spent passively spectating others' skills, not enjoying our own activities.[2] Our leisure now is rare and low-grade: playful at best, hardly ever thoughtful.

So Russell argued that we have both insufficient quantity of leisure and low quality leisure, with the result that our lives are impoverished on a number of fronts. In particular, the encroachment of utility on areas of our lives whose true value is non-utilitarian has had dramatic effects on our psychologies and our ethics: 'there was formerly a capacity for light-heartedness and play which has been to some extent inhibited by the cult of efficiency. The modern man thinks that everything ought to be done for the sake of something else, and never for its own sake.'[3]

Russell's view is certainly not anti-work, but he does think that work and leisure are quite distinct activities, that work is more subtle than pure utility suggests, that the two must be balanced sensitively, and that modern life has failed to achieve this. Part of Russell's fear was of what we now call 'workaholism' – epidemic in the 1980s, and with urban outbreaks still in the third millenium. Yet while many suffer from workaholism – and some suffer willingly – others suffer the effects of involuntary unemployment. As Rowan Williams recently put it: 'the working situation is skewed in two ways. Either there is no possibility of finding a way in the world of serious economic acquisition and negotiation; or that world takes on an obsessive character – unsurprisingly, considering the bleakness of the alternative.'[4]

Russell's view raises two questions. What is the appropriate balance of work and leisure for individuals? And how best can we secure this balance today? The background to this question is that many in industrialised, consumerist society who need work – meaningful work – are deprived of work, and many who need leisure are deprived of leisure. Furthermore, work frequently seeps into leisure time destroying the distinctive quality of our leisure (undermining play, or calm reflection), and leisure – or rather, our unfulfilled leisure needs – can seep into work time destroying our energies for and interest in work (for example, the problem of personal internet and email usage in the office).[5]

This deprivation of, and destruction by, work and leisure has complex effects. Deprivation and destruction of *leisure* does not just reduce the amount and quality of recreation in our lives, but also means that we can experience difficulties in attending to work which we see as cheating us of the leisure that we need. Thus research in 2004 indicated that Australians are sacrificing sleep for more leisure time because of the problem of work impinging on free time.[6] Meanwhile, deprivation and destruction of *work* does not just affect our employment and productivity, but also means that we have difficulty, as a society and as individuals, in taking adequate leisure which we can see as cheating us of work opportunities. One result of this is that, according to researcher Kay Hymowitz, thirty-somethings today flee to work for the fun and escapism that their parents thirty years before sought in drugs and rock and roll: 'for the young, ecstatic capitalist work is not work; but then leisure is not leisure.' This new work ethic of 'ecstatic capitalism' offers 'the blurring between work and play, the youthful energy and intensity, the sense of both individual meaning and recovered community in a fragmented world.'[7]

This collapse of a real distinction between work and leisure may turn out well for some, but will disadvantage others. Also, deprivation and destruction of work/leisure affects not only our attitudes to and aptitudes for these, but also our participation in other crucial activities. For example, in the contemporary context when people do read, think, socialise, attend concerts, lectures, political debates, or religious services, this is more and more dependent upon their perception of these activities as either 'recreational' or 'useful', leisure or work. Thus activities which possess intrinsic value of their own are reinterpreted as the leisure or work we lack and need, and so get where and how we can.

To address Russell's problem of the work/leisure balance and how to secure it requires an account of the relationship between work and leisure. This account will have to explain the distinctness of work and leisure so as to capture their complex interrelation, and give some guidelines for the proper integration of work and leisure in the lives of busy people and societies. The account should also explain the special obligation to provide for work and leisure and should clearly assign this obligation to a particular obligation-holder: there is little value in talk of 'obligation to provide' (or 'right to have') work and leisure if this talk leaves it unclear just *who* has the obligation to provide, why he has it, and how he must discharge it.[8] But the ethics of work and leisure must be more than just an account of governments' duties or workers' rights. It should also discuss our general attitudes towards creation-through-work and recreation-through-leisure, and the particular emotions these two activities elicit from us. It may well turn out that our attitudes and emotions concerning working and playing are extensively disordered in a consumerist setting; which may help to explain some of the difficulties many people have today in identifying and balancing work and leisure.

Prolegomenon

Different types of people will respond differently when they find an unexpected gap in their timetables. Some will immediately fill it with more work, others will get excited at the unexpected bonus and start planning a holiday, yet others will take a cautious, more balanced approach. But what does constitute balance here? 'All work and no play makes Jack a dull boy' is true; but so is 'the Devil makes work for idle hands', along with 'a stitch in time saves nine' and numerous other nineteenth century encouragements to industry and prudence. Balance is not necessarily fifty-fifty; it is something to be estimated after an analysis of the concepts and what is at stake.

First, what is work? The major ends of work are manufacture and systems of idea – work is either manual, or cerebral. The former is sometimes judged inferior, possibly on the grounds that it possesses only instrumental value. But the fact that manufactured *goods* are instrumental does not mean that manufacturing *work* is instrumental; indeed, manual work may be intellectual work's superior in some respects.[9] In a deeply hierarchical culture – a caste or slave culture, for example – manufacture is generally degraded, servile, contemptible to those dependent on it, and resented by those reduced to it. But a hierarchical culture can also regard intellectual work too as a sad and reprehensible waste of human talents. As late as Jane Austen's day, trade is a disgrace – but the learned professions are only a little better. In most modern cultures, however, and largely due to the influence of the Christian ethic, work is generally regarded as valuable, a basic right, a social responsibility, even an expression of human dignity.

This does not mean that in modernity the mere fact of having work is ethically positive: human work can still be degraded or 'sweated' labour. But it is not degraded because it is manufacture: work is degrading where the worker or his tasks are treated as pieces of machinery or implements, objects that do not initiate skilful manual activity but simply respond, unintelligently, to others' wills. The existence of degrading work is one of the unsolved puzzles of contemporary work, technology, and politics. Just as in the pits and steelyards and factories of old, the tools can so easily become the masters, and the sufferings of the operators invisible. The needy worker is incorporated into the tool-kit, or the software, no more than a servant of the profiteers who now own and direct him, his opinion no more valued, sought, or heeded than the opinion of the spanner or the keyboard mouse.

The ethics of work covers such topics as the nature and purpose of our (manual and thoughtful) labour; the exercise of important human capacities – especially, intelligence, imagination, and sociability – through manufacture or cerebral work; the limits to be placed on the content and duration of work; the relations of workers to machines and technology, and to colleagues, managers, owners, and shareholders; society's opinion of thoughtful work and manual work and those who undertake it; conditions at work and the negative effects these conditions can have on workers; the rationality and morality of the opportunities for both manual and thoughtful work that are available, and so on.

I have argued above that the major effect of leisure is to recreate ourselves through restful play and re-vitalising reflection. Of course, work too can have recreational value. This, however, is secondary to work's productive role – as production of needed objects and ideas is secondary to leisure's recreative role. In work, producing items of utility or ideas of value is what counts; in leisure, what counts is finding ways in which to rest and re-make ourselves.

Because of their different relations to human nature and fulfilment, leisure and work raise some different ethical challenges. Leisure, like ethics, focuses primarily on forming the self; work, unlike ethics, focuses on results. This means there are different ethical problems involved in our working and play lives. For example, good results at work can be achieved at the cost of others' or my own wellbeing: an ethics of work must therefore seek to explain work as not just achieving results at any cost; it must relate work to workers', and others', wellbeing. Good labour ethics should also offer guidelines for how we are to respond when work does subordinate persons to the pursuit of manufacture and systems of ideas. Meanwhile, focus on the self in leisure can also come at the cost of well-being; for focus on self always involves the possibility of self-indulgence, partiality, loss of objectivity. Leisure ethics will thus offer guidelines for dealing with play or reflection that becomes selfish, extreme, compulsive, and detrimental to some person's wellbeing.

To achieve this, leisure ethics will appeal to recreation in order to demonstrate that leisure is more than just selfish indulgence, or living for the moment, or for 'no. 1': leisure is justified because it is achievement of something objectively valuable. Using this principle, we can develop guidelines for how to respond when leisure does tend towards subjectivism and hedonism. Meanwhile, labour ethics must appeal to creativity and intelligence and to the real needs of human nature and culture in order to demonstrate that work is not just labour in the service of productivity: work is justified as creative and intelligent response to real human needs. And again, such an objective account of work will enable guidelines for how to respond if work does become dehumanising, meaningless, or otherwise unethical. An objective account of work will argue against self-instrumentalisation, and suggest what we might do if we encounter danger of this.

Leisure ethics/labour ethics

Our perceptions of work and leisure may not have kept pace with social change; or quite possibly, social change may have out-paced our objectively correct perceptions of work and leisure. Practices of work and leisure have new and significant effects on each other today. For example, consumerised leisure has given birth to service industries providing work for many; leisure often requires hard work and expense if people are to 'enjoy' their leisure, and is often framed in terms of personal achievements, goals, pushing the boundaries, and other hard-work notions. Meanwhile, work is an essential part of many people's identity, represents their personal choice, and is often a major source of reassurance and familiarity: work is for many people the environment in which they are most relaxed, stimulated, most themselves; it has taken over leisure time for many professionals (hence, the new phenomenon of 'leisure sickness'[10]).

What suggests a clear distinction between work and leisure nonetheless is the fact that leisure is the normal means to recreation, and work the normal means to needed products and services. This in no way hinders people from achieving recreation at work – or creating useful products during their leisure. Rest and renewal can be achieved through other means than play or reflection, including work; and products can be achieved through other means than manual or intellectual work, including leisure: leisure can be fruitful. Nevertheless, there is a real difference, for both recreation and products are required for a good life, and ordinarily these are achieved by, respectively, our leisure activities and our daily work.

If there is an important distinction between work and leisure, we then face Russell's problem of how we should most appropriately balance or integrate them. I will suggest that a good balance of work and leisure in an active life requires effective creativity, solidarity, and amateurism in both our work and play.

Creativity and solidarity

The most satisfying leisure and work for the agent will be the most creative forms of each. Creativity is the work of the imagination. The imaginative capacity to create, store, and select images is a normal part of everyday, psychological functioning; here, imagination works on data gathered by our senses, forming and arranging from these images true to the data but also peculiar to the individuals that we are: for example, we both see the forest, but to me this is a dark image of fear and nightmare, to you a bright symbol of ecological hope. But imagination is also the capacity to construct complex fictions and fantasies – to build images we recognise as meaningful but removed from what we take to be literal truth. Such vivid imagining is not only for the sake of art – vivid imagination is also an important source for worthwhile work and leisure. It suggests ways of creating, and ways of viewing what we create, that challenge the mindless 'work' of check-outs and

'leisure' of compulsive gambling. Moreover, the introduction of imagination to work and leisure is symbolically powerful in consumerist
culture, showing up and challenging the cults of efficiency-first and
me-first.

Unimaginative work quickly becomes over-laborious, humanly unre-
warding, hard to sustain, even if efficient in terms of productivity;
unimaginative leisure becomes trivialised, repetitive, compulsive, even
if enjoyed, as we see with consumerist leisure. There may be nothing
wrong *per se* with triviality, or with working purely for survival; but
these are far from the richest forms of human activity and experience.
At their very best, work and leisure have a common root: they will
draw deeply from human creativity, and where they do, agents have
greater opportunities for fulfilment.[11]

How much work and how much leisure do we need for a good life?
What is the appropriate balance for a life and for a society? An obvious
thought is that people should be deprived of neither, and certainly
never deprived intentionally; a second is that we must not allow work
or leisure to dominate to the extent that it begins to harm us by affecting our participation in the other, or in anything else worthwhile and
important. What more can be said than this?

First, modern people are deeply sensitive to the perception that they
have no work or no meaningful work; it is thought to be degrading
and a sign of failure. The perception that we do not play, however,
carries no shame and can even be a source of admiration: people boast
about their out-of-control work lives and lack of spare time. Gini
records that in the US, busy-ness is part of the moral fabric of society –
active life and work is held to be clearly superior: 'In this society,
workaholism is considered to be a clean addiction, one prized by business and corporations.'[12] Aristotle's and Aquinas's great debate about
whether the active or the contemplative life is superior is firmly
answered here on the side of activity, but activity as building things,
not building a character. In this context, if both work and leisure are
necessary, then many modern people need more leisure, better leisure,
and greater respect for leisure. At the very least, people need sufficient
leisure to avoid the stress and tension that affects their work, and other
parts of their lives, due to lack of regular, quality recreation.

Secondly, the work-play balance must provide enough of each to
allow us to regard ourselves as usefully employed and well rested and
refreshed. Self-image and the strong emotions consequent upon it
(pride, shame, guilt, remorse, envy and so on) suffers if we cannot
regard ourselves as doing work of some use and having sufficient

private time to rest and to sense that our efforts and commitments are reviewed, renewed, or refined. Modern societies seem to be losing a religious understanding of the person; if so, there is all the more reason for finding ways of retaining a balanced view of human life as useful and rational, and not simply buying and dying. Making a social contribution and having freedom to care for the direction of our own lives are basic ingredients of a happy, fulfilled existence.

This means that societies which intentionally deprive people of reasonable work and leisure opportunities are simply corrupt; and societies that do so unintentionally, as a side-effect of their other policies, would require very strong arguments indeed to justify these policies: tolerating mass unemployment or unimaginative employment, lack of leisure opportunities or of imaginative leisure opportunities, would require threats as serious as invasion, natural disaster, economic crisis... Societies and groups that allow work to dominate and perhaps to destroy leisure, or leisure to dominate and threaten work demonstrate contempt for people: people need the products of work and the activity of work, and people need the experiences of recreation and the activities of leisure. Societies that settle for a permanent imbalance of work and play leading to (individual or social) unrest, anxiety, tension harm the common good and risk undermining individuals' effective and satisfactory exercise of their basic capacities.

Mention of the common good raises the question of assigning the obligation to provide a good work/leisure balance. As with most obligations, stating an obligation to provide for leisure and work is of little use if society does not endorse, assign, and require the performance of the obligation. If I am un(der)employed, or exhausted and anxious, simply pointing out to me in a loud voice that I have a right to work and duty to play does little good. Satisfactory employment and recreation are possible where work and reflection are made available, widely advertised and encouraged, and individuals trained to choose and perform these activities for themselves. If the individual is to find work, be encouraged to take leisure, and to strike an appropriate balance between the two, society must help; and if society is to provide work, enable leisure, and uphold the balance, then policies and structures must enable, monitor, and enforce this. The obligation to provide work and leisure, and also to study and correct the balance between the opportunities for these, rests then with political bodies. And as things presently stand, these are not up to the task, for consumerist economies and ideologies have proved to be no safeguard of work, leisure, and an education in the ideal of a balanced life.

This is not to say that 'it is all government's responsibility'. Work and play require individual motivation, continuing education, the cultivation of personal excellence in a balanced, happy life, and support for this from family and other social systems and agencies than the political. But this is often not possible except with government support: the virtues required for work and play, and motivation in these areas require a public culture of education, support, and encouragement. This is not simply the development of more job creation schemes and the building of bigger sports stadiums as low-aiming governments often think (bread and circuses indeed). Rather, it is to oppose the many trends of deprivation and destruction in work and leisure now routinely accepted in consumerist society. These include: acceptance of a permanent, drugged, unemployable underclass; the drudgery of much mechanistic or technologised work; expansion of casual work that keeps people permanently tense about their employment; expansion of consumerist leisure at hands of corporate giants, often accompanied by growth in consumerist addiction and ill-health of one form or another; lack of criticism of forms of leisure that exhaust and hold people back, instead of resting them and encouraging them to look a-fresh at their lives; public endorsement of lifestyles based on glamorous free time and work time instead of quality recreation and imaginative employment. An interested government would be honest about the problems of consumerism – even if it felt that it could not tackle the total logic – and so would help to drive back into the twentieth century the overwhelmingly sad vocabulary of 'stress', 'tension', 'anxiety' and their cognates that has been the post-WW II generation's main contribution to labour/leisure ethics. A good government might convene a new standing forum on the work/leisure balance now.

But how can we justify such a vast obligation on society and on government in the face of the practically infinite demands of health-care, education, law and order, defence, the economy, environment, and so on? Is not attaining the ideal work/leisure balance a luxury, an intellectual indulgence or utopia, compared to these bread-and-butter necessities? I think not. Public health, education, law and order, the economy, and our other major political and social commitments suffer more because of deficiencies in employment and recreation and the lack of a healthy balance of these activities shared widely and fairly among the population. The common good does not suffer piecemeal ('in country X: education is good, health not so good, peace very good, work bad...'); rather, when deprivation or destruction of any necessary activity occurs, negative effects are felt throughout our other human capacities.

Lack of leisure or work incapacitates a society for achieving the common good. Seeking the common good, and seeking the good of individuals, is sharing in a number of vital activities each of which has reciprocal effects on our performance of the others. The political organism, like the human organism, is one and it is harmed and helped by major changes in any of our vital activities. The obligation to spend in the areas of work and leisure is therefore simply justified: improvement in the common good demands it.

Amateurism

The difficulties of persuading governments and voters that the work/ leisure balance matters as much as does the economy, healthcare, or the education system is partly addressed by the fact that our personal experience of work and leisure itself helps to correct imbalances in our choices. Work and leisure are complementaries – not in the sense that they fulfil opposite, unrelated needs, or the same needs in opposite ways; but rather because part of their proper function is to subvert each other whenever one or the other becomes an inappropriate fixation, a compulsion, or an ideology. This subversion is different from the wanton destructiveness of work by leisure, or *vice versa*, noted above. Subversion is a useful check on any unbalanced tendencies within our active lives. Hence, when we over-work, our need for recreation will call us to more leisure, and when we overplay, our need for employment, or for productivity, will summon us to work. Of course, we may not be in a position or have a will to answer the summons; but complementarity will issue a warning, pulling gently on our fear, guilt, or shame until we recover a more reasonable perspective.

Today, the conveyor-belt lines we often think of as an outrage from the past are re-created in the vast open-office spaces, check-outs, and call-centres of the present; and the leisure we once regarded as primarily learning, team play, and building fit, healthy people becomes solitary game (or role) playing, often on screen, with few on-going benefits for health, fitness, stamina, intelligence, or imagination. Against this background, our need for recreation will eventually speak up against extremities of soulless work, as our need to take part in productive work speaks up against repeated, free time self-indulgence. Where work or leisure become increasingly fanatic or compulsive in individuals, or become ideologies for whole societies, leisure and work themselves will prompt people to play or to produce, more or better. Thus (human) nature itself helps to expose unbalance and to correct unreasonable activity of one sort by pulling us towards its complementary.

To avoid things reaching such extremities people can learn from the traditions of amateurism. In an age that really only takes professionalism seriously, true amateurism is regarded as eccentric but still a safeguard against excessive utilitarianism at work and pure hedonism at play. Amateurism in work or play requires having confidence and taking delight in our imaginative contributions: in other words, these should be a matter of real love for us. The love of true amateurs for their activities helps to prevent work reducing itself (and us) to utility, and leisure reducing us to gratification.

The modern work environment can fight strongly against amateurism. Everyone, from CEO to office cleaner, is exhorted towards, and threatened for offences against, professionalism. Of course, expertise and professionalism matter, but where they are presented as the highest or sole standards at work, there is danger that workers will cease to love their trade, its history and standards, and the imagination and excellence that it involves, and start to love instead their own success at performing tasks, their status, their projects, and to seek the rewards work brings as more important than the good work does. Whole teams of management consultants may be brought in to inculcate such attitudes today – and to 'rationalise' the workforce, removing 'deadwood' job lovers, old-style workers, and grading everyone in terms of efficiency, commitment, and 'performance'. This may be called 'professionalism' (usually found coupled with 'transparency' and 'accountability' towards someone or other), but is often as much a blow to those who truly profess their work standards, as to those who love their work.

Leisure systems too will often oppose amateurism. The goal for a gifted sportsman (writer, musician, fisherman and so on) today is unquestionably to become a professional. Of course, the mythology is still that he loves his sport and that this love governs all his efforts; but success, fame, and rewards are undeniably powerful motivators. And sport is certainly not the only leisure activity presented as anti-amateur. Performers jetting from city to city, landing for several days of frantic rehearsal and performances; gamblers who gamble not as contributory recreation but as an attempt at systematic income-earning; obsessive gym enthusiasts; compulsive shoppers; internet and TV addicts – these all demonstrate lack of love for leisure activity. Self-indulgence and love of gain ('no pain, no gain') are always signs that leisure has been turned on its head, 'professionalised', and is now a business, hard work, one thing more to become anxious about.

How can people retain love for their work and play in a culture desperately yearning to label every junk-food waitress a 'professional' and to chase adolescents into malls, machine arcades, and gambling halls – and more sinister venues too – as soon as they are old enough to have any dollars to spend? I have two thoughts here.

George Eliot wrote: 'Leisure is gone – gone where the spinning wheels are gone, and the pack-horses, and the slow wagons, and the peddlers, who brought bargains to the door on summer afternoons. Ingenious philosophers tell you, perhaps, that the great work of the steam-engine is to create leisure for mankind. Do not believe them: it only created a vacuum for eager thought to rush in. Even idleness is eager now.'[13] Her point is that the world truly has changed; it always is changing, of course, but the modern world is a time of very rapid change. We cannot seek our recreation now according to the patterns of the 1920s, and we cannot seek to hold back work inside '9 to 5, with a month off every year' limits. So it is from within our modern structures and norms that we must discover satisfactory work and leisure. Since consumerism will be here for many years, we should seek ways in which to minimise drudgery and self absorption. This will very probably mean altering the time we spend at, and training for, each, and our attitudes towards full-time and free-time. This is a critical work for thinkers today, as well as workers, players, and providers.

Secondly, we should remember that manufacture and recreation are indeed necessities: that we *require* to transform natural resources into products, and to transform ourselves, in order to survive and flourish. An amateur's love of work, leisure, and his search for a healthy balance cannot then threaten *unproductiveness* in work or *unreflectiveness* in leisure. Amateurs must keep their eyes on the final goals of production and recreation. Truly to have an amateur's interest in our jobs or our play is not to see these as part-time or unimportant but to seek and admire the highest standards attainable in each. The great difference between the amateur and the professional is that the amateur will always respect and support all those, perhaps including himself, who have *low* success rates, but who do endeavour to serve the high standards of the activity and who do make a productive contribution or achieve some personal recreation. Ultimately, the meaning of amateurism is that the 'reign of love' will always appear more satisfying to people than the alternative 'reigns' of utility or hedonism.

Experience of working

Every choice has reflexive effects upon the agent and so implications for his character and future choices. So work choices are not simply productive: as with any choice, they are also self-productive. The unique challenge that work poses is how to balance the production of some resource with an activity productive of self: how to make things or ideas, which are the goals of work, without making yourself just a maker, of no more significance than one of your own products, or your capacity for making these? Choices to recreate, start a family, study, vote for a party, socialise are not choices to manufacture something of purely utility value (though they may include elements of this, if they involve some work); work choices, however, are for the sake of utility, and this means they run a high risk of workers (employers, colleagues, customers and so on) treating themselves or other workers solely as a means.

Can we secure work's existence as a fulfilling and human choice, a dignifying activity, while acknowledging that work exists primarily to create objects and ideas that are useful? To great extent this depends on the type of work at stake, but to some extent too it depends on our attitude towards work. There are many ways in which to produce a piece of coal, a book, a new piece of legislation, or a symphony. Some of these possibilities will damage or threaten the body, or the will, the emotional life, imagination, the senses, the intelligence, our relationships or families, our conscience, health, faith, reason, or our very lives. When unethical processes of manufacture or cerebral work endanger the exercise of our most basic human capacities, we are inhibited from establishing excellence in our own lives and impeded in our search for fulfilment.

Often when this happens, work or product has been prioritised over the wider life of the worker; the worker is treated as expendable, valuable only for the sake of the product or the labour – something which may happen equally in the dockyard or in the law firm.

Of course, doing any job that requires exercising certain skills involves ignoring, failing to develop, perhaps even diminishing other skills: by typing and thinking each day I fail adequately to maintain physical health, fail in communication with certain others, perhaps in passion, or in relationships, duties to family, and so on. So how do we distinguish necessary failure to exercise some human capacities from abusive denial or diminishment of human capacities?

This distinction is perhaps best explained in terms of the q-basic and basic goods enabled by exercise of each basic capacity. It is one thing to prioritise exercise of some capacity over others; it is quite a different matter to exercise one capacity to such an extent that our share in the goods associated with other basic capacities drops to harmful levels. Choosing to write for a month (or for nine hours a day, or three months a year) is acceptable so long as this does not exclude the individual from adequate share in such goods as emotional tranquility, delight in the senses, creativity, love, health, moral uprightness, and so on, offered by other activities than work.

'How much is adequate?' There is no simple answer, but the fewer and the less of such goods people share in, the greater is the chance of them harming themselves. And this harm will be serious when it consists in impairment of (any) of the underlying human capacities from whose exercise human good results. When people accept a decrease in overall function for the sake of work, the most important question to ask then is: is exercise of any human capacity thereby impaired or seriously threatened? If so, then further questions can be asked to establish whether the harm is intended or just foreseen, temporary or permanent, extensive or limited, questions which will have important implications for identifying the particular wrong committed. But the main issue is self-harm. Where workers harm themselves for the sake of work, they reduce themselves to productive means, and so miss out on many good things, and may fail even with respect to work.

Relevant too to describing our experience of work are our personal and emotional attitudes towards working. Attitude differences can be great between different individuals and different cultures, even in the consumerised world. Niall Ferguson has recently discussed the well-known fact that Americans work longer hours, with fewer holidays, than Europeans. Recreation is seen as moral indulgence by many Americans, whereas work is an obligation – together with family, the supreme obligation.[14] In the UK and Australia, culture and leisure are more of a right, less an indulgence; while in much of Europe, they are an obligation. Hence, in Europe, Aristotle's 'work is for the sake of leisure' is often heeded; while in America, all other activity is directed towards work and success; and in the UK and Australia, there is something more like the ideal of subversion of work and leisure by one another: both a sign of underlying imbalance, and grounds for a belief in future improvement.

Of course, such broad social generalisations also co-exist with strong emotional differences. Two of the strongest emotions affecting working practices in the west are ambition and fear. The marks of ambition are eagerness to succeed, excessive hunger for promotion, worry about success (understood as increase in status or reward). High ambition is part of the mythology of consumerism; though in fact, for all but the wealthy few who can seek the highest rewards, it is mute envy not ambition that tends to motivate in consumerist society. Meanwhile, fear is built into the hierarchical nature of work today (employers and employees, job-givers and receivers, superiors and inferiors). Major financial commitments – generally, the mortgage – tie people in to life-long or career-long dependence. From this dependence flows the fear that keeps people's heads down permanently over the keyboard, never admits to being slack but always claims busyness, and drives middle aged people to run anxiously through the crowds in case they are seconds late back from lunch. Everywhere, there is fear of displeasing employers and greater surveillance of employees; as a result, discipline, service, and trust are rarer and rarer, and only ambition, or fear, keeps many of us obedient.

Ambition and fear can be healthy responses: when someone is in a job that does not exercise his talents, ambition is appropriate; when there is threat of danger to which he has no ready or guaranteed response, fear is natural. But where these emotions come to define the experience of working, they are symptoms of a lack of care by employers or of personal dysfunction in employees. This is so if fear and ambition begin to affect health, relationships, will, thought, creativity, family, and so on – if in other words, they extend beyond the workplace. Other work emotions too can indicate problems. Some people feel hate towards their work situation because of the tasks or relationships it involves them in, or because it is simply pure drudgery. Others feel resentment that they have to work at all, or work in this way, or at this level. And then there are the positive work emotions too: pleasure at work done efficiently and fast; satisfaction in achievement; reassurance and fascination through work that suits my interests and abilities. The range of emotions felt at and through work indicates that though justified by our need for goods and services, work has also become a major contributor to our peace of mind, and happiness generally.

Status and dignity

In consumer culture, work has extraordinary status because it is the usual key to consumption, which is the key to social life. The anxiety that this high status of work breeds amplifies the temptation to over-work. Practically, this can be best resisted by investment in a wide range of activities that exercise our various natural capacities and by regularly reviewing and perhaps varying our priorities; emotionally, it can be resisted, first, by reflecting that work is not our nature but exists to produce what we need, and secondly, by increasing our involvement in and passion for leisure.

In certain ancient cultures people derived their social status largely from leisure. Today, at least in most industrialised societies, status comes largely from work. At the beginning of the modern period, Descartes, Rousseau, and Kant tried in their different ways to suggest an intrinsic human status, a status not established by group membership or function – and they succeeded, at least in terms of the modern world's political and human rights rhetoric. Nevertheless, most people in the post-Communist world do not accord status by humanity but by job, position, title, affiliation, prospects. And in the post-modern but still consumerist world, the lifestyle that a good job makes possible is perhaps awarded even greater status than the job itself.

Determining social status by work tends to confer greater value upon some work and workers than others: if facts about work determine social status, then since status is graded, work too must occur at various grades of importance or significance. The particular value of someone's work depends on the type of work, their position, degree of training or talent, remuneration, level of responsibility, and so on. Thus all work may be instrumental but some work is instrumental to other work, and not just to the product made at the end of the day; hierarchically lower tasks involve subservience not just to products, but also to others' work and others' decisions.

Problems with superior/inferior social status have caused some to relate work not to social but to human status: human status is all-or-nothing, not a matter of grade. Thus Pope John Paul II has argued in a series of Encyclicals for the fundamental dignity of work as a sign of humanity, and the primacy of the worker over capital.[15] The Pope argues in *Laborem Exercens* that work is not just a nuisance, not a distraction from more important things: it is itself one of the important 'goods' that give shape and value to our lives. This is so because it is intelligent activity: it is good use of reason.[16]

If work is intelligently fashioning physical nature and using our own minds so as to serve our purposes and satisfy our needs, then that is indeed a dignifying activity, if done with reason and compatible with our other obligations. But it is not easy to reconcile the Pope's high theology of work with the fact that work, when it comes down to it, is about making what we need. Certainly, there is more to employment than just the product, but the 'something more' is not the exercise of a basic capacity called 'work', but the combined exercise of other basic capacities. Art, science, healthcare, exercise, politics are about fashioning ourselves in various ways; but work is about producing what we need through exercise of body, intelligence, and our other capacities. The capacity to make what we need – though perfectly natural and highly valuable – is not exercised for its own sake but for the sake of the things needed, and so, ultimately, for the sake of the capacities whose fulfilling exercise requires the use of these things.

But if work is not an intrinsically valuable human activity, its value is not purely instrumental either: persons should not, and generally do not, treat themselves or each other for eight hours a day simply as tools. Work is valuable because workers satisfy human needs by exercising and excelling in some of their most basic human capacities. Work does not fall happily into the 'either-intrinsic-or-instrumental' dichotomy, for working is utilising capacities of intrinsic value because of their instrumentality in satisfying our fundamental needs. Perhaps we need a new term for the value of activities that responsibly call on intrinsically valuable activities in the service of some further end.

Work then remains an indicator of social rather than human status. In many ways this is reasonable: work is an accurate indicator of talents and gifts, and also of training and qualifications, personal exertion and effort, achievement, others' esteem; thus it is one important sign of our standing in society. But status can take many forms, and in consumerist society the status we receive from work is frequently identified with the wealth and commitment to the consumer lifestyle that work makes possible. Thus someone who works well, with integrity and honour, industry and honesty, initiative and cooperation may not be recognised as enjoying high status, if he is not in search of or possession of a fortune and an approved lifestyle. Deriving social status from work may be reasonable, but there is better reason still to interpret this as valuing someone because he is a morally responsible employee, trusted colleague, team player, or thoughtful manager, rather than a high-earner with a taste for the high life.

Social status is also sometimes derived from leisure choices. It is true that there is danger here of embracing class as marker of status: 'reading and classic music indicate higher social status than TV watching and pop listening'. But familiar class divisions can be more perception than reality: snobbishly attending the symphony or reading Proust to look good indicate higher consumerist values than does watching nature programmes on TV and taking a serious interest in pop culture. Leisure should suggest status not because of class, but because of what leisure choices imply about commitment to personal recreation and the extension of this throughout all sections of society.

Where someone is committed to play or to reflection and living out this commitment in ways appropriate to his situation and responsibilities, this does suggest something important about his scale of values. Balanced leisure lovers love doing things just for their own sakes, not for what they achieve in rewards or immediate gratification. They choose to play in interesting and enjoyable ways that allow them to rest from their more productive activities; they may also play in ways that cause them to reflect upon the meaning of what they do and who they are, knowing that this will allow them to approach life refreshed and with new heart, greater enthusiasm, deeper insight. Necessarily, leisure lovers will have to make decisions about the relation between leisure and work in their lives. They will usually act responsibly at work, but they will also rest and reflect sufficiently to allow them to approach their work, family, friendships, study, religion, and other central activities with the dedication and effort they deserve.

Thus the lives of balanced leisure lovers will show they do not value exercise of one human capacity above others, but do value rest and renewal of all their capacities for the sake of integrated functioning and greater fulfilment. In particular, their lives will show that people can value work and the reality of important needs that must be satisfied, without treating work as the highest end or as a higher end than leisure. Those who value their work because of desire to increase wealth and personal property far beyond needs and to secure a social status based on ownership and lifestyle will often be affronted by real lovers of leisure. For by casting leisure into the determination of social status, we imply that the highest status of all requires a change in consumerist lifestyle and the adoption of selective deafness by many already wealthy people in the presence of their investment managers.

9
Recreating the Arts

In her treatment of leisure Elizabeth Telfer extends Aristotelian contemplative leisure to embrace other intrinsically worthwhile activities, including aesthetic creativity and the contemplation of beauties. In my account of reflective leisure too the arts have high recreational value. Of course, the arts are not just another leisure activity (like sport or travel): for they also celebrate a distinct dimension of human nature and wellbeing (artistry and appreciation, not just relaxation and rejuvenation). In this respect, they are like study or worship or exercise; they can exercise more than one human capacity: recreation as well as intellect, or spirituality, or health. The arts are part of leisure because of their capacity to stir reflection and to use and extend our play skills. Committed artists and arts lovers also take part in play and develop reflective insights through their aesthetic activities; thus the arts add to the leisure profile of a society serious about leisure, and not only to its aesthetic profile.

In fact, the arts will benefit from people more fully recognising their leisure potential – provided that, as with work and leisure, the autonomy of art and leisure and their different relations to the human good are respected. Respect here means not creating and valuing art just for purposes of recreation (or politics, religion, health and so on), but always too for purposes of developing the imagination and our appreciation of the meanings of imaginative creations. But since artistic creation and appreciation also call upon sophisticated forms of play and stimulate sophisticated forms of reflection, involvement with the arts will almost certainly lead to greater and better leisure. Thus, as with most valuable human activities, more than one human capacity can be exercised by the activity, and a number of forms of human good shared in when we perform the activity well.

Beauty is central to art, as free activity is central to leisure. Natural and artificial beauty surrounds us, often unrecognised. Perhaps the truth behind the otherwise unhelpful maxim 'beauty is in the eye of the beholder' is that we can easily become blinded to beauties by familiarity, and then will recognise beauty only in novelty, extravagance, surprise, or melodrama. And if we recognise beauty only where there is spectacle and excitement, there is danger that beauty as a notion and an experience will vanish from our thought on art or nature, to be replaced by a simpler and less rewarding interest in the spectacular and the exciting.

Within the generic category 'art', the performing arts are the most eye-catching; thus they run the highest risk of substituting spectacle and thrill for beauty. Yet genuine beauty in performance matters to us all – whether we are arts lovers or not. Discussing beauty with reference to the performing arts has certain risks: few will admit to caring for it; fewer still may recognise that it is beauty they are responding to in their favourite films or performances. The term where used at all today is more naturally used of the visual arts. But performing arts are most people's experience of great art and so of beauty; and in a world in which festival, liturgy, and the symbolic life generally are fast vanishing, the performing arts will matter very much, and should become a standard of, and even an educator in, beauty.

The arts in general matter because they direct human imagination towards opportunities for aesthetic contemplation, understanding, and delight. The performing arts do so by focussing our attention on the skilled performances of people who have researched, prepared, and rehearsed their roles. This is sufficient justification for the performing arts (and for their public financing): performing art focuses the attention of individuals and society on performances that lead to experiences of aesthetic delight, understanding, and contemplation. To deny importance or funding here would be to query aesthetic experience itself as a necessary part of human wellbeing; it would be to claim either that the imagination does not matter, or that it can be exercised sufficiently without the aesthetic stimulation of regular performance. It is hard to see how anyone could soberly do this, though of course they may try.

There are people whose aesthetic sense and taste is undeveloped in the direction of performance, and people too in whom the aesthetic life in general is undeveloped (as knowledge, religion, emotion, relationships may all be undeveloped in some). But these people too have reason to support or participate in the performing arts. For activities in which we engage primarily for aesthetic reasons can also promote our more fulfilling engagement in other activities, which exercise a range of capacities and open up a number of human goods important to us. Thus theatre, music, opera, ballet, street theatre, and other modes of performance can also promote increased leisure, new knowledge, a better understanding of relationships, inner peace, good health, spiritual experience – all of which may be reasons for people to support and learn more about performance. The arts, and in particular the performing arts, have positive effects on the human good generally, including recreation, and not just on the aesthetic life.

The arts and the good life

A vibrantly aesthetic culture will add to people's share of the good and will encourage a more diverse share in the good(s). To take some examples, we tend to think of good health as fitness and stamina served by diet and exercise, but of course, at least as important is mental health: emotional balance and good cognitive functioning. As thinkers from Aristotle onwards have noted, part of the benefit of artistic performances is the opportunity to express and explore powerful emotions and beliefs in safer and more controlled environments than real life generally allows. The *katharsis* of emotion is not just 'letting off steam': it is feeling deeply so as to learn more about our emotional ranges and limitations, and preparing ourselves for situations and people that might otherwise overwhelm us if met unprepared in real life. Thus art can help people to maintain good psychological and emotional health.

Performance does not only train emotion; it also trains thought. The complexity of thought aroused by the multiple levels of a Mozart symphony, a Shakespearean tragedy, a work of contemporary dance, or a Janacek opera provides in a relatively undemanding and enjoyable context something of the mental sustenance that complex poems, classic novels, scientific lectures, and good sermons once brought many people. We may not be as literary a culture as hitherto; but good performance can feed the mind and inspire clear and deep thinking, along with emotional satisfaction, even where books are rejected.

One of the most significant forms of human wellbeing supported by the arts is contemplation.[1] Aesthetic contemplation usually begins by encountering new ideas. Reflection on these ideas is difficult when actually following a dramatic narrative, so aesthetic reflection tends to take place subsequently to performance. A live performance is also an education in human capacities for emotion, sensibility, and will – the

implications of choice. Contemporary education theory sometimes rec-
ommends taking children away from systematic studies to 'empathise'
with 'ordinary' or 'actual' people's lives and choices. A regular diet of
good theatrical performance can cater for what is worthwhile in
this trend without compromising the need for classroom education. To
this end, theatres are rightly visited regularly by school parties; concert
halls less so (why are matinee concerts so rarely offered?).

An obvious fact about performances is that they are directed towards
groups of people: they are social events; even during my native city's
Edinburgh Fringe Festival the phenomenon of the single-member audience is rarely other than a myth. Regular arts attendees know that the
experience in which they take part is very different from that of spending time alone at home with even the very best audio-visual equipment: the stage performance is unrepeatable, and so are the members
and attitudes of the audience. Occasionally, this is brought sharply
home to us; as when a performance is given at a time of public tragedy,
triumph, or with references to topical or local concerns. On a more
intimate scale, Maria Callas's performances of operatic tragedies were
sometimes occasions in which the tragedies and traumas of her own
life and her relations with impresarios and audience (particularly at
La Scala) were turned towards the dramatic purpose of the stage.
She would sacrifice some aspect of universal meaning to make a
personal point – which sometimes, though not always, was aesthetic
validation of a *new* universalism she had discovered in the work performed. Meanwhile, the experience of individual audience members is
also dependent in various ways on the wider social circumstances of
the performance. For example, those who are seated alone need
courage to withstand the fact that the social 'rites' accompanying the
performance (like the rights of holiday-making) are tailored towards
the couple-or-group mentality; though of course, the solitary audience
member may well be in more intense relationship to performers,
directors, composers, and audience than are those in couples or groups.

Significant peace of mind and of conscience can also occur through
performances; and indeed, they can unite in a particular way. Performances have both logic and affect: to participate in them is to follow a
coherent, logically related series of incidents and to be affected emotionally by this progression. The better the performance, the more our
emotional experience is also intellectual gain, and the greater the sense
of personal integration of the two. But a truly great performance
will make a claim not just upon our psychologies, but also upon our
moral judgement: a first class performance of even an inferior work

will challenge us to endorse a certain moral perspective. And whether or not the attitude of the work itself (writer, director, performers) is one we endorse, the performance will help to clarify what *is* our own moral position on the issues raised. In other words, a great performance will restore or enhance peace of conscience – harmony between my thoughts and deeds and the way I believe I *ought* to think and act; it will not only achieve peace of mind (harmony between my thoughts and deeds, and my emotions). One of the greatest experiences in the theatre or concert hall is contemporaneous emotional satisfaction (psychological peace) and conscientious elevation (moral peace) through the performance of a great work.

Such is a great artistic experience – but not the greatest. Even the least religious people recognise in their reactions to the very greatest performances something they may, even if only with reluctance, describe as 'transcendent', 'spiritual', 'sublime'. Theatre and music can assist people to expose or to recover friendship and union with God and interest in transcendent matters and questions of ultimate destiny. This can be difficult to distinguish from purely psychological or moral re-integration (they are hardly unconnected, after all!). But it does exist as participation in a distinct, identifiable human good: an achievement of transcendence, and not just of psychology or conscience. Some confirmation of this is the possibility of witnessing a performance of, say, Beethoven's *Missa Solemnis* which unsettles me, for one, emotionally, and actually adds to my moral confusion by introducing a perspective I can neither confirm nor deny. Yet despite the fact that it disturbs my (psychological and moral) peace, a great performance of this masterpiece, part of whose magnificence is its very potential to unsettle, causes me to revisit my religious beliefs, the possibility of return to God in prayer, and my eternal destiny. The performing arts at their greatest, then, bring about experiences of transcendence.

The arts exist for the sake of aesthetic creativity and appreciation; this is the responsibility with which artists are charged. But fulfilling participation in the arts clearly has effects upon other parts of our wellbeing too. Even those whose aesthetic experience is imperfect and unsatisfying and who therefore receive little by way of on-going aesthetic benefit can be led to significant share in other fundamental human goods by exposure to the arts. If supporting theatre is good for my health, mind, relationships, religion, state of mind (and recreation – see below), I have good reason to support the theatre – and then there is very good reason too for governments and others to support it. Nevertheless, people will find their support for the arts more rewarding in all sorts of ways if they come to richer aesthetic appreciation and a greater knowledge and love for human creativity.

Performing arts and leisure

There is a rather snobbish view that our spare time can be spent either in enjoying the arts or at leisure but not at both. In fact, attending performances is an important and natural leisure activity for many people: few concert-goers attend for the sake of contemplation, health benefits, or an experience of transcendence; more will attend for the sake of aesthetic appreciation – more still perhaps for socialising. But I suspect many people attend the performing arts as their preferred way to spend their leisure time. Is this a bad thing? Certainly not; but there can be some risks.

There are risks that the goals towards which the arts are most naturally directed – enhanced aesthetic experience and creativity – might be downgraded; that the objective becomes solely leisure in enjoyable performance-attendance rather than aesthetic experience. There is increased danger of this with a commercialised view of leisure: in consumer culture, the arts are often presented as just another personally satisfying, or socially useful, or status enhancing commodity. But there is certainly nothing wrong *per se* with supporting the arts as means to deeper recreation – any more than there is a problem with attending performances so as to socialise more meaningfully, get a broader education, restore one's faith, and so on. Also, arts attendance may be instrumental in establishing a taste for reflective leisure more broadly, particularly against a background of less penetrating leisure alternatives.

Opera, to take just one case, has been a form of leisure and of art throughout its history. It has offered beauty, and it has also provided an experience of play, fun, and festivity, and an opportunity to meditate upon, in particular, love and loyalty. Modern opera performance has done well to open up its territory of lyricism and drama to huge new audiences, but it teeters on the edge of accepting the consumerist view of leisure – noticeable in tame repertoire, arena-scale productions, the creation of (almost identical and image-heavy) glamour 'stars' by US music academies, and manic publicity statements and advertising claims. But opera can offer the purposeless experience of play in place of social 'relevance', and the opportunity for deep reflection rather than desire 'satisfaction'. It is worthy of reflective leisure, though vulnerable to consumerist leisure, and so is a good barometer of the arts/leisure relationship today.

One great contribution operatic performances make towards leisure is their sheer extravagance. The extravagance of opera is part of its message: the performance announces more obviously than any other aesthetic form 'look, all of this just because we can *do* it!' Opera performances, like firework displays, train us in the half-forgotten but sometimes necessary virtues of magnificence, excess, flamboyance, spirited generosity. Giving us a taste for these on appropriate occasions is playful and invigorating: it gives a sense of the good things in life, the generosity of life and of people, and the need to have a lavish hand; food for reflection indeed. Good promotion of opera as leisure would promote periodic operatic indulgence as needful not wasteful, public indulgence not self indulgence, social celebration not social consumption; and would quietly forget the 1980s obsession with political relevance or 'correctness' and the need for a message, the pseudo-cost we were then required to pay for indulging ourselves in spectacle.

Straight theatre too can serve as leisure – plays are a sort of play, and the fictions and fantasies that drama crafts can give audiences material for subtle reflection. Theatre today has to be aware of what is happening in television. Thanks to TV, we now have distant corners of Alaska and fairytale castles of Bohemia in our own living rooms; this familiarity desensitises people, and therefore, theatre must seek new ways of engaging. One way in which theatre responded to TV's takeover of the fabulous and exotic was by choosing to concentrate more on domestic issues, personal dramas, local scenes. Thus 1950s and '60s theatre responded to TV's advent by focussing on relationships, class, kitchen-sink drama. This gritty realism might have threatened to reduce the leisure potential of theatre (*leisure* in everyday-ness, or squalor and depression?), but audiences, bizarrely, enjoyed escaping their own daily grind – for the identical daily grind of their neighbours. TV quickly saw the potential of this as easily-produced, cheap entertainment, giving birth to the phenomenon of the soap opera. 'Escapism' today need not mean the Bahamas or Never-Never Land: the street next door works just as well; in fact, as gossips have always known, imagining our neighbours' vices is more titillating than imagining those of distant strangers.

This phenomenon has now developed into intrusive, fly on the wall 'investigations', docu-dramas, and, lately, reality TV, in which we see our *real* neighbours placed in embarrassing positions and held up, all too willingly, to scrutiny. Unfortunately, these are generally so staged and so corny that the only obvious arts connection is with vaudeville. Also, practically no opportunities for meaningful recreation are offered by such programmes since playfulness is replaced by cruelty or intrusiveness, and reflection is sacrificed for curiosity.

Theatre meanwhile has held its own after the kitchen-sink experiments of the '60s. Many classic and contemporary companies have developed strong markets, without compromising our need for aesthetic appreciation of beauty and human creativity. In particular, festival theatre and fringe theatre succeed in attracting vast, new, and often youthful audiences, exposing them to the pulse-racing fun or fury of drama, from Euripides to Shakespeare to Pinter, losing neither the integrity of the works nor their (original) power to galvanise whole populations and not just wealthy arts elites. It is probably true that the multicultural experiment has yielded more significant results in world theatre (and perhaps cookery) than in social integration.

Contemporary dance performance has also discovered whole new audiences for dance, though romantic and classical ballet remains a minority interest and a relatively low cultural presence. Contemporary dance engages with leisure in a number of ways (for example, by forging links with modern music, gymnastics, aerobics, social dancing, fashion, and the wider gym-and-health cult; this has certainly broadened its appeal. There is more to dance than leisure, of course, but it is a form of stylised leisure in all cultures and so an art form that can easily integrate with the search for recreation.

Classic ballet's leisure potential is more restricted; yet classical ballets have always filled a celebratory role – as annual Christmas time performances of *Sleeping Beauty* still show. If Tchaikovsky ballets remain aesthetic museum pieces compared to, say, Verdi operas, that must be partly the fault of impressarios and promoters, for the works and scores are magnificent. Better promotion of an art form centred on the power and beauty of the human body and on voice-less communication might well lead to interesting links with other recreational activities in this body and image-focussed age. A recent staging of *Swan Lake* with an all-male cast was a tremendous international success, drawing audiences and critics not by shock-value but through physical beauty, breathtaking images, and the aesthetic challenge. Contemporary opera has not separated itself form classic opera as contemporary dance has from ballet; and there is perhaps a lesson to be learned here by today's ballet impresarios.

Orchestral performances intersect most obviously with leisure through music's capacity to relax and to excite; but music has a role too in stimulating thought as well as play. Live musical performances can arouse and satisfy emotions more immediately and more intensely than any other forms of performance. This is part of what the ancient Greeks saw as the very real danger of music for health, education, contemplation, religion, and peace. But where someone also listens to music intelligently, there are substantial benefits with regard to the intellectual, and the spiritual, life.

Good musical performances are successful at achieving a balanced response between playfulness and thoughtfulness in their audiences: a good listener at a good performance is absorbed in the features of music that excite (dynamic extremes, virtuosity) and those that tranquilise (rhythm in particular, but also melody and harmony). Where a work or a concert programme is well balanced, play and reflection will support each other so that the leisure experience offers a rich recreational balance of enjoyment, relaxation, and rejuvenation. Listening attentively to great music is confirmation of the hypothesis that recreation is a broadening of the mind promoted, and not hindered by, pleasurable, playful activity.

Practical benefits of aesthetic leisure

If we accept the leisure potential of the arts as a genuine, if secondary, reason for enjoying them, there will be some predictable practical benefits. For one, the still common view of the arts as 'not for the likes of us' might be confronted in new and effective ways. Suspicion of the arts is the result of incomprehension or unfamiliarity. But even when extra knowledge and exposure to the arts is provided, some people continue to feel art alien – a different matter to finding it 'not to my taste'.

Probably everyone feels the difficulty of explaining aesthetic experience or appreciation to people uncertain about it: even the words sound pretentious; though I can do no better. Perhaps we should be trained in aesthetics, given seminars in beauty, as people attend healthcare consultations, relationships counselling, religious education, work training, sports classes, and so on. All people do enjoy beauty, and most contribute in some way to the creation of beauty; so it should not be a difficult task to progress people's enjoyment of cultural and natural beauties (for example, in the environment, clothes, architecture, food, movies and so on) to an interest in the arts. In this endeavour, presenting the arts as legitimate leisure-time activity, and encouraging people to see them as a source of recreation, as well as of aesthetic pleasure, may help rather than hinder.

Why does it seem such a leap for many people from well-presented food and well-cut designer shirts to the performing arts? Here are three reasons. First, there are financial costs. Performances cost a great deal to attend, and to mount. This question is more complex than simple hesitation about altering spending patterns. In our consumerist society, what people are willing to do with their money helps to reveal their characters. At one time, our choices in relation to religion were the main revelation of our selves, who we were and where we stood: today, we reveal ourselves by what we buy and how much we spend on it. Linked to income-disposal are questions about what work we do and which types of people we associate with; but these too tend to be economic questions: we ask about people's jobs because of what this says about their income bracket and spending habits, and we ask about their friends because of what this says about their choice of job and pattern of income-disposal. If people invest financially in the arts – in the form of tickets, subscriptions, recordings, books – this reveals something rather unusual about their characters. Arts lovers are still popularly thought to be very slightly eccentric; they have staged a mini-rebellion against prevalent tastes and are enjoying something rather subversive, anti-consumerist.[2]

We may live in a relativised culture, but the only opinions given mass endorsement are the pseudo-truths of consumerism; a choice to be different is a risk. If we could break or fracture the leisure/arts divide so that arts became a legitimate and popular leisure activity, then more people might come to think that spending ninety dollars on a ticket to an opera is perfectly intelligible and actually says something interesting about a person, and then more people might do it. If arts organisations more imaginatively promoted the (reflective) leisure potential of the arts as fully compatible with their (primary) aesthetic goal, the consumerist mentality here could be turned against itself. Pop culture is all about (consumerist) leisure; classical culture might become an icon of reflective leisure. For managers worried about numbers, offering something new and distinctive like this might just 'sell'.

Secondly, there are social costs of supporting the arts: novices feel socially, as well as economically, challenged. How do arts organisers break down the them-and-us effect? Much more could be done here to improve the environment of performances. If we keep the leisure model in mind, some of the more stuffy accompaniments that are now either archaic or only associated with the tastes of the super-rich, politically important, fashionable, aesthetes, and other elites could be swept away, or at least justified in terms intelligible to new-comers. Concerning the lay-out of theatres, for example: they should look grand since something very special happens in them; but if grandness means physical discomfort, bad sidelines, or exclusivist seating, the old should give way to the new. Again, the design of concert halls is determined by the need for excellent accoustics; but the public gets to hear little of this fascinating science, which would help to explain much about why we have to go to huge buildings with few overhanging balconies and keep very quiet in order to hear music well performed.

Audience manners and conventions can be more serious sources of discomfort than building design to arts novices. Dressing and behaving grandly, socialising noisily, and criticising performers ostentatiously are not necessary to aesthetic experience; on a leisure model they could be quietly discouraged by offering in-house, informal presentations from artists, academics, and popular figures able to relate arts to popular culture. Casual clothing is a sensible norm, given the need to find new audiences: anything suitable for church today should be suitable for theatre. And as long as audience members do not distract others by making noise or interrupting sightlines, they should do as they please (in this latter respect, it is *not* like attending church).

Newcomers are also by definition outsiders: the company's PR welcomes them, the company's audience too rarely does. Companies cannot instruct audience members to change their spots, but they can alter the lay-out and appearance of crush areas, reconsider what is available to eat and drink, provide imaginative interval events, and abolish, disguise, or segregate corporate hospitality. Conventions of applause too are often silly: applause, and criticism, should be genuine. There is no need for repeated curtain calls after an indifferent performance; also, there is no justification for the semi-fascist termination of curtain calls so as to save on overtime costs after a superb performance. If you invite someone to a party, you do not specify the finishing time – especially if the guest is paying.

Thirdly, there are emotional costs. How do we persuade people to sustain deep emotional shocks, find them important, think about them, enjoy them, and come back for more? Most people are used to experiencing deep emotion only in very private matters and private places. In many cultures, emotions are embarrassing, and public display of emotion unthinkable. On a leisure approach to the arts, it should be easier to suggest connections between aesthetic emotions and the deep, if more primitive, emotions felt at such familiar leisure activities as sports contests, gambling, cinema, night clubs, and so on.

By recognising common leisure emotions and deepening or varying these by means of arts performances we might gradually popularise aesthetic emotional experiences that are intense but more subtle, enduring but more varied, shocking but safe. There is nothing tame about a good performance of Euripides' *Bacchae* or Mozart's *Don Giovanni*: the arts offer a richer, more diverse (and safe!) range of experience, and can do so by sacrificing none of the wildness that other leisure forms offer.

From the perspective of the entrepreneur and the arts CEO there is a further benefit of relating the arts more explicitly to leisure. More corporate money is spent on sports sponsorship than on the arts. If the leisure/arts divide were successfully tackled, the recreational potential of the arts could help to attract sponsorship money currently earmarked for the recreation portfolio. At the moment, despite high profile corporate givers, arts sponsorship is more usually philanthropy and individual-based than advertising or corporate-based, and sports sponsorship the reverse. In some ways this is good news – it helps to protect the integrity of the arts' primary purpose and the autonomy of artists. But there is less regular and guaranteed money in philanthropic and individual sponsorship than in advertising and corporate sponsorship. A good presentation of arts as leisure – one that does not compromise the aesthetic nature and purpose of the arts but skillfully makes the connections with a rich leisure life and active life generally – might make arts sponsorship more attractive to corporate givers and advertising budgets. But making this argument effectively would rely on certain changes in social attitude, changes in the way in which people understand and value performance.

How likely are such changes of attitude? One encouraging factor is that the leisure/arts divide is relatively modern. In general, 'inter-good qualification' – the idea that sharing in any form of human good has positive implications for our sharing in other human goods – was more deep-seated and more widely recognised in earlier times. Those able to attend the arts would not have made the distinction we make today between art and leisure, imagination and recreation.

In this respect, the divide is an example of our modern elitism and specialism. Basic human capacities are genuinely distinct, but our reasons for pursuing their exercise need not be as heavily segregated from each other as they generally are in our individualist, compartmentalised culture; they are, after all, constitutive aspects of the one, integrated nature. It would be in many ways truer to the spirit, ethos, and history of the performing arts to work for the closure of the arts/leisure divide and to link art, with leisure, more closely, and more fearlessly, to the refreshment and revitalisation of the human spirit. In particular, we could assist the increase and quality of reflective leisure by creating partnerships between leisure and the arts; art is a greater stimulus to reflection than is commerce. And there may be very real benefits at stake for audience members and arts organisations in making art more leisurely.

Making the arts more leisurely

Travel, music, reading, sport, and other traditional leisure activities are so commercialised that turnaround towards reflection will be very difficult. A more realistic beginning may be dialogue between leisure providers and arts providers: arts are less commercialised; and a push towards reflection-through-leisure would also help to combat any tendencies towards dumbing-down or selling-out in our arts companies. To take one obvious example, cinema has remained both an art and a leisure activity; but it has developed in ways that are now helping to kill both leisure and art. The spread of huge multi-screen suburban cinema complexes has contributed towards the death of some more traditional, and local, forms of leisure now starved for participants and support. Cinema itself is narrowed down to US-format movies in multi-screen chains, with private operators who support non-action 'arthouse' movies squeezed out of business or out of their specialties; number and times of sessions are set so as to maximise profits, not to suit customers; the whole experience is sold with popcorn gimmicks and usher-less, self-service 'theatres', often built inside the still-visible wreck of former theatre balconies.

Instead of the reductionism of dollar-driven vision, the great powers of cinema could consider brief flights in the teeth of (present) commercial wisdom. If leisure and art were to remarry (or renew the wedding vows they first made in the '20s) in the context of modern cinema, cinema could offer, occasionally, films that went against mass public taste and addressed local, not Hollywood-global, issues. Cinema could also contribute something of the celebration and extravagance that marked early screen performances for decades before economic rationalism won. Early cinema contained a huge number of works of art that were watched by vast audiences as their primary recreation. And it was also presented as a true, public, week-end celebration, with glamour, local news stories, and a varied programme; the very opposite of a formulaic 120 minute, all-action film to be quickly consumed before the next 'session' starts. Classic leisure cinema did not simply aim at numbers. Attracting vast numbers is not proof of popularity: popularity is being loved by the people, not just being paid by them.

'The arts have their natural place within festivals', wrote Josef Pieper.[3] Of course, what Pieper understood by festivals were those occasions when people turned aside from profit and commerce for a few days to celebrate their traditions and, as with the Greeks and Romans, joined in community discussion and debate about profound and pressing public matters. What on earth would Pieper have made of every other small country town today holding a 'festival' designed exclusively to bring in cash and sell its local products!

If the performing arts regularly pursued festivity – celebration of what we hold to be of greatest importance about our way of life – and did so on a vast and accessible public stage, they could regain mass popularity without compromising integrity and greatness. This was possible, after all, for Aristophanes, Shakespeare, and Verdi. And if leisure-conscious politicians, academics, and providers actively pursued a closer relationship with the arts, festive celebrations of what we feel most deeply about might become successful recreation as well as great art. The Millenium Dome in London was a disaster, but there is still time to succeed where it failed in a meeting of art and leisure. The great danger is to avoid confusing leisure with shallow populism, and art with short-term relevance. In leisure and in art, wise people can enjoy exposure to universal themes and the chance to think about the deepest questions.

What would everyday leisure facilities like gyms and casinos look like according to this new picture? Much the same, but there would probably be fewer of them and they would offer different activities catering much less to vanity and greed, and more to developing good health and good relationships; they would prioritise play that allows people to rest and relax – afterwards too, and not just in the forgetfulness of the leisure activity; and they would support rather than undermine or compete with our capacity to reflect upon what really matters: sadly, the title of a recent book, *The Philosophy Gym*, only succeeds today because of the pleasurable oxymoron. In more traditional language, the vices that have now become perverted leisure 'virtues' (indulgence, pride, aggression, arrogance, envy, acquisitiveness – also frequently disguised with new, 21st century 'virtue' labels: 'personal care', 'self-respect', 'drive', 'ambition', 'self-confidence' and so on) would be recognised as clearly vicious once again; and our leisure opportunities would more often acknowledge and promote moderation, courage, self-respect, fairness, wisdom, generosity, hospitality, and the other true virtues of a fulfilled life.

The virtues that most help us to excel at leisure – those that constitute the ideal of *eutrapelia* – are out of fashion. Leisure – like all forms of activity, now dependent upon commerce, the master-activity – openly flaunts its association with the vices ('you too can look like her!', '$17 million jackpot this week!', 'Go on: you deserve it!'). A chief effect of a more aesthetic leisure is the restoration of the traditional 'excellencies' or virtues to our play lives: play becomes a fine and noble thing once again. An early sign that this is taking place would be our ceasing to feel embarrassed about using the traditional virtue terms to describe our own recreational choices and interests.

Reclaiming leisure

My major concern throughout this book has been that we are failing to understand, pursue, and sufficiently educate people in fulfilling habits of leisure; that leisure is commercialised and infantilised in ways that are harmful for individuals and cultures given our very human need for fulfilling recreational activities. This is a concrete, social claim, and, though basically philosophical, my project has had the practical purpose of change. Nevertheless, it is necessary in conclusion to admit that one result of improving the quality of leisure would be to incline us towards becoming a more reflective, a more philosophical, society. Another result would be to alter our view of play: to make our play more restful, less compulsive; but that would not seem to raise the suspicions caused by making us more philosophical.

Modern societies are deeply imperfect in terms of opportunities for, and institutions supportive of, thoughtfulness. This helps to explain growing illiteracy and intellectual insensitivity (despite the publishers boom), isolationism and cultural insensitivity (despite the tourist boom), philistinism and emotional insensitivity (despite the CD boom), competitiveness and physical insensitivity (despite the professional sports boom). Thoughtfulness and wonder – the conditions for a sustained contemplation – were maintained historically by Church and academy. What has happened to these today? And what can leisure now offer to retrain us in human wisdom?

What happened to the churches and the universities was not just the 1960s; in fact, it is surprising that 'the '60s' took so long to arrive). Perhaps if the western world had remained at peace for a longer period after the 1914–1918 World War, society might have had time to mature gradually; instead, there was international and political turbulence and eventually, inevitably, the devastating all-in-one rejection of traditions felt in the '60s. In other circumstances, that decade might have ushered in a mature rethink and even revival of key traditions, perhaps along the lines of the Islamic and Christian traditions' reinvention of themselves (in the literal sense, a 're-finding') at the beginning of the second millenium. But modern people rarely possess the wisdom – or the patience – of the medievals, or their insight into the power of traditions and culture.

Thus when the '60s did occur, many religious and academic thinkers reflected to little purpose and with little patience on the revolutions, both violent and peaceful, of the age, finding few pointers for how to re-invent their traditions but simply new resources for being anti-tradition. In some cases, churches and academies willingly transformed themselves into cradles of subjectivism, and later relativism, and then sat down to wait – until the eventual social endorsement in the '80s of anti-ethics or 'economic rationalism' stirred them to postmodernism. Religion and scholarship are still reeling from the effects of this new rationalism and the growth of post-modernism. Opportunities for quiet spiritual or scholarly contemplation in these circumstances are few.

Theology and philosophy seem to have reached one of their periodic lows. Meanwhile, however, freelance spirituality and the new professional ethics flourish and give people some reminder of the need for reflection and depth in their lives. But deprived of the forms offered by religion and collegiality, new spirituality and self-help philosophy can quickly deteriorate into instances of the consumerism and subjectivism they were designed to interrogate.

At the same time, certain churches and universities try to buy into the new subjectivism and consumerism, usually with disastrous results. Some religions now define themselves largely by involvement in popular social work causes and initiatives designed to locate and punish their failing leaders; and the contemporary world is comfortable with these 'well behaved' churches. And some universities define themselves by inter-varsity competition (not of students as in the past, but *for* students) and strong public image – matters which their administrators can easily disguise to themselves as necessary accountancy, new funding strategies, more responsible management, and so on. In this new situation, a necessary question for both churches and universities today is whether they would willingly accept the loss of their reputations and popularity rather than deviate from their (sacred and profane) traditions and obligations. But sadly, martyrs for faith or for reason are uncommon.

In this environment in which worship and study are ceasing to be great public goals actively served by religion and education, the reflective life is not seriously encouraged or pursued by congregations or students. While this has serious and obvious consequences for our community's knowledge and faith, it has more subtle consequences for our recreation. For without regular reflection, it is difficult to rebuild our selves systematically and to query the direction of our lives wisely. Since reflection is rarely taught, publicised, or practiced as a major goal in mainstream academic or religious life, it is important now that it is reintegrated with at least some popular leisure activities.

It may seem unlikely that people will ever agree to make their leisure more thoughtful. But first, consumerist leisure's own literature and practice are already rich in relevant rhetoric and techniques – self-discovery, self-help, meditation, alternative therapy, rejuvenation, de-stress, anti-tension, recovering holistic balance and so on. Admittedly, this is often pure jargon backed up by no systematic body of thought or practice; and often it simply reflects a (lucrative) business taking itself far too seriously. But the rhetoric and the approaches are very successful, which suggests that in responding to the deep inclination to recreate ourselves many do still turn to ideals of reflection, contemplation, inner depth, and thinking that is greater, if less immediately rewarding, than everyday thinking. It should be possible to re-think and re-present from first principles the contemplative dimension of leisure, but to remove the egotistic, self-indulgent, and superstitious edges from contemporary recreation rhetoric.

And secondly, why should physical exercise, games, reading, dancing, and butterfly-spotting not assist reflection on life, our selves, our relationships, God, truth, justice, meaning, and so on? Leisure activities involve removing ourselves from the pursuit of external purposes and simply enjoying locating ourselves within freely chosen activities. The freedom of mind this brings is playful, and the relaxation of spirit it offers suitable for the deeper thinking we find it difficult to engage in at other, busier times – difficult today even in study and religion. And whereas pure freedom from activity is often a hindrance to thought, something which makes thought seem too confronting, in leisure we are free *but still active*. Who has not known the benefit of thinking through some complex matter 'with their feet' as they walk, or sorting out a practical problem 'with their hands' as they knit or paint? And if modern leisure time is reclaimed for reflection, people may also be encouraged to try a more reflective approach to their faith and their studies, as well as to their recreation.

In good experiences of recreation we truly re-build parts of our lives that are incomplete or tired or broken. The sort of quiet reflection needed for this is not always or best catered for by more formal education and better study structures: there is today more formal education than ever before, but less philosophical wisdom and less evidence of sustained contemplation than previously. We should, then, take advantage of the self-forgetfulness of play and do what we can to make our leisure time more quietly reflective as well as fun. For doing so will improve our recreation, and this will decrease tension and stress.

Leisure was once the prerogative of a few who, to their credit, did tend to honour and seek leisure in virtuous ways. Now leisure is commonplace but its nobility and its virtues are ignored, unknown, denied, or ridiculed. The redemption of leisure for modern people will demand, or will be part of, a greater sacrifice: in particular, the break-up of the consumerist empire and the vices that it depends upon. We may not be willing to pay that price for many years; and perhaps not at all. But until it is paid, recreation will often be uncertain, life more stressful, and happiness less likely. Reclaiming leisure from consumerist leisure is the most important way in which we can serve recreation today, and one very important way in which we can serve human nature and culture. For a new reflective leisure will mean that people are contributing more towards their own recreation and so towards the quality of life in their societies.

Notes

Introduction

1. For a good philosophical cure for workaholism, see Al Gini *The Importance of Being Lazy* (New York: Routledge, 2003). For the particular anxieties that concern a person's social status, together with some traditional philosophical responses, see Alain de Botton *Status Anxiety* (London: Pantheon, 2004). And for the various 'slow' movements responding to our addiction to speed, efficiency, and the consequent stress, see Carl Honore *In Praise of Slowness: how a worldwide movement is challenging the cult of speed* (San Francisco: Harper, 2004).
2. St Thomas Aquinas, trans. Fathers of English Dominican Province *Summa Theologiae* (New York: Mcgraw Hill, 1963), 2-2, 35, 1.
3. For discussion of the evidence regarding both sides in this debate, see H. G. Koenig, M. E. McCullough, and D. B. Larson *Handbook of Religion and Health* (Oxford: Oxford University Press, 2001).
4. For studies of the range of benefits, physical, psychological, and social, that can be received from a good leisure life, see B. L. Driver, Perry Brown and George Peterson (eds) *Benefits of Leisure* (State College PA: Venture, 1991).
5. For a fascinating history of the concept of leisure, see Sebastian de Grazia *Of Time, Work, and Leisure* (New York: Twentieth Century Fund, 1962).
6. Johan Huizinga *Homo Ludens* (Boston: Beacon, 1971).
7. Josef Pieper *Leisure: the basis of culture* (Southbend IN: St Augustine's Press, 1998).
8. I build here on the distinguished attempt by Elizabeth Telfer to develop, as well as defend, an Aristotelian view of leisure, see Elizabeth Telfer 'Leisure' in *Moral Philosophy and Contemporary Problems* (Cambridge: Cambridge University Press, 1987). I have opted for 'reflective leisure' rather than 'serious leisure', partly because the latter is used and used in a different sense by Robert Stebbins *Amateurs, Professionals, and Serious Leisure* (Montreal: McGill University Press, 1992). By 'serious leisure' Stebbins means voluntary, amateur, and hobbyist pursuits, as opposed to such 'casual leisure' activities as watching TV, visiting shopping malls, and so on. While my account implicitly rejects Stebbins' view, it is no part of my argument to deny the seriousness of the important activities he opposes to casual leisure – however, many of them are not particularly playful or reflective.
9. Elitism seems hardly the appropriate charge in any case since the change involved is not based on class or wealth but on changes in education and reflection on what really matters.
10. James Schall *On the Unseriousness of Human Affairs* (Wilmington DE: ISI, 2001) also tries to justify a change of mind and heart here, basing his appeal on literary and theological insights.

11. See John Kelly and Geoffrey Godbey *Sociology of Leisure* (State College PA: Ventura, 1992); Geoffrey Godbey *Leisure in Your Life* (State College PA: Venture, 2003); John Robinson and Geoffrey Godbey *Time for Life: the surprising way Americans use their time* (University Park PA: Pennsylvania University Press, 1997); Gerald Fain 'Moral Leisure' in Gerald Fain (ed.) *Leisure and Ethics* (Reston Virginia: American Association for Leisure and Recreation, 1991).
12. Bertrand Russell *In Praise of Idleness and Other Essays* (London: Routledge, 1994). Also, see Paul Western 'More Praise for Idleness', *Philosophy Now*, Oct/Nov 2000.
13. de Grazia *Time, Work, and Leisure* Ch. 1 argues that removing leisure from Aristotle's thought at any point would be radically to distort his meaning.
14. Mihalyi Csikszentmihalyi *Flow: the psychology of optimal experience* (New York: Harper and Row, 1990).

Chapter 1   Philosophers on Play

1. Aristotle *Prior Analytics*, 68a39-b6, see A. W. Price *Love and Friendship in Plato and Aristotle* (Oxford: Oxford University Press, 1989), Appendix 4. For all references to Aristotle, see Jonathan Barnes (ed.) *The Complete Works of Aristotle* (Oxford: OUP, 1984).
2. Aristotle *Nicomachean Ethics*, Bk 1. 5.
3. Aristotle *Nicomachean Ethics*, 1177b4.
4. Aristotle *Politics*, 1334a4-15.
5. Aristotle *Nicomachean Ethics*, 1154b21-31, 1176b33-36; *Politics*, 1137b40-1338a1.
6. Aristotle *Politics*, 1337b31-1338a3.
7. Aristotle *Politics*, 1326b30-31; 1329a1-2.
8. Telfer 'Leisure', p. 158.
9. In Telfer's own Aristotelian theory, these activities include contemplation, aesthetic creation, research, enjoying personal relationships, and work undertaken for the benefit of others. On virtue and leisure, see too Aristotle *Politics*, 1334a15-34.
10. Aristotle *Nicomachean Ethics*, 1178a6-10, 1178b24-32.
11. Aristotle *Nicomachean Ethics*, 1177a21-b4; *Metaphysics*, 1072b14-26.
12. See Gabriel Lear *Happy Lives and the Highest Good* (Oxford: Princeton University Press, 2004) for excellent discussion of contemplation and leisure in Aristotle. Also, see Nancy Sherman *The Fabric of Character* (Oxford: OUP, 1989), pp. 99–100.
13. Aristotle *Metaphysics*, 1074b38-1075a5.
14. Sarah Broadie *Ethics with Aristotle* (Oxford: OUP, 1991), p. 419.
15. Cf. Broadie *Ethics with Aristotle*, p. 419: 'Excellent practice aims for and ideally results in at least some leisure for itself.'
16. See Christine Korsgaard 'Aristotle and Kant on the Source of Value', *Ethics* 96, 1986, pp. 486–505.
17. Victor White O. P. (ed.) *How To Study* (London: Bloomsbury, 1947).
18. Augustine *City of God*, 19: 19, quoted in Aquinas *Summa*, 2-2, 182, 1 *ad* 3.
19. Gregory the Great *Moralia*, 6: 37, quoted in Aquinas *Summa*, 2-2, 182, 4 *ad* 3.

20. *Nicomachean Ethics*, Bk 2, 7; 4, 8.
21. Aquinas *Summa*, 2-2, 168, 2, *ad* 3.
22. Aquinas *Summa*, 1-2, 32, 1, *ad* 3.
23. Aquinas *Summa*, 2-2, 168, 2, *ad* 3.
24. Simon Tugwell (ed.) *Albert and Thomas: Selected Writings* (New York: Paulist Press, 1988), p. 527. Though, admittedly, elsewhere Aquinas comes close to downgrading play, eg., *Summa*, 2-2, 168, 4.
25. Aquinas *Summa* 2-2, 168, 2-4.
26. Augustine *On Music*, 2, 15.
27. Aquinas *Summa*, 2-2, 168, 2, *ad* 3. See Ch. 2.
28. Aquinas *Summa*, 3, 40, 1 *ad* 2.
29. Aquinas *Summa*, 1-2, 3, 8; *Commentary on the Sentences* Book 4, 49, 1: 1.
30. Aquinas *Summa*, 2-2, 175, 3; though also see 2-2, 180, 5 where Paul is said to have beheld the divine essence but not at the very highest level of contemplative experience.
31. For discussion of Thomas's ambivalence about the philosophers despite his 'official' line on philosophical contemplation, see Mark Jordan 'Theology and Philosophy' in Norman Kretzmann and Eleonore Stump (eds) *The Cambridge Companion to Aquinas* (Cambridge: Cambridge University Press, 1993), pp. 234–5.
32. Aquinas *Summa*, 1-2, 3, 5 & 6; 2-2, 180, 4.
33. Aquinas *Summa*, 1-2, 4, 7. Aquinas explains how contemplative happiness can be lost or limited by external pressures such as overwork, illness, forgetfulness, 1-2, 5, 4.
34. Immanuel Kant, trans. Lewis White Beck *Critique of Practical Reason* (Indianapolis: Bobbs-Merrill, 1956), 129.
35. Immanuel Kant, trans. H. J. Paton *The Moral Law* (London: Hutchinson, 1985), 426, 442: empirical principles cannot determine a rational will, and (418) happiness is an utterly empirical matter.
36. Kant *The Moral Law*, 405.
37. Kant, trans., Norman Kemp Smith *Critique of Pure Reason* (London: Macmillan, 1963), p. 131.
38. Kant *The Moral Law*, 415, 430.
39. Immanuel Kant *Critique of Judgement*, trans. J. Bernard (New York: Hafner, 1951), 209.
40. Kant *Critique of Judgement*, 450-451; Immanuel Kant, trans. Lewis White Beck *Critique of Practical Reason* (Indianapolis: Bobbs-Merrill, 1956), 108–10, 128–9.
41. See the work undertaken in defence of this proposition by Marcia Baron *Kantian Ethics Without Apology* (Ithaca, NY: Cornell University Press, 1995).
42. 'The apathy Kant is most interested in is not absence of emotion, but absence of sentimentality and *tyrannising* emotions', Nancy Sherman *Making A Necessity of Virtue* (Cambridge: Cambridge University Press, 1997), p. 119.
43. And this subordination is not a banishment since well-regulated emotions are themselves partly constitutive of the moral life. See Sherman *Making a Necessity of Virtue*, Ch. 4.
44. All of this is well discussed in Victoria S. White *Kant on Happiness in Ethics* (Albany, NY: State University of New York Press, 1994).

45. See Kant *Critique of Practical Reason*, 21-3. Cf. *The Moral Law*, 393.
46. Kant *The Moral Law*, 423. See the discussion of this in Onora O'Neill *Faces of Hunger* (London: Allen and Unwin, 1986), pp. 141–63.
47. Kant, trans., Mary Gregor *The Metaphysics of Morals* (Cambridge: Cambridge University Press, 1991), pp. 191–2.
48. Kant, trans., Louis Infield *Lectures On Ethics* (New York: Harper and Row, 1963), p. 6.
49. See Ray Monk *Ludwig Wittgenstein: the duty of genius* (Harmondsworth, Middlesex: Penguin, 1990), p. 13.
50. He also did have playfulness – of a sort. 'Wittgenstein had a sense of humour, a capacity for playfulness, that does seem to have had precisely a childlike quality to it. A favourite joke went like this: a fledgling leaves the nest to try out its wings. On returning, it discovers that an orange has taken its place. "What are you doing there?", asks the fledgling. "Ma-me-laid", replies the orange', David Edmonds and John Eidinow *Wittgenstein's Poker* (London: Faber and Faber, 2001), p. 159.
51. For example, see Cyril Barrett *Wittgenstein on Ethics and Religious Belief* (Oxford: Blackwell, 1991), Ch. 6.
52. Ludwig Wittgenstein, trans, G. E. M. Anscombe and R. Rhees *Philosophical Investigations* (Oxford: Blackwell, 1953), 2, 23.
53. Wittgenstein *Philosophical Investigations*, 66.
54. Of course, some think that families too are not 'bounded', for example, one parent families, same sex families, the family of nations etc.
55. For a wonderful and idiosyncratic account of Wittgenstein on rules, see Saul Kripke *Wittgenstein on Rules and Private Language* (Oxford: Blackwell, 1982).
56. Wittgenstein 'Remarks on Frazer's Golden Bough', in C. Luckhardt (ed.) *Wittgenstein: Sources and Perspectives* (Ithaca NY: Cornell University Press, 1979), p. 7: 'When we watch the life and behaviour of people all over the earth, we see that apart from what we might call animal activities, taking food etc., people also carry out actions that bear a peculiar character and might be called ritualistic.'
57. Hans-Georg Gadamer, trans., Nicholas Walker *The Relevance of the Beautiful and Other Essays* (Cambridge: Cambridge University Press, 1977), p. 10.
58. Gadamer *The Relevance of the Beautiful*, p. 22.
59. Gadamer *The Relevance of the Beautiful*, p. 23.
60. See Gadamer *Truth and Method*, 2nd ed. (New York: Continuum, 1989), p. 108: 'Play is really limited to presenting itself. Thus its mode of being is self-presentation.'
61. Gadamer *The Relevance of the Beautiful*, p. 35.
62. Gadamer 'The Play of Art' in Walker, trans., p. 130.
63. Bernard Williams *Ethics and the Limits of Philosophy* (London: Fontana, 1985), p. 6.
64. Thomas Nagel *The View From Nowhere* (Oxford: Oxford University Press, 1986), p. 107.
65. Nagel *The View from Nowhere*, p. 218 ff.
66. Nagel calls this 'non-egocentric respect for the particular', p. 222.
67. Nagel *The View From Nowhere*, p. 223.
68. Alasdair MacIntyre *After Virtue* (London: Duckworth, 1985), p. 187: 'by a "practice" I am going to mean any coherent and complex form of socially

established cooperative human activity through which goods internal to that form of activity are realised in the course of trying to achieve those standards of excellence which are appropriate to, and partially definitive of, that form of activity, with the results that human powers to achieve excellence, and human conceptions of the ends and goods involved, are systematically extended.'

69. MacIntyre *After Virtue*, pp. 190–1.
70. MacIntyre *After Virtue*, p. 187.
71. MacIntyre's work on practices is often invoked by writers on recreation and sport, see, for example, William Morgan *Leftist Theories of Sport* (Chicago: University of Illinois Press, 1994).
72. Alasdair MacIntyre *Dependent Rational Animals: why human beings need the virtues* (London: Duckworth, 1999), p. 85.
73. MacIntyre *After Virtue*, p. 216.
74. MacIntyre *After Virtue*, p. 219.
75. Particularly good introductions include: on Aristotle, J. O. Urmson *Aristotle's Ethics* (Oxford: Blackwell, 1988); on Aquinas, Ralph McInerny *Ethica Thomistica* (Washington DC: Catholic University of America Press, 1997); on Kant, Roger Sullivan *An Introduction to Kant's Ethics* (Cambridge: Cambridge University Press, 1994); on Wittgenstein, Anthony Kenny *Wittgenstein* (Harmondsworth: Penguin, 1973); on Gadamer, Robert Dostal (ed.) *The Cambridge Companion to Gadamer* (Cambridge: Cambridge University Press, 2002); and on Williams, Nagel, and MacIntyre see their own works discussed here.

Chapter 2   Reflective Leisure

1. See John Kelly and Geoffrey Godbey *Sociology of Leisure* (State College PA: Venture, 1992), Ch. 8 for the development of mass leisure and the problems caused by commodification and democritisation of leisure.
2. Recently, a critical philosophical history of consumerism appeared in De Botton *Status Anxiety*, Ch. 3 (perhaps somewhat ironically, given the level of advertising, TV specials, videos, and other promotions behind de Botton's book).
3. Juliet Schor, quoted in Gini *The Importance of Being Lazy*, p. 85. Gini's Ch. 5 'Shopping as Leisure and Play' makes for disturbing but fascinating reading.
4. Gini *The Importance of Being Lazy*, p. 83.
5. Martin Davies 'Another Way of Being: Leisure and the Possibility of Privacy' in C. Barrett and T. Winnifrith (eds) *The Philosophy of Leisure* (London: Macmillan, 1989), p. 117.
6. de Grazia *Of Time, Work, and Leisure*, p. 294.
7. de Grazia *Of Time, Work, and Leisure*, p. 432.
8. John Robinson and Geoffrey Godbey *Time for Life: the surprising way Americans use their time* (University Park PA: Pennsylvania University Press, 1997).
9. Gerald Fain 'Moral Leisure' in Gerald Fain (ed.) *Leisure and Ethics* (Reston, VI: American Association for Leisure and Recreation, 1991).
10. Cyril Barrett 'The Concept of Leisure: idea and ideal' in Barrett and Winnifrith *The Philosophy of Leisure*.
11. See Kelly and Godbey *The Sociology of Leisure*.

12. Mihalyi Csikszentmihalyi *Flow: the psychology of optimal experience* (New York: Harper and Row, 1990). Flow is 'a psychological state based upon concrete feedback which acts as a reward in that it produces continuing behaviour in the absence of other rewards', Mihalyi Csikszentmihalyi *Beyond Boredom and Necessity* (San Francisco: Jossey-Bass, 1975), p. 23.

13. Kelly and Godbey *The Sociology of Leisure*, p. 508.

14. See Robinson and Godbey *Time for Life*, p. 308.

15. For an exploration of the connections between leisure, contemplation and the 'day of rest' in Christian tradition, see Dennis Billy 'The Call to Holy Rest', *New Blackfriars* 82, 2001.

16. Pieper *Leisure: the basis of culture*, p. 43.

17. Josef Pieper *Happiness and Contemplation* (London: Faber and Faber, 1958), pp. 76–9.

18. Pieper *Leisure: the basis of culture*, p. 46.

19. Robinson and Godbey *Time for Life*, p. 305.

20. Anecdotally, parents report that playing with babies and young children, particularly when tired and flat, restores energy and leads naturally to thought on the meaning and blessing of the relationship, and the meaning and value of life generally.

21. John Hemingway 'Leisure and Democracy: incompatible ideals?' in Gerald Fain (ed.) *Leisure and Ethics*. I do not, however, think Aristotle would have any problem understanding why Aquinas and Pieper would naturally assign his category of contemplation to religion. Pieper argues in Ch. 10 of *Happiness and Contemplation* that there is no non-religious contemplation but that awareness of God can be kindled by virtually anything encountered. When the meanings of these words had been explained, I think Aristotle might well have agreed. What would trouble him is Pieper's thought that all religious contemplation is directed towards knowledge of Christ's Incarnation.

22. Emmanuel Mounier, founding figure of French personalism, shared Pieper's deep reverence for reason in the face of totalitarianism and mass consumerism. Like Pieper, he argued for the need to revive culture by understanding leisure as life rooted in a sense of spiritual richness, see Brian Rigby 'French Intellectuals and Leisure: the case of Emmanuel Mounier' in Barnett and Winnifrith *The Philosophy of Leisure*.

23. Elizabeth Telfer 'Leisure' in J. D. G. Evans (ed.) *Moral Philosophy and Contemporary Problems* (Cambridge: University of Cambridge Press, 1987), p. 154.

24. Telfer 'Leisure', p. 162.

25. Telfer 'Leisure', p. 159.

26. Telfer 'Leisure', p. 159, 162.

27. Gini *The Importance of Being Lazy*, pp. 74–5.

28. Gini *The Importance of Being Lazy*, pp. 151–6.

29. Geoffrey Godbey *Leisure in Your Life*, quoted in Kelly and Godbey *The Sociology of Leisure*, p. 505.

30. R. T. Allen 'Leisure: the purpose of life' in Barrett and Winnifrith *The Philosophy of Leisure*.

31. Among those who do, is Aristotle, who views recreation instrumentally, and so thinks it possesses lower status than leisure (see, for example, *Politics*

1339b40, 1342a1). Schall *The Unseriousness of Human* Affairs, p. 103, also argues that recreation – though not leisure – is for the sake of return to work. I argue that recreation means restoring and renewing the whole self, and that this is not instrumental to work, but is one of our most crucial, human activities and is of intrinsic value.

32. In fact, the idea of something chosen for the sake of an independent good and sought as desirable in itself is a basic feature of Aristotelian ethics, and a topic with which every scholarly interpreter must come to terms. For a recent investigation of activity that is chosen for its own sake and for the sake of some more ultimate good, see Lear *Happy Lives and the Highest Good*, Ch. 2.

33. MacIntyre *Dependent Rational* Animals, p. 85.

34. Huizinga *Homo Ludens*, p. 13.

35. Gadamer *Truth and Method*, p. 102.

36. Cf. Mary Midgley *Heart and Mind* (London: Harvester, 1981), p. 144: 'play is found pervading our most important concerns; play insists on being taken seriously.'

37. Hugo Rahner *Man At Play, Or: Did You Ever Practice Eutrapelia?* (London: Compass, 1964), p. 65.

38. Rahner *Man At Play*, p. 28.

39. Rowan Williams *Lost Icons: reflections on cultural bereavement* (Edinburgh: T & T Clarke, 2000), p. 56.

40. Gini *The Importance of being Lazy*, p. 32.

41. 'All play has somewhere deep within it an element of the dance; it is a kind of dance around the truth', Rahner *Man at Play*, p. 66.

42. Rahner provides a marvelous illustration of play and the contemplative life joining hands. He recounts how after the Mass of Easter Day it was the tradition in parts of medieval France for the bishop and his clergy to play a ball game in choir, following a strict dance measure. 'Moving in solemn dance step...the bishop and the clergy of Auxerre would throw the Easter ball to one another, rejoicing like children in their redemption, for this was the evening of the day which had celebrated the victorious sun of Easter', Rahner *Man at Play*, p. 86.

43. Aquinas *Summa*, 1-2, 37, 2.

44. Aquinas *Summa*, 1-2, 38.

45. Aquinas *Summa*, 2-2, 35, 2.

46. Aquinas *Summa*, 2-2, 20, 4.

47. Aquinas *Summa*, 2-2, 35, 1.

48. Julie Edwards and Nicole Rotaru (eds) *I Will Remember These Things Forever* (Melbourne: Outreach Grief Services, 1999), p. 1.

49. Gini *The Importance of Being Lazy*, pp. 2–4.

Chapter 3   Reflective Leisure and Recreation

1. John Hemingway 'Leisure and Democracy: incompatible ideals?' in Fain (ed.) *Leisure and Ethics*.

2. See, for example, Michael Casey *Meaninglessness: the solutions of Nietzsche, Freud, and Rorty* (Melbourne: Freedom, 2001); Roger Scruton *An Intelligent*

Person's Guide to Modern Culture (South Bend IN: St Augustine's Press, 2000); Susan Haack *Manifesto of a Passionate Moderate* (Chicago: University of Chicago Press, 1998); Martha Nussbaum *Sex and Social Justice* (Oxford: Oxford University Press, 1999). Meanwhile, full, modern versions of natural law theory have been provided by German Grisez, and collaborators John Finnis and Joseph Boyle, as well as a range of supporters and challengers from within natural law ethics, including Ralph McInerny, Benedict Ashley, Robert George, Russell Hittinger, and others.

3. Aristotle *De Anima*, 415a16-22.
4. See Philippa Foot *Natural Goodness* (Oxford: Oxford University Press, 2001), especially Ch. 3, for a recent (though different) response in the same tradition as the present work.
5. See R. Sokolowski *Introduction to Phenomenology* (Cambridge: Cambridge University Press, 2000) for a discussion of phenomenological method.
6. Aquinas *Summa*, 1-2, 94, 2.
7. For clear presentation of the new natural law, see German Grisez *The Way of the Lord Jesus* Vol. I (Chicago: Franciscan Herald Press, 1983); John Finnis *Natural Law and Natural Rights* (Oxford: Oxford University Press, 1980) and *Fundamentals of Ethics* (Oxford: Oxford University Press, 1983); Joseph Boyle, John Finnis, and Germain Grisez *Nuclear Deterrence, Morality and Realism* (Oxford: Oxford University Press, 1989); and Robert George (ed.) *Natural Law Theory: contemporary essays* (Oxford: Oxford University Press, 1992).
8. Different versions of the method of reflection on one's own (and others') life and choices have been utilised in contemporary natural law thinking. For example, see Finnis *Natural Law and Natural Rights*, Chs 3 and 4, Timothy Chappell *Understanding Human Goods: a theory of ethics* (Edinburgh: Edinburgh University Press, 1998), Ch. 2, and George *Natural Law Theory*, Ch. 2. For intelligent discussion of lists of basic human goods, see Sabina Alkire 'The basic dimensions of human flourishing: a comparison of accounts' in Nigel Biggar and Rufus Black (eds) *The Revival of Natural Law: philosophical, theological, and ethical responses to the Finnis-Grisez school* (Aldershot: Ashgate, 2000).
9. See Justin Oakley *Morality and the Emotions* (London: Routledge, 1992) for a straightforward presentation. Martha Nussbaum *Upheavals of Thought* (Cambridge: CUP, 2001), Ch. 1 and *Hiding from Humanity: disgust, shame, and the law* (New York: Princeton University Press, 2004) offers the sharpest presentation of this ancient view (also discussed in Sherman *Making a Necessity of Virtue*, Ch. 2).
10. Aquinas *Summa*, 1, 59, 4. See Aidan Nichols *Discovering Aquinas* (London: Darton, Longman, and Todd, 2002), Ch. 6 for recent discussion of angelology.
11. McCabe *Law, Love and Language* (London: Sheen and Ward, 1969), p. 74. My account in this section is heavily indebted to McCabe's 'plain English' and Wittgensteinian reading of Aquinas. For more, see his *God Matters* (London: Geoffrey Chapman, 1987) and *God Still Matters* (London: Continuum, 2002).
12. McCabe *Love, Law and Language*, p. 76: 'with the linguistic animal the media of communication are created by the animal itself.'

13. Cf. the attempt by his great admirer MacIntyre to close the gap between species in his *Dependent Rational Animals*.
14. Schopenhauer, trans., E. F. Payne *The World As Will and Representation* (New York: Dover, 1969), 2: 18. Schopenhauer can be read instructively alongside Nagel's work on the objective and subjective perspectives, including *The View From Nowhere*.
15. Elizabeth Anscombe *Intention* (Oxford: Blackwell, 1957), p. 68.
16. See, for example, Aquinas *Summa* 1, 82, 4; 2-2 58, 4. See Robert Pasnau *Thomas Aquinas on Human Nature* (Cambridge: CUP, 2002), Chs 7 and 8 for an account of the will. The alternative view – that will is a purely psychological response to intellectual apprehension of the good – would require the body to be motivated instrumentally so as to act upon our willing. But human beings are psychophysical unities, and their bodily pursuit of ends is not *caused* by mental attraction but is the natural embodiment or enactment of mental attraction.
17. See Jean Porter *The Recovery of Virtue* (London: SPCK press, 1990) for good discussion of justice and the will for the common good.
18. See Anthony Kenny *Aquinas on Mind* (London: Routledge, 1993), Ch. 4; Christopher Martin *The Philosophy of Thomas Aquinas* (London: Routledge, 1988), Ch. 5.
19. For an excellent range of views, see A. Mele and P. Rawling (eds) *The Oxford Handbook of Rationality* (Oxford: University of Oxford Press, 2004).
20. Aristotle *Politics*, 1253a2
21. Aristotle *Nicomachean Ethics*, 1156b8-10.
22. A current ideology argues same sex couples can do this by inventing same sex marriages and families. I think the confusion here is more a matter of misunderstanding the idea of setting up a home than misunderstanding the urge for sex. Nominalist worries apart, such analogical senses of 'marriage' and 'family' could only succeed where one man acts or pretends to act as a woman. But the only human capacity this type of cross-over would seem to represent is close friendship. And same sex couples ought to be able to find more creative and fulfilling ways of being close friends than using the forms of married couples.
23. This use of *'phronesis'* as both virtue and part of our nature is expertly analysed by Finnis in *Natural Law and Natural Rights*, Ch. 5.
24. For fascinating discussion of the implications of this, see Nagel *The Last Word*.
25. There is still no better discussion of conscience as *con-scientia* than Eric D'Arcy *Conscience and Its Right to Freedom* (London: Sheed and Ward, 1961).
26. For example, see Pope John Paul II *Fides et Ratio* (Sydney: St Paul's, 1998), 81, on the need for philosophy to 'recover its sapiential dimension as a search for the ultimate and overarching meaning of life.' And see the discussion of this by John Haldane in 'The Diversity of Philosophy and the Unity of its Vocation' in Anthony Fisher OP and Hayden Ramsay (eds) *Faith or Reason: friends or foes in the new millennium?* (Hindmarsh, SA: ATF Press, 2004).
27. Aristotle *Nicomachean Ethics*, 1128a5-10.
28. Rahner *Man at Play*, p. 91.
29. Aquinas *Summa*, 2-2, 168, 2; also see 168, 3-4, and *Commentary on the Nicomachean Ethics*, 2: 9, 4: 16, and 8: 2.

30. Rahner *Man at Play*, p. 91.
31. The new growth in 'reality' TV shows, however, suggests that all too often the ideological life is engaged in (vicariously, or not?) as people's 'real' life, with their own home life increasingly the illusion. An aunt used to make the TV announcer a cup of tea, but that was in the early 1950s: today, he may be more likely to make her one first.
32. This requires some honesty and self-criticism. In a review of Carl Honore's *In Praise of Slow*, Frank Campbell *The Australian*, Review Section, July 17–18, 2004 p. 12, writes of consumerist society: 'we are hoist on our own petard: we don't want to abandon cornucopia for utopia.'

Chapter 4   Playing by the Book

1. *1 Thessalonians* 4: 11.
2. The *Sydney Morning Herald* June 7 2004 p. 10 included the headline: '*Iliad* cut back for text generation'. The Herald went on to report that Microsoft has translated the first five books of the *Iliad* into thirty two lines of SMS text language, for example, 'Ares helped da Trojans but Athena helped Diomedes 2 spear im.'
3. See Martyn Lyons 'New Readers in the Nineteenth Century' in Guglielmo Cavallo and Roger Chartier (eds) *A History of Reading in the West* (Cambridge: Polity, 1999).
4. See Jacqueline Hamesse 'The Scholastic Model of Reading' in Cavallo and Chartier (eds).
5. See, eg., Timothy Chappell *Understanding Human Goods* (Oxford: Edinburgh University Press, 1998), Ch. 4.
6. See Anthony Fisher and Hayden Ramsay 'Of Art and Blasphemy', *Ethical Theory and Moral Practice* 3, 2000.
7. See, for example, Hildred Redfern *Questions in Aesthetic Education* (London: Allen and Unwin, 1986).
8. Alberto Manguel *A History of Reading* (London: HarperCollins, 1996), p. 189.
9. Plato *Protagoras*, 320b.
10. Manguel *A History of Reading*, p. 21.
11. Timothy Radcliffe 'Tradition and Creativity: the Paradigm of the New Testament', *New Blackfriars* 70, 1989, p. 59.
12. Radcliffe 'Tradition and Creativity', p. 58.
13. T. S. Eliot 'Tradition and the Individual Talent', in *Selected Essays* (London: Harcourt, 1950).
14. Harold Bloom *The Western Canon* (London: Macmillan, 1994).
15. Bloom *The Western Canon*, p. 3.
16. I say 'western' here, though Bloom writes: 'if we could conceive of a universal canon, multicultural and multivalent, its one essential book [would be] Shakespeare, who is acted and read everywhere, in every language and circumstance', p. 38.
17. Bloom *The Western Canon*, p. 40.
18. Bloom *The Western Canon*, p. 94.
19. Schall *On the Unseriousness of Human Affairs*, p. 96.
20. See Raimond Gaita 'Truth As A Need of the Soul' in *A Common Humanity: thinking about love and truth and justice* (Melbourne: Text, 1999).

21. An excellent contribution here is Hubert Dreyfus *On the Internet* (London: Routledge, 2001) who argues powerfully that increasing exposure to the Net means losing our sense of what is truly relevant, and so increasing our incapacity to identify what we need to know. Dreyfus also argues that the sense of invulnerability and of independence the Net gives disables our impulses towards risk-taking and apprenticeship and so undermines our capacity to learn.
22. For an even-handed treatment, see Gordon Graham *The Internet: a philosophical enquiry* (London: Routledge, 1999).
23. The phrase is St John's (1 John 2: 16), and it is discussed by St Augustine at *Confessions* 10: 35.
24. Gilbert Meilander 'It Killed the Cat: the vice of curiosity' in *The Theory and Practice of Virtue* (Notre Dame IN: Notre Dame University Press, 1984).
25. Meilander 'It Killed the Cat', p. 139.
26. Aquinas *Summa* 2-2, pp. 166–7.
27. For a more optimistic assessment here, again see Graham *The Internet*.

Chapter 5   Playing Abroad

1. John Carroll *Ego and Soul* (Sydney: HarperCollins, 1998).
2. Carroll *Ego and Soul*, p. 142.
3. Carroll *Ego and Soul*, p. 143.
4. Carroll *Ego and Soul*, p. 149.
5. As one young person puts it: 'We're such a multicultural society and we don't really have an identity, so I think for a lot of people it's about finding where you come from', from 'Young and Fearless Keep an Industry Aloft', *The Sunday Age*, 21 July 2002, p. 9.
6. Cf. Alain de Botton *The Art of Travel* (London: Hamish Hamilton, 2002), p. 20: 'A momentous but until then overlooked fact was making its first appearance: that I had inadvertently brought myself with me to the island.'
7. De Botton *The Art of Travel*, Ch. 5.
8. Jonathan Margolis 'Leisure', in *A Brief History of Tomorrow* (London: Bloomsbury, 2001), p. 191.
9. 'Hospitality as commerce...the founding principle of a sea-side resort', Maggie Lane *Jane Austen and Food* (London: Hambledon, 1995), p. 139.
10. De Botton *The Art of Travel*, p. 124.
11. See the response to the Pope by Libby Purves, *The Times*, Tuesday July 10, 2001, p. 14. She describes how the fact that tourists were visiting Croatia meant that *someone* knew what was happening to the city of Dubrovnik during the recent war.
12. The range of topics covered in perhaps the first large-scale academic work on tourism makes clear how irrelevant the travel/tourism distinction generally is today. See Jim Davidson and Peter Spearritt *Holiday Business: tourism in Australia since 1870* (Sydney: Miegunyah, 2000).
13. 'And when we *do* return, it shall not be like other travellers, without being able to give one accurate idea of anything. We *will* know where we have gone – we will recollect what we have seen...Let *our* first effusions be less insupportable than those of the generality of travellers', Jane Austen *Pride and Prejudice* (London: Dent, 1958), p. 135.

14. Josef Pieper *In Tune with the World: a theory of festivity* (Chicago: Franciscan Herald Press, 1965), p. 3.
15. Pieper *In Tune with the World*, p. 26.
16. See, for example, May Lee Nolan and Sidney Nolan *Christian Pilgrimage in Modern Western Europe* (Chapel Hill and London: University of North Carolina Press, 1989), pp. 47–53.
17. MacIntyre *After Virtue*, p. 219.
18. De Botton *The Art of Travel*, pp. 225–6.

Chapter 6   Playing in Tune

1. As Aristotle says at *Politics*, 1340a6, music is not only pleasure and relaxation: it has influence over the character and soul. He argues that unlike tastes and touches and the visual arts, music has – and causes – moral qualities.
2. Alan Merriam *The Anthropology of Music* (Evanston: Northwestern University, 1964), p. 219.
3. Cf. Aristotle *Politics*, 1338a21: 'The use of music for intellectual enjoyment in leisure.' For scholarly discussion of the point, see Thomas Christensen 'Introduction', pp. 1–23, and Calvin Bower 'The Transmission of Ancient Music Theory into the Middle Ages' in Thomas Christensen (ed.) *The Cambridge History of Western Music Theory* (Cambridge: Cambridge University Press, 2002).
4. For Boethius's work on music, see Henry Chadwick *Boethius: the consolations of music, logic, theology, and philosophy* (Oxford: Oxford University Press, 1981).
5. Hence, twentieth century philosophy's focus on the relation of music to the emotions is focus on a modern question: a question for a psychologised age, one that looks to Freud, William James, Hume, and ultimately Descartes' work on the passions, to understand profound experiences. Before Descartes and his account of the passions (including his treatment of music), performance, listening, and the effect of music on people were not scholarly concerns. Now, of course, at the other extreme, looking at emotion is the only (or the major) way in which most philosophy of music proceeds. See, for example, Nussbaum *Upheavals of Thought*, Ch. 5; Roger Scruton *The Aesthetics of Music* (Oxford: Oxford University Press, 1997); Malcolm Budd *Music and the emotions: the philosophical theories* (London: Routledge, 1985); Aaron Ridley *Music, Value, and the Passions* (Ithaca: Cornell University Press, 1995).
6. See William Weber*The Rise of Musical Classics in Eighteenth Century England: a study in canon, ritual, and ideology* (Oxford: Oxford University Press, 1992).
7. He wrote 'Musique d'ameublement' (1920), for piano, three clarinets, and trombone (!).
8. On this, see Robert Philip *Performing Music in the Age of Recording* (New Haven CT: Yale University Press, 2004).
9. Except in the Ethiopian Orthodox Church where liturgical dance plays a unique role, recalling King David who danced before the Ark of God.
10. After writing this I encountered the following lines from Roger Scruton 'The Decline of Musical Culture', in Neill and Ridley, p. 123: 'In a very important

sense the dances observed on the stage, as in a ballet, are not real dances, but representations of the dance. And while there are places where you can go for waltzes, polkas, or highland reels, you do not so much dance there as "dance" in inverted commas, conscious of your separation from the real life of the body in modern conditions.'

11. Christopher Ballantine *Music and Its Social Meanings* (New York: Gordon and Breach, 1984), Ch. 1, p. 5: 'In various ways and with varying degrees of critical awareness, the musical microcosm replicates the social macrocosm.'

12. For a different, and always stimulating, view, see Peter Conrad *A Song of Love and Death: the meaning of opera* (London: Hogarth Press, 1989). He begins his analysis with the different forms of self-understanding that opera demonstrates – the archetypes of Orpheus, Dionysius, Eros, Mephistopheles, and Dagon (song, sensuality, sexuality, the devil, and religion).

13. Cf. Rupert Christiansen *The Spectator*, 16/23 December 2000, p. 25, on his conversion to opera: 'What compelled me was the sense that opera was something, as it were, on the top shelf – dangerous, arcane, complex and, as Dr Johnson supposedly said "exotick and irrational". Now I worry that, by making opera so officially "accessible", all the well-meaning, friendly work...actually neutralises those qualities, making what should be subversive and potently strange seem like nothing more alluring than an approved sidebar of the National Curriculum.'

14. Honorius of Autun 'A Picture of the World' in John Wippel and Allan Wolter (eds) *Mediæval Philosophy: from St Augustine to Nicholas of Cusa* (New York: Free Press, 1969), p. 183.

15. Aquinas *Summa*, 2-2, 91, 2, *ad* 4.

16. For discussion of Schopenhauer's view of music, see Malcolm Budd *Music and the Emotions: the philosophical theories* (London: Routledge and Kegan Paul, 1985), Ch. 5; Bryan Magee *Wagner and Philosophy* (London: Allen Lane, 2000).

17. See Norman Lebrecht *When The Music Stops* (London: Pocket Books, 1996) for critical and fiery discussion of the classical recording business. As a response to limitations in that business, several famous orchestras have inaugurated their own record labels in 2004.

18. 'To me there is no pop or classical. That which we call classical today was popular culture in its time. There's only good work and bad work, a great story and a not-so-great story', Baz Luhrmann, *Opera* 53, Nov. 2002, p. 1312.

19. See, for example, Bruce Baugh 'Prolegomena To Any Aesthetics of Rock Music', *The Journal of Aesthetics and Art Criticism* 51, 1993, 23–31.

20. The issue of the nature and standards of popular music is hotly contested by sociologists and philosophers of aesthetics. See for example the debate between Baugh and James Young, *Journal of Aesthetics and Art Criticism* 53, 1995, 78–83; Simon Frith *Performing Rites: on the value of popular music* (Cambridge, Mass.: Harvard University Press, 1996); Donald Clarke *The Rise and Fall of Popular Music* (New York: St Martin's Press, 1995); John Covach and Graham Boone (eds) *Understanding Rock: essays in musical analysis* (Oxford: Oxford University Press, 1997).

21. For discussion of the culture that forms and is supported by the simple music of rock and pop, see Roger Scruton *An Intelligent Person's Guide to Modern Culture* (South Bend, IN: St Augustine's Press, 2000), Ch. 10.

22. Colin Bostock-Smith, 'What Is It That Makes Us So Sad When A Rock Star Dies?', *The Spectator* 13th July 2002, p. 10, recalls years ago meeting an ex-member of the *Rolling Stones*. As the others argued about which group was best: '(Ian) Stewart paused for a moment, and, balancing an amplifier on his broad shoulders, listened to us. Then he gave us the benefit of his inside knowledge. "They're all crap", said the one-time Stone. "All of them. Crap."'
23. One of the most shameful moments of my own life is, as a 12 year old, sweating in a music class while the teacher asked each pupil in turn what was his favourite music. As boy after boy answered 'Mud', the band of the moment, I took a deep breath and answered – 'Mud'; my fear of their contempt too great to allow me to mention Smetana's *Vltava*, which I had just heard for the first time.
24. Simon Frith 'Towards an Aesthetic of Popular Music' in R. Leppert and S. McClary *Music and Society: the politics of composition, performance and reception* (Cambridge: CUP, 1987), p. 143.
25. Frith 'Towards an Aesthetic of Popular Music', p. 137.
26. Christopher Ballantine *Music and its Social Meanings* (New York: Gordon and Breach, 1984), p. 9.

Chapter 7   Playing by the Rules

1. Heather Reid *The Philosophical Athlete* (Durham NC: Carolina Press, 2002).
2. For discussion of thinkers from Plato to Sartre on play in sport, see William Morgan and Klaus Meier (eds) *Philosophic Inquiry in Sport* (Champaign ILL: Human Kinetics, 188), pp. 1–76.
3. Jan Boxill (ed.) *Sports Ethics: an anthology* (Oxford: Blackwell, 2003), p. 1.
4. For athletics as reminder of our mortality, training the body and soul, and homage to the gods, see Stephen Miller *Ancient Greek Athletics* (New York: Yale University Press, 2004).
5. This idea comes from Anthony Skillen 'Sport is for Losers' in J. McNamee and S. Parry (eds) *Ethics and Sport* (London: E. and F. Spon, 1988), pp. 180–1: 'because it is one of the few domains in which humans are engaged to stretch to their limits, sport has the potential to teach us to live with such limits, and at the same time, because we have to be "given" a game by the person who beats or is beaten by us, sport has the capacity to teach us to live within the limits of a human fellowship informed by awareness of common frailty. Good sports have much generous wisdom in their bones.'
6. Cf. Robert Simon *Fair Play: the ethics of sport* (Boulder CO: Westview, 2004), p. 27: the principal value of sport lies not in winning, but in overcoming the challenge presented by a worthy opponent. That is, competitions are a 'mutually acceptable quest for excellence through challenge', not a 'zero-sum game'.
7. Heather Reid 'Sport, Education, and the Meaning of Victory', Twentieth World Congress of Philosophy, Boston, Massachusetts, from August 10–15, 1988 http:www.bu.edu/wcp/Papers/SporReid.htm
8. Jan Boxill 'The Ethics of Competition' in Boxill (ed.) *Sports Ethics*, pp. 107–16.
9. Stephen Miller *Arete: Greek sports from ancient sources* (Berkeley: University of California Press, 2004), p. ix: 'The word "arête" has imbued ancient athletics with an aura of the quest of man for perfection.'

10. Russell Gough *Character is Everything* (Fortworth TX: Harcourt Brace, 1997), p. 30.
11. Carroll *Ego and Soul*, p. 39.
12. John Hoberman *Mortal Engines* (New York: Macmillan, 1992).
13. Hoberman *Mortal Engines*, p. 103.
14. Claudio Tamburrini 'What's Wrong with Doping?' in Torbjorn Tannsjo and Claudio Tamburrini (eds) *Values in Sport: elitism, nationalism, gender equality, and the scientific manufacture of winners* (London: E. and F. Spon, 2000).
15. Hoberman *Mortal Engines*, p. 192.
16. *Beyond Therapy: biotechnology and the pursuit of happiness* A Report By The President's Council On Bioethics (New York: HarperCollins, 2003), Ch. 3.
17. *Beyond Therapy*, p. 125.
18. *Beyond Therapy*, p. 126.
19. *Beyond Therapy*, p. 128.
20. In her Address to the World Congress of Philosophy, p. 5, Heather Reid argues that doping indicates lack of appreciation for the value of learning about oneself and natural human capacities, or one's carefully crafted maximum performance: 'If you've made sure that your victory is inevitable, ask yourself how it could possibly be a victory at all' (to which some contemporary athletes will doubtless reply: 'money', status', 'fame').
21. For general discussion of TV and sport, see Ellis Cashmore *Making Sense of Sport*, 2nd edn (London: Routledge, 1990), Ch. 10.
22. Hoberman *Mortal Engines*, p. 284.
23. Torbjorn Tannsjo 'Introduction' in Tannsjo and Tamburrini *Values in Sport*, p. 10.
24. *Beyond Therapy*, pp. 155–6.
25. See Michael Smith 'What is Sports Violence?' in Boxill (ed.) *Sports Ethics*.
26. John Heeley 'Leisure and Moral Reform' in *Journal of Leisure Studies* 5, 1986, pp. 57–67.
27. See Carwyn Jones and Mike McNamee 'Moral Development and Sport: character and cognitive developmentalism contrasted', in Boxill (ed.) *Sports Ethics*.
28. Skillen 'Sport is for Losers'.
29. Paul Gomberg 'Patriotism in Sport' in Tannsjo and Tamburrini (eds) *Values in Sport*.
30. William Morgan *Leftist Theories of Sport* (Chicago: University of Illinois Press, 1994).

Chapter 8   Work and Leisure

1. Bertrand Russell 'In Praise of Idleness'.
2. Russell *In Praise of Idleness*, p. 19.
3. Russell *In Praise of Idleness*, p. 18. For recent discussion see Paul Western 'More Praise for Idleness', *Philosophy Now* 29, Oct/Nov, 2000, pp. 26–8.
4. Rowan Williams *Lost Icons*, p. 62.
5. Williams *In Praise of Idleness*, p. 62: 'The surrounding environment freights economic activity with so much anxiety that the interruptions of the game seem threatening, not liberating; anxiety and violence are carried over into

what is meant to be play....The skewed character of work in our society is intensified all the time by the lack, the thinness or the impotence of the remaining social rituals that embody charity.'

6. See report in Sydney *Sun-Herald*, October 10 2004, p. 23.
7. Kay Hymokvitz 'Ecstatic Capitalism's Brave New Work Ethic, see http://www.city-journal.org/html/11_1_ecstatic_capitalisms.html.
8. I owe this point to Onora O'Neill. See for example, Onora O'Neill *The Bounds of Justice* (Cambridge: CUP, 2000), *Faces of Hunger* (Cambridge: Cambridge University Press, 1986), and *A Question of Trust* (Cambridge: Cambridge University Press, 2002).
9. For example, Yves Simon *Work, Society, and Culture* (New York: Fordham University Press, 1971) argues for the high place of manual work in upholding ideals of honesty and perfection for intellectual workers.
10. Sarah Marinos *Qantas, the Australian Way*, June 2004, pp. 65–7 discusses the research of Ad Vingerhoets of Tilburg University who first diagnosed leisure sickness after study of 1900 Dutch sufferers. Leisure sickness affects 3–4% of the Dutch population. These are people ill at the weekend or start of a holiday because they see their work as a vital part of their identity, and therefore regard leisure with guilt feelings. On this sort of view, presumably the weekend is like a cold, holidays like serious illness, and redundancy or retirement like death.
11. It cannot be denied that leisure and work are unequal partners. For leisure is more 'basic' than work: it is the normal means to exercising a basic human capacity, while work is the normal means to the products utilised in exercise of basic human capacities. Thus, as Roger Scruton puts it in his Preface to Josef Pieper *Leisure: the basis of culture* (South Bend IN: St Augustine's Press, 1998): 'work *may* be creative. But only when informed by leisure', xii. The creativity of leisure is naturally prior to that of work.
12. Gini *The Importance of Being Lazy*, p. 22.
13. George Eliot *Adam Bede* (London: Dent, 1960), p. 497.
14. Niall Ferguson *The Weekly Telegraph* No. 681, 2004, p. 24. Ferguson explores and contrasts Americans' long working hours and high level of religious practice, with Europeans much shorter working hours and longer holidays, and their commitment to atheism.
15. See Pope John Paul II's Encyclicals *Laborem Exercens, Solicitudo Rei Socialis, Centesimus Annus.*
16. John Paul II *Laborem Exercens*, 6.

Chapter 9   Recreating the Arts

1. The relations between appreciating beauty and pondering truth are complex. For good discussion, see Ronald Hepburn *Wonder and Other Essays* (Edinburgh: Edinburgh UP, 1984).
2. In fact, the dependence of economies on the arts and of the arts on economies is complex. For a different approach, see the argument in Tyler Cowen *In Praise of Commercial Culture* (Cambridge, Mass.: Harvard University Press, 1998).
3. Pieper *In Tune With The World*, p. 40.

Index